# Developing Early Years Practice

LOAN

S... art time studen...

# Linda Miller, Carrie Cable and Jane Devereux

The Open University

David Fulton Publishers

David Fulton Publishers Ltd
The Chiswick Centre, 414 Chiswick High Road, London W4 5TF

www.fultonpublishers.co.uk

First published in Great Britain in 2005 by David Fulton Publishers.

10 9 8 7 6 5 4 3 2 1

Note: The right of the individual contributors to be identified as the authors of their work has been asserted by them in accordance with the Copyright, Designs and Patents Act 1988.

*British Library Cataloguing in Publication Data*
A catalogue record for this book is available from the British Library.

David Fulton Publishers is a division of ITV plc.

ISBN 1 84312 317 7

Typeset by RefineCatch Limited, Bungay, Suffolk
Printed and bound in Great Britain

Also available

**Foundation Degree Texts**
Understanding Children's Learning: A Text for Teaching Assistants
*Edited by Claire Alfrey*
*1−84312−069−0*

Supporting Learning and Teaching
*Edited by Christine Bold*
1−84312−127−1

Successful Study: Skills for Teaching Assistants
*Christine Ritchie & Paul Thomas*
*1−84312−106−9*

Additional Educational Needs: Inclusive Approaches to Teaching
*Edited by Sue Soan*
*1−84312−149−2*

# Contents

# About the Authors

**Linda Miller** is Senior Lecturer in Childhood Studies at the Open University and is Chair of the Early Year Sector Endorsed Foundation Degrees Delivery Network. She has worked both with and for children throughout her professional life. Her research and publications include the areas of literacy development, the early years curriculum and professional and training issues in the early years workforce.

**Carrie Cable** is a Senior Lecturer in Education at the Open University where she is involved in developing courses for teaching assistants and early years practitioners. She has worked as a teacher and advisor and has contributed to national training and development initiatives for teaching assistants and teachers particularly in the field of English as an additional language. Her research interests and publications include the learning and teaching of EAL, and the roles of bilingualism and bilingual teaching assistants in children's learning.

**Jane Devereux** is a Senior Lecturer in Education at the Open University where she has chaired courses for the Early Years Sector Endorsed Foundation Degree in Early Years. She has worked as a teacher, advisory teacher and a teacher educator in primary and early years. Her research interests and publications include the professional development of primary and early years practitioners in the UK and South Africa, children's learning, observation and assessment of learning and developing subject knowledge, particularly in primary science.

# Acknowledgments

The authors would like to gratefully acknowledge the contributions of the following people to the writing of the original Open University course materials that have been drawn on in writing this book.

## External consultants

Helen Bilton
Ann Bridges
Mary Briggs
Nicola Davies
Linda Pound
Mary Stacey
Angela Underdown
Colleagues at Manchester Metropolitan University

## OU academics

Hilary Burgess
Deirdre Cook
Janet Collins
Anna Craft
Ian Eyres
Roger Hancock
Alice Paige-Smith

# Foreword

This is a timely book written by forward thinking authors who are writing at a time of almost unprecedented change as the remodelling of the early years workforce is planned and is beginning to take shape. It is vital for the sake of young children and their families that at this time of change, practitioners are equipped to meet the new challenges and enhanced expectations that form part of their expanding occupational and professional roles. Whilst recognising that titles across the UK may vary, this book is designed primarily to support the training and development of the 'Senior Practitioner'. The development of this role is an important step in bringing about workforce change and in meeting the needs of young children and their families in the 21st century. The book will also be of value to a wider audience including those undertaking Early Childhood Studies Degrees or Initial Teacher Education Courses, in offering the underpinning of knowledge and understanding required for such courses.

The Open University Courses on which the book is based have created accessible routes into Higher Education for large numbers of early years practitioners and are supporting the development of well trained, highly skilled senior practitioners. Many practitioners who have completed these courses will go on to complete the Sector Endorsed Early Years Foundation Degree and other relevant training ensuring a supply of competent people both into, and within, the workforce who have practical skills as well as knowledge and understanding that is securely rooted on a firm theoretical basis. The book is up to date and draws on both new research and well established research highlighting the need for evidence based practice.

Research has indicated that the outcomes for children are better when the staff involved have higher qualifications and a good understanding of child development and learning. The ability of practitioners to stand back and reflect on their practice is also central to continuous improvement and the bringing about of a step change in the experience of children in early years settings. This book supports and encourages reflective practice and provides case studies and practical examples of activities and tasks to support reflection.

A key strength of this book is its UK wide approach. It reflects the differences and changes in social and educational policy affecting early years that have come about in each UK Home Country. This ensures its relevance to the widest audience.

The book is broad in its approach to early years practice and covers issues in a logical and readable manner. The first section includes empowering environments, multi-agency working, positive learning environments, listening to and safeguarding children, partnerships with parents: all of these are important issues affecting the development of the workforce. Section 2 moves on to ways of learning, and covers learning through play, birth to three, assessment and inclusion. Finally, Section 3 moves through to more detailed consideration of the curriculum for the early years, covering self esteem and identity, creativity and ICT, literacy and mathematical development and exploring the world.

This is an innovative and thoughtful book which should play an important role in training and developing existing practitioners and the early years practitioners of the future. At all times it leads the practitioner back to their own situation and practice, stimulating thinking and placing the child and family at the centre. I have no hesitation in recommending this book for a wide range of audiences who will have their understanding of effective early years practice supported and deepened.

Maureen Smith
*External Adviser to the Open University Early Years Sector Endorsed Foundation Degree*

# Introduction

The authors of this book have spent a large part of their professional lives developing courses and providing training for practitioners across the fields of early years education and care and in primary education. All three authors share a particular commitment to encouraging and supporting students who may be new to study, particularly at Higher Education level. We know that the majority of early years practitioners are mature women who may be experienced practitioners who have worked with young children for many years. These practitioners will have built up considerable 'knowledge in action' – an idea we examine in Chapter 5 of this book – but may now want to explore more deeply their understanding of how children learn and develop and delve into the theory that informs such understandings.

This book started life as two courses offered by the Open University, leading to a Certificate in Early Years Practice. The certificate forms part of the Open University's Sector-Endorsed Foundation Degree in Early Years. As the authors of this book, we have been fortunate in working with authorities in the fields of study covered by the book who contributed to the Open University courses, and we acknowledge their contribution to the book. The material on which this book is based has been 'tested' in the field by practitioners in their workplaces and drafts of the original material were read and commented on by 'critical readers' who work in the field of early years education and care. These critical contributions challenged our thinking and understandings and helped us to convert the course material into what we hope is an accessible and informative text.

In Chapter 1 of this book we refer to a 'climbing frame' analogy of professional development to describe the ways in which early years workers progress from lower to higher level qualifications (Abbott and Hevey 2001). This analogy represents the ways in which early years workers enter training and qualifications at different points in their professional lives, bringing with them different experiences and qualifications at each entry point. This book is written with these people in mind. We acknowledge that some people reading this book may be new to or returning to study. A primary aim of the book is that it will provide a core introductory text for the many early years practitioners who are embarking upon or are part way through a course of study such as a Foundation Degree in early years education and care, an Early Childhood Studies Degree or an Initial Teacher Education course. We hope that the book will empower such people in the early stages of their professional development to develop the knowledge, skills and understandings required to reflect upon and develop their practice.

The book therefore aims to:

- support early years practitioners in the early stages of higher education study;
- enable early years practitioners to understand the influences which impact on their work, both internal and external to the workplace, and on the well-being of the children and families with whom they work;
- contribute to the knowledge and understanding of early years practitioners in relation to the theoretical perspectives which underpin their work;
- encourage early years practitioners to take a reflective stance in relation to their practice.

This book is organised into three parts:

- Creating empowering environments
- Ways of learning
- Curriculum in practice.

Each chapter in the book outlines the aims for the chapter, has activities to support learning and reflection, and many include illustrative case studies. At the end of each chapter is a review of the content, questions for reflection, and suggestions for further reading.

Part 1 of this book includes chapters which consider the ways in which both the internal and external environments impact on early years practitioners and the young children and families with whom they work. It also considers the professional development of early years practitioners in a time of great change. In Part 2 the chapters focus on how children learn, how practitioners can support and extend this learning and how all children can be included. In Part 3 the chapters consider different aspects of the early years curriculum. The final chapter considers different perspectives on curricula and the ways in which these can influence how practitioners work with children and understand and promote their learning and development.

We hope that readers will enjoy this book and that it provides a useful starting point for a lifelong learning journey.

## Reference

Abbott, L. and Hevey, D. (2001) 'Training to work in the early years: developing the climbing frame,' in Pugh, G. (ed.) *Contemporary Issues in the Early Years: Working Collaboratively for Children*, 3rd edn, London: Paul Chapman Publishing, pp. 179–93.

# Part 1

# Creating Empowering Environments

# Introduction to Part 1: Creating Empowering Environments

Part 1 of this book is concerned with both internal and external changes in the environment. It considers how these changes are impacting on early years practitioners' day-to-day working practices and on the lives of young children and the families with whom they work. The five chapters cover the themes of: recent policy changes, changes in service provision and in employment roles in the field of early years education and care; ways of working with other professionals; developing partnerships with parents; the role of positive and inclusive environments for learning, and the personal and professional development of early years practitioners.

The first chapter focuses on the external environment and charts how early years education and care has become a high priority on the agenda of government. It goes on to consider how new policy and legislation is influencing the organisation of service provision. At the level of practice, the chapter describes how developments such as Sure Start and new inspection and regulation legislation are opening up new and additional employment opportunities for those wishing to work with young children and their families. The chapter also describes how new opportunities and progression routes, such as Foundation Degrees, are being created, where early years education and care is a key focus of study. The move towards multi-agency working is a major feature of this changing scene, as is the need for a new core worker who can work across professional boundaries.

The theme of working with other professionals is continued in Chapter 2, where we consider how the ethos and environment in early years settings can set the scene for the development of the mutual regard needed for successful teamwork. We go on to consider some key aspects of working with others, such as developing the important skills of listening and communicating. We also consider the impact of external developments such as changes in legislation and policy on working together in early years settings, for example in relation to equality issues. Creating partnerships with children's parents and carers is seen as an important aspect of working with others.

In Chapter 3 we explore the contribution that parents can make to children's learning, development and well-being in an environment where working with others is truly valued. We discuss the form that partnerships can take and consider what is feasible, given the diverse nature of a parent body, and the complexity and range of children's needs. We consider the challenge for practitioners of reaching out to parents who may feel unable or reluctant to work in close collaboration with them and explore practices that might foster ways of working together for the benefit of children.

In Chapter 4 we consider why early years practitioners have a responsibility to create an ethos where both children and adults can learn and develop together. We discuss the benefits of positive learning environments, where children are listened to and their rights are respected. We see this as an important aspect of protecting children and keeping children safe. We also discuss the need for environments where children can try out new things, where practitioners allow them to explore and take some risks and so enable them to become both competent and confident learners.

A key aim of this book is to empower early years practitioners through increasing their knowledge and understanding of their practice. In Chapter 5 we consider the professional development of early years practitioners. Alongside this developing knowledge, we explore the intuitive knowledge that practitioners bring to their practice and discuss the place of 'knowledge in action'. Practitioners are encouraged to stand back and to reflect upon their practice. However, we recognise that in a world where increasing accountability features, such reflection is not sufficient and we discuss the need for practice to be supported by evidence. We consider the role and nature of this evidence. Finally the reader is asked to consider his or her own professional development and to identify some future goals for this professional journey.

# 1 Changing Times: Early Years Practitioners Today

## By the end of this chapter you will have:

■ explored changing roles and professional practices in working with young children and their families;

■ considered current and future changes in ways of working with young children and their families;

■ increased your understanding of other professionals, their roles and responsibilities.

## Introduction

> Practitioners in today's early childhood institutions are maybe facing some of the most demanding challenges in the history of their profession . . . Profound and interrelated change in our social, economic, political and technological environments, combined with a fundamental shift in the nature of work and employment patterns, are impacting on the lives of children and families.
>
> (Oberhaumer and Colberg-Schrader 1999, cited in Abbott and Hevey 2001: 179).

The past decade has been both a challenging and exciting time to be working with young children. In this chapter we discuss the changing external environment, which is opening up new roles, responsibilities and opportunities for early years practitioners, which will require broader and higher levels of knowledge and skills. The working contexts and professional roles of early years practitioners are evolving fast. Policy makers are increasingly focusing on how the workforce is organised and trained. Over the past century the need for childcare and early years education prior to school has grown, as more and more women have entered paid work outside the home. This has led to a need to provide quality service provision to children and families, as well as meaningful career routes and progression for early years practitioners. In this chapter we discuss this background of policy developments and in particular how professional work in the early years is changing.

## How is professional work in the early years changing?

There have been many forces for change within the early years education and care sector. We outline the most significant changes below.

### The National Childcare Strategy

The National Childcare Strategy, launched in England in 1998, aimed to increase the quality, accessibility and affordability of early years education and care provision. Developments in Wales, Northern Ireland and Scotland paralleled many of the changes proposed in England. The formation of Early Years Development and Childcare Partnerships (EYDCPs) meant that early years services were planned in each Local Authority. EYDCPs were identified as having a key role in developing and training the workforce to support these services.

### Integrated provision

Integrated provision is a key policy development of government and the government's aim is to have a Children's Centre in every community in England. Children's Centres bring together under one roof early education and care, family support, health services, employment advice and specialist support for parents and easy referral between services. The DfES Children's Workforce Unit, in collaboration with the National College for School Leadership (NCSL), has developed a 'National Professional Qualification in Integrated Centre Leadership' aimed at Children's Centre Heads and Deputies (DfES 2004b) to provide leadership training for the leaders of these new centres.

### Sure Start programmes

Sure Start programmes operate in all four countries in the United Kingdom (UK) and bring together health, early learning and parenting, with the common aim of coordinating early years services and tackling child poverty and social exclusion.

### Extended schools

Extended schools are an initiative which began in Scotland and are planned in England in 1,000 primary schools by 2008. They are aimed at supporting working parents and will provide 'wrap-around care' childcare at either end of the school day. In addition schools will offer sports and art activities, family learning and parent classes and extra study support for children.

## National Children's Service Framework

A National Children's Service Framework (NSF) will establish new national standards for children across the National Health Service (NHS) and Social Services and will interface with Education (DfES 2003b).

## Children's Trusts

Children's Trusts will bring together a range of partners, including the voluntary and community sector, to integrate the planning of children's services (DfES 2003b).

## Early years education

All four countries in the UK have developed initiatives for expanding early years education. In England a framework for working with children from birth to three has been developed (Sure Start Unit 2002) and a single framework for childcare and learning from birth to five is proposed (HM Treasury 2004). The Scottish Executive has extended part-time education to all three-year-olds and has extended the educative role of practitioners. National guidance relating to the care and education of children from birth to three, 'Care and Learning for Children from Birth to Three', will be published in 2005 (LTS Scotland 2004). In Wales a draft framework for children's learning has identified the need to consider changes relating to a learning curriculum for children aged 0–7 (National Assembly for Wales, Learning Wales 2004). In Northern Ireland a play-based 'Enriched Curriculum' is being piloted in Year 1 classes for four- and five-year-olds (Sproule 2004). All four UK countries have introduced published curriculum frameworks or guidance documents, identifying areas of learning for children aged three to five.

## Inspection and regulation

In the past decade there has been new legislation, which underpins inspection and regulation requirements in all four UK countries, with the aim of improving and monitoring early years provision. These new requirements have implications for the workforce in relation to the type and level of qualifications required to work with young children. In England a more coherent and integrated approach to inspection and regulation is planned for early education and childcare services (HM Treasury 2004).

## Workforce reform

Workforce reform is crucial to providing a quality service for children and parents. Research shows that the quality of provision in early years settings is clearly linked to the quality of staff that work in them (Sylva *et al.* 2003). The establishment of the Learning and Skills Council in April 2001 is an indicator of the government's intentions for a skilled and qualified workforce. This body was set a target to enable 230,000 people to achieve new or higher childcare qualifications by March 2004. A review of National Occupational Standards for Early Years Education and Care funded by the Department for Education and Skills (DfES) will report in late 2004 (Smith 2003). The revised standards will reflect changes in the sector in all four UK countries and, in particular, changes relating to the key roles undertaken by early years workers. New professional standards for Higher Level Teaching Assistants (HLTA) working in schools have been introduced in England (DfES 2004a). A common core of skills, knowledge and competence is being developed and a complementary set of qualifications for all those who work with children, young people and families (DfES 2003b).

The Green Paper *Every Child Matters* (DfES 2003b) outlines plans for a workforce reform strategy, as does the ten-year strategy for childcare, 'Choice for Parents, the Best Start for Children: a ten year strategy for childcare' (HM Treasury 2004). The strategy is intended to improve the skills and qualifications of the children's workforce in partnership with employers and staff.

## Training and qualifications

All four UK countries have attempted to rationalise a confusing array of qualifications within this sector by developing a national framework covering vocational and occupational qualifications in early years education, care and playwork, and clearer progression routes to higher level qualifications. This has been under development since 1999 in England (QCA 1999) and the Northern Ireland Qualifications Authority has linked with QCA to accredit qualifications within this framework. In Wales the Learning and Skills Council is developing a training framework for early years education and care and in Scotland the Scottish Credit and Qualifications (SCQF) framework is in place, which encompasses the respective levels and types of qualification from school to university (Scottish Social Services Council 2004).

In England, the ten-year strategy (HM Treasury 2004) proposes a professionally led workforce with a strengthened qualification and career structure. A graduate-qualified early years professional leading in full day-care centres is proposed, and increased qualifications for home-based carers. A Children's

Workforce Development Council will lead the reform of the early years and childcare workforce. These policy developments, leading to new forms of services, will require a range of workers at all levels to provide high quality services for young children and their families. Increasingly this work will take place in multi-disciplinary and multi-agency contexts and will both enable and demand multi-agency working where health, social care, and education services work together.

## Multi-agency working

The need for joined-up services such as those described above is illustrated by the case study of Adam (DfES 2003a).

### Case Study: Adam's story

Adam was born a full-term healthy baby. At four weeks old he developed meningitis and spent the next three months battling for survival.

Adam is now 13 months old. He has a combination of disabilities.

Adam has had 315 different service-based appointments in the last nine months, in 12 different locations. His family have found it extremely difficult to access information, specialist equipment, financial help, support from local or national groups, or coordinated services.

Some of the things his family would like include: information; access to assessment; an appointment system that recognises the complexity of Adam's needs and brings some appointments together; a break from caring; help with future planning; a key worker.

(adapted from 'Together from the Start', DfES 2003a: 5)

The Green Paper *Every Child Matters* (DfES 2003b) aims to address the issues raised in Adam's case in relation to multi-disciplinary and multi-agency working and proposes a more universal approach across services. The consultation framework focused on four main areas:

- early intervention and effective protection;
- supporting parents and carers;
- accountability and integration – locally, regionally and nationally;
- workforce reform.

Additionally a Minister for Children, Young People and Families has been created.

Both the Welsh Assembly and the Scottish Executive have expressed a keen interest in the issues raised in the Green Paper and will consider which parts of the approach adopted in England they will seek to adapt respectively.

## Activity 1.1 Multi-agency working

Multi-agency working may pose a particular challenge, particularly if you are working in a home-based setting like Naima below. Write down which other professionals you work with, what their roles are, and how you work together. Note what works well and what does not.

## Case Study: Naima

I am mostly home based as a childminder with some access to a playgroup as a volunteer. When working at home I do not come into contact with many other professionals. I have met with health visitors but this doesn't really include working together. As a volunteer in a playgroup, the other professionals I meet are people with playgroup qualifications or occasionally a visiting specialist such as a speech therapist. In this situation plans are written down for all the staff to follow. This has changed from when I worked full time some years ago. It works better now, with definite plans written down for everyone to share. I have noticed the Special Educational Needs Coordinator shares plans with the other staff and this seems to work well in providing a coordinated approach to working with individual children.

How you work in relation to other agencies will depend on your own role. If you are a childminder or a nanny, you may find you work with other agencies such as social services or health workers as and when necessary. However, in a day-care, nursery, playgroup or school setting, there may be a number of established ways in which you link with health and social services and education. The ways you work with other agencies will affect all children in your care. For example, you may be supporting a child who works regularly with a speech and language therapist and taking advice about how best so support the child. Some multi-agency work will involve an expert opinion being passed on in one direction, and in others it may involve more collaborative work, as in the case of Children's Centres. Key factors in successful multi-agency working have been identified as:

- commitment and willingness;
- understanding roles and responsibilities;
- common aims and objectives;
- communication and information sharing;
- dissemination of information;
- leadership and drive;
- involving relevant people;
- access to resources.

(Atkinson *et al.* 2002)

You may find it helpful to compare your own thoughts about what works well with a colleague or someone who knows your work well.

## Professional responsibility: working with others

It is important to understand the roles of other professionals that you work with, as we discuss in Chapter 2. Communication is very important and rests on accurate and mutual understandings of roles and responsibilities. We need to be aware of making stereotypical assumptions about the roles and responsibilities of others with whom we work, which may be based on their work roles, gender, racial origins, disability, and age. Group dynamics are a significant aspect of working with others, whether or not the setting is a multi-agency one. An important aspect of working in a multi-agency environment is sharing information and skills with other colleagues (DfES 2001a: 46). To do this, you will need to be familiar with your setting's policy and practice and you will need to network with others.

### Multi-agency working and increased professionalism for early years practitioners

In a National Foundation for Educational Research (NFER) study involving an evaluation of multi-agency working, Atkinson *et al.* (2002) suggested that collaboration leads to improved services and prevention of potential problems through better identification of gaps in provision. For the individuals involved, working in a multi-agency context was seen as stimulating and rewarding; however, it also often led to higher work pressure. Practitioners interviewed for the study commonly reported that working alongside other professionals broadened their own perspective and increased their understanding of how other agencies operate.

Moss (2003) has questioned whether the ways in which we currently understand and organise childcare and education are sufficiently holistic, and whether they adequately reflect the needs of families and children. He reports that most parents feel there is a lack of affordable childcare, which he attributes to government seeing childcare as a private service that parents should purchase, rather than something that the state should invest in heavily to make it affordable. He contrasts the situation in England to that in Denmark and Sweden, where public money is used to subsidise the costs.

He also discusses the problem of retaining early years practitioners, the majority of whom are traditionally women and poorly paid. As increasing numbers of women become better educated and have wider employment opportunities, he questions whether or not they will wish to continue working in low-paid occupations associated with this sector. Moss predicts a crisis of care, which could lead to radical reform. We have seen the beginnings of such reforms in the Green Paper *Every Child Matters* (DfES 2003b) and the ten-year strategy for early years and childcare (HM Treasury 2004), for example better integration of services and new roles for 'core workers' capable of working across services. Moss offers examples of the core worker model – the 'New Teacher' model from Sweden, New Zealand and Spain and the 'Pedagogue' model from Denmark – which works holistically and brings together education and care. This model also offers better qualifications and an enhanced role to early years practitioners in those countries.

## Activity 1.2 Reflecting on your experience

We would now like you to think about your own role and career to date and whether you see it as taking place largely in the field of education or care, or a mixture of both, often referred to as 'educare'. Outline your past, present and future work as an early years practitioner. You may like to draw a diagram to represent this.

Here is how one person completed this activity.

PAST: (when children were young)
Education: playgroup assistant; joint owner of playgroup; teaching assistant in a primary school
(Break for other work)
Care: Part-time nanny to twins
Care and education: day-nursery worker
During this time gained qualifications as an NVQ tutor/assessor.
PRESENT: Care and education: Playgroup leader and part-time NVQ assessor.

FUTURE: Care and education: Continue as a Playgroup leader and have enrolle
Foundation Degree in Early Years at my local FE college.

You may have found yourself reflecting on the different options and possibilities that have been available to you at times in your own career and those which you consider to be open to you now. As we have seen, there are now clearer progression routes for early years practitioners' career development than at any other time in our history. Current options might include taking or progressing along a vocationally related route via NVQs/SVQs, or enrolling for a Foundation Degree with possible progression to Qualified Teacher Status (QTS). More recently, a new professional route has opened up, which we discuss below.

## The role of the Senior Practitioner

In 2001, following consultation within the sector and training providers, the DfES published a 'Statement of Requirement' (DfES 2001b), which set out the content and delivery of Early Years Sector-Endorsed Foundation Degrees (EYSEFD) leading to the new role of Senior Practitioner (SP). This was to provide a new professional level for practitioners engaged in the care and education of young children who wished to continue working directly with children, rather than moving into the position of manager or on to teacher training. This Foundation Degree could also lead to QTS through employment-based and part-time routes. The Early Years Sector-Endorsed Foundation Degree is aimed at practitioners with considerable skills and experience but whose level of formal qualifications may be relatively low and is designed to allow practitioners to continue working whilst studying for higher-level qualifications. Thus it could help the sector retain talented and experienced practitioners, whilst also providing a career progression route not previously available. This would be achieved through part-time study routes, flexible modes of delivery, recognition of work-based learning and prior study and broad-based academic learning.

> It will be a badge of professional excellence and can act as a springboard for those who want to progress towards qualified teacher status as an early years specialist.
>
> (DfES Press Notice 2001/0352)

The 'Statement of Requirement' represents the sector's recommended content for inclusion in any qualification that prepares people for recognition as a Senior Practitioner and is used by universities and partner institutions, such as Further Education Colleges, to design their Foundation Degrees if they wish to achieve Recognition Status. This status is approved and monitored by the DfES. At the time of writing, these degrees are available in England and are offered in Wales and Northern Ireland, funded by the relevant funding councils and subject to the devolved administration arrangements.

The introduction of the Senior Practitioner (SP) role recognises the importance of those working with young children being trained to high professional standards, and that training and qualifications should support the development of an integrated sector. In January 2004 a DfES Senior Practitioner Working Group (SPWG) was established to develop a definition of the Senior Practitioner role, to source case studies and to work towards promoting the SP role within the sector. The group is made up of representatives from the DfES, HEI Providers of EYSEFD, sector organisations such as SkillsActive, NDNA, NCMA and Topss, and other interested parties such as GTCE, NHSU and Unison.

The SP definition shown below is on the Sure Start website.

A Senior Practitioner is a reflective, experienced professional who:
- understands and demonstrates high quality practice;
- integrates this with appropriate research and theoretical knowledge;
- is able to apply this to enhance her/his own personal, professional practice and the professional development of others;
- contributes to improvement and innovation within a setting; and
- can lead by example in a variety of settings.

(www.surestart.gov.uk)

An outcome of the working group will be a document to communicate this definition to employers, prospective students and other interested parties to explain how Senior Practitioner status is awarded, what it means in the workplace and what a Senior Practitioner can do.

What is less clear is how this role links to government proposals 'for a new profession combining learning with care, along the lines of the continental "pedagogue" model' (HM Treasury 2004: 46), for which new training is envisaged.

So, what do all these developments mean in practice? This will depend on your setting, your job and the age range that you work with, and your ambitions and intentions, as we discuss in the next section.

## Your professional development

In the past in many parts of the childcare and education sector, career routes were limited. During the 1990s, six separate workforce surveys highlighted a growing workforce increasingly expected to operate at a professional level, but at the same time not well qualified. Abbott and Hevey (2001) identified three types of reason why the sector is perceived as under-trained and under-valued:

- Training is often short-term, low level and not part of a coherent course and therefore does not provide a basis for progressing to higher-level qualifications.
- Insufficient resources – the size of many early years settings means that many practitioners have to fund themselves on a low income.
- Issues relating to availability and flexibility in options and access.

A 'climbing frame' rather than a ladder analogy has been used to present progression from basic to higher-level qualifications in the early years sector. Early years workers enter the climbing frame at different points and have often gained experience and qualifications in unrelated fields (Abbott and Hevey 2001). As we have discussed in this chapter, new opportunities are opening up for improving skills, transferring job roles, for example into teaching or social work, and for progression to higher-level qualifications. These include:

Foundation Degrees;

Early Childhood Studies Degrees;

S/NVQs at level 4;

Early years routes into teaching;

Leadership and management training;

New roles within the sector.

It seems likely that change will continue rapidly for some time to come (Moss 2003). Given this changing context, it is likely that your future professional development will need to encompass additional training and qualifications and opportunities to engage in multi-agency working in order to reflect this change.

In the final activity for this chapter we encourage you to review your own professional development and consider any implications for you and your workplace.

## Activity 1.3 My professional development

Now think about your own professional experience. Choose a recent period of your professional life and write a paragraph or two describing your role and the ways that you carry it out. Then highlight places where you think you might begin to develop your role.

In your account you may have noted how you acquired your current knowledge and skills, perhaps 'intuitively' through years of practice or within a 'community of practice'. You may have noted the influence of parents and families of the children you have encountered on your professional journey. More recently it is likely that your role has been affected by explicit policies and priorities in your setting, which in turn will have been influenced by national policies. You may have recently undertaken or be considering formal learning opportunities such as studying for a Foundation Degree. You may have also noted possible obstacles to your professional development, such as difficulties in funding your studies.

We return to your professional learning and development in Chapter 5.

## Review

We need a new type of worker for these services: a worker who can combine many tasks and work with the whole child and her family; a worker who is a reflective practitioner, able to think and act for herself, rather than a technician trained to do as she is told; a worker on a par with teachers in terms of training and employment conditions.

(Moss 2003: 5)

In this chapter we have outlined possible future changes for early years practitioners and the children and families who use care and education services. We cannot be sure what these changes will be, but we, can be sure that change is happening in this sector and that it will continue, and that there will be increasing movement and flexibility across job roles, settings and services. This will require new forms of training and qualifications, like the new Foundation Degrees, to bring together practice and more formal academic learning. Practitioners working with young children and their families will need to be trained to high professional standards, whether through training in the workplace or through routes leading to more formal qualifications. We wish you well on this exciting journey towards a new professionalism.

## Questions for reflection

1 How do you think the changes and developments outlined in this chapter will impact on your current and future work roles?

2 What steps will you need to take to keep abreast of these changes?

3 In what ways do you think the changes described will affect the families and children you work with?

# References

Abbott, L. and Hevey, D. (2001) 'Training to work in the early years: developing the climbing frame', in Pugh, G. (ed.) *Contemporary Issues in the Early Years: Working Collaboratively for Children*, 3rd edn, London: Paul Chapman Publishing, pp. 179–93.

Atkinson, M., Wilkin, M., Stott, A., Doherty, P. and Kinder, K. (2002) *Multi-Agency Working: A Detailed Study*, Slough: National Foundation for Educational Research.

Department for Education and Skills (DfES) (2001a) *Schools: Building on Success*, London: HMSO http://www.dfes.gov.uk/everychildmatters/ (accessed April 2005).

Department for Education and Skills (DfES) (2001b) *Early Years Sector-Endorsed Foundation Degree: Statement of Requirement*, London: HMSO.

Department for Education and Skills (DfES) Press Notice 2001/0352 (1 October 2001) http://www.dfes.gov.uk/pns/DisplayPN.cgi?pn_id=2001_0352 (accessed April 2005).

Department for Education and Skills (DfES)/Department of Health (DH)(2003a) *Together From the Start – Practical guidance for professionals working with disabled children (birth to third birthday) and their families*, Executive summary, London: DfES Publications.

Department for Education and Skills (DfES) (2003b) *Every Child Matters*, London: DfES.

Department for Education and Skills (DfES) (2004a) *Professional Standards for Higher Level Teaching Assistants, September 2003*, London: Teacher Training Agency.

Department for Education and Skills (DfES)/National College for School Leadership (NCSL) (2004b) *National Professional Qualification in Integrated Centre Leadership*, London: National College for School Leadership.

HM Treasury (2004) in conjunction with Department for Education and Skills (DfES), Department for Work and Pensions (DWP), Department for Trade and Industry (DTI), *Choice for Parents, the Best Start for Children: a ten year strategy for childcare*, London: HMSO, www.surestart.gov.uk/aboutsurestart/strategy/ (accessed April 2005).

LTS Scotland (2004) *Care and Learning for Children from Birth to Three* [online], http://www.LTScotland.org.uk (accessed April 2005).

Moss, P. (2003) *Beyond Caring: the Case for Reforming the Childcare and Early Years Workforce*, London: Daycare Trust, The National Childcare Campaign.

National Assembly for Wales, Learning Wales (2004) *A Foundation Phase in Wales: A Draft Framework for Children's Learning* [online], http:www. learning.wales.gov.uk/foundationphase (accessed April 2005).

Qualifications and Curriculum Authority (QCA) (1999) *Early Years, Education, Childcare and Playwork Sector: A framework of nationally accredited qualifications*, London: Qualifications and Curriculum Authority.

Scottish Social Services Council (2004) *Qualifications Criteria for Phase Two Registrants – Early Education and Childcare Workers* [online], http://www. sssc.uk.com/SSSC.Web/Documents/QUALIFICATION%20CRITERIA.pdf (accessed April 2005).

Smith, M. (2003) *Draft Report on Occupational Mapping of the Early Years Care and Education Sector in the United Kingdom*, unpublished paper, FutureWise Solutions Ltd.

Sproule, A. (2004) 'A quality curriculum in the early years: A Northern Ireland Perspective', paper delivered at 14th Annual Conference on Quality in Early Childhood Education: *Quality curricula: the Influence of Policy and Praxis*, University of Malta, 1–14 September.

Sure Start Unit (2002) *Birth to Three Matters: A framework to support children in their earliest years*, London: Department for Education and Skills (DfES).

Sylva, K., Melhuish, E., Sammons, P., Siraj-Blatchford, I., Taggart, B. and Elliot, K. (2003) *The Effective provision of Pre-School Education (EPPE) Project: Findings from the Pre-School Period: Summary of findings*, London: Institute of Education/Sure Start.

## Further reading

Muijs, D. Aubrey, C., Harris, A. and Briggs, M (2004) 'How do they manage? a review of research on leadership in early childhood', *Journal of Early Childhood Research*, 2 (2), 157–69.

O'Keefe, J. and Tait, K. (2004) 'An examination of the UK Early Years Foundation Degree and the evolution of Senior Practitioners – enhancing work-based practice by engaging in reflective and critical thinking', *International Journal of Early Years Education*, 12 (1), 25–41.

Pugh, G. (2001) 'A policy for early childhood services', in Pugh, G. (ed.) *Contemporary Issues in the Early Years: Working Collaboratively for Children*, 3rd edn, London: Paul Chapman Publishing, pp. 9–22.

Rodd, J. (1998) *Leadership in Early Childhood: the pathway to professionalism*, 2nd edn, Buckingham: Open University Press.

## Website references

http://www.ncsl.org.uk – for information on National Professional Qualification in Integrated Centres Leadership Programme.

www.teachernet.gov.uk – for information relating to achieving Qualified Teacher Status.

www.dfes.gov.uk – links to *Every Child Matters* and Children's Workforce Unit (commoncore).

www.surestart.gov.uk – links to Early Years Sector-Endorsed Foundation Degrees; Statement of Requirement and Senior Practitioner role; 10-year strategy for early years and childcare.

# 2 Working with Other Professionals

## Introduction

Early years practitioners take on many roles and responsibilities related to the provision of care and education for children, which involves collaboration with parents and carers, and liaison with other child- and family-focused professionals. Many early years practitioners bring experience and intuitive understandings to their work with children. The great majority are women, and many are parents and bring a great deal of their personality and individuality to the work they do. Moyles (2001) suggests that 'the people working in this area often display a "deep and sound commitment" which can amount to feelings of "passion" for the work and the role' (2001: 81). Early years practitioners are required to take on a vast range of issues and develop appropriate skills and knowledge through a range of different learning experiences, which include training and further study, if they want to provide the best possible service for the young children in their care. Much of this will involve working with others – colleagues, parents, carers and children. We begin this chapter by investigating teams – the people in them and how they can work well together. We then look at ways in which communication and listening skills can be made more effective. We explore ways of developing mutual regard within early years settings;

in particular, by ensuring that we foster the right ethos and environment in our settings; and pay attention to issues of equality and empowerment.

Most roles in care and education are carried out within a social matrix of personal interaction and formal and informal working relationships. Our ability to do this well is, to a considerable extent, dependent upon how we relate to work colleagues and parents and carers. Some teams gel together easily and enable everyone to make a contribution; others run into problems that may have an impact on the performance of the team and individuals and on the care and education of children.

## Professional behaviour

It is possible to identify two basic aspects of professional behaviour. The first is *personal* qualities – professional attributes that are of particular value in education and care settings, such as commitment, conscientiousness and humanity. The second aspect relates to competence, knowledge and specific skills developed through professional practice. These tend to be used and practised over time so that they can be effectively employed with different children across a range of contexts. These include valuing children, observing and knowing about how children learn and about resources that help children grow and learn. However, professionalism often means that a practitioner is able to move thinking and practice beyond what may normally (or naturally) be done by those working outside the profession and/or field of knowledge. There is evidence that those working with children tend not to 'sing their own praises' enough. Brown and McIntyre (1993) found that educational practitioners 'routinely achieve a great deal which they so take for granted as to not even notice' (1993: 110).

We need to consider how adults learn in the workplace and how professionalism can be developed. Our interactions with children and their parents should provide us with opportunities to improve our practice. Children's reactions and our observations of their progress will enable us to gauge if we are being successful. Some parents will give us helpful feedback about their children's experiences. Workplace colleagues, too, can provide invaluable support and comment, especially if they feel they can take on the role of 'critical friend'. Training and study are also important means by which we can better understand what happens at work and take steps to increase our professional effectiveness.

## Roles and responsibilities within teams

The terms 'roles' and 'responsibilities' refer to the positions held by people within an organisation and the activities they carry out. So, in early years settings, a person's *role* may be that of centre manager, team leader, a team member in different settings such as a reception class or a parent-helper. That person's *responsibilities*, on the other hand, will vary in relation to the setting and her or his position within the organisation: for example, a centre manager's responsibilities may include the efficient management of the staff and resources; oversight of children's experience and learning; as well as tasks as varied as risk assessment of the building, development planning, liaison with other agencies and child protection.

For many people, one way of identifying their role and responsibilities may be through a contract or job description. For less formal work arrangements, however, there may be policies or protocols that explain roles within a setting. A nursery nurse may have a job description which includes responsibility for a number of children, looking after specific areas of the nursery, setting up and clearing away, making observations and keeping records. The following activity invites you to reflect on your daily work, and the role and responsibilities you undertake.

### Activity 2.1 Your daily work

Think about your role and responsibilities within your team or setting. Make a list of these. Opposite each one, indicate whether or not it is included in your job description or whether you have chosen to do it. Is there any formal identification of the extent, boundaries and responsibilities of your role? If your role is identified less formally, how do you know the extent and limits of your role and the responsibilities that fall to you?

Defining the roles and responsibilities within any organisation or setting is an important part of good management. Each member of a working team needs to know her or his role and place within the team. The expectations that others, including management, have of each team member's role are important in helping individuals to understand the requirements of their job. Confusion, duplication, omission and ineffective delivery of services will often be the result when team members are unsure of their role, its purpose, boundaries and their responsibilities.

## Working in teams

Early years practitioners do not work in isolation: whatever the context, there will be links and relationships with others. Some professional contacts may be easily recognised as operating within the spheres of education, health or social services. However, increasingly, many early years practitioners and other professionals operate under a multi-disciplinary umbrella within an holistic environment – for example, in Children's Centres and SureStart groups. In the consultation document *Every Child Matters* (DfES 2003) this approach is being strongly proposed to ensure that children receive 'joined up care and education'. This means that the services available to children and their parents and carers work together to ensure the needs of the child as a whole are met and are not received piecemeal.

Whether you work in your own home as a childminder caring for one child, or in a large day-care centre, nursery or primary school caring for large numbers of children, you will have links with a variety of people and agencies because of your work with young children.

Figure 2.1 shows some groups and people you may come into contact with in the course of your work. You may find it interesting to highlight those you interact with regularly and think about others not included in this diagram. Each worker in a setting may belong to a slightly different core team, depending on their role, the children in their care and the type of setting.

It is also quite possible for parents to become part of the early years team as many parents work as volunteers; indeed, some nurseries and playgroups rely on them to help staff their settings on a rota basis. These parents then become

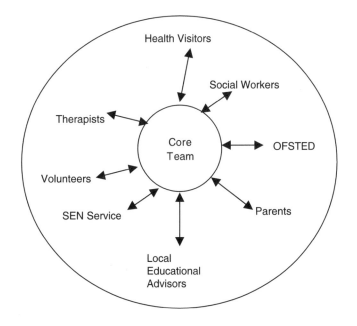

**Figure 2.1** Team relationships

members of the team, but not necessarily the core team. A childminder working in her/his own home, caring for only one child, may view the parent or carer with whom he/she has daily contact as a core member of her/his 'team'. For all settings, there will be a range of agencies and people that could be considered part of the wider team. These wider links are essential in providing advice, security and support, but developing a working relationship with these people is not always easy and can take time to establish.

## The multi-disciplinary team

As we saw in Chapter 1, multi-agency ways of working are being encouraged and developed to provide holistic and joined-up services for children and families (DFES 2003). As we move towards such integrated services, it is increasingly likely that your perception of your daily work may not be the same as that of your colleagues. One of the features of early years settings is diversity. In multi-disciplinary teams, practitioners will often come to their setting having attained different levels of professional competence and from a variety of fields – social work, education, health, business and administration. As a result, each team member sees the world from a different perspective because of her or his own specialist training and experience and is in a position to make a unique contribution to the work of the team.

However, there are also potential challenges if team members have different priorities or conflicting points of view. Working together effectively to meet the needs of children and families means being prepared to listen to different interpretations of what is happening, and to modify practice if appropriate. It is vital, therefore, that professionals have regular opportunities to share their knowledge, values and beliefs, and to develop sound understanding and knowledge of what children need to grow and learn. This requires good communication skills by all.

## Communicating with others

Communication within early years settings is fundamental and, as Rodd (1998) suggests:

> Working in an early years setting, whether it is large or small, involves many interactions between adults and other adults and between adults and children. These may be informal or more formal. But these interactions are regarded as the building blocks of the service and the outcome of the service.
>
> (Rodd 1998: 42)

Most definitions of communication suggest that it involves:

- the exchange of information, ideas or feelings;
- more than one person;
- writing, gesture, speech and other means, including electronic devices;
- information or ideas being willingly or unwillingly given and/or received.

Effective communication is part of good teamwork and depends on being able to share successes and to handle conflict openly and fairly. Everyone in the team should feel that they are able to contribute to the smooth working of the setting and that they can voice differing views. It is essential, therefore, that the setting fosters the kind of ethos and atmosphere that enables such exchanges to take place: '... better relationships are considered to develop out of feelings of safety, security and trust and are characterised by openness and sharing between people' (Rodd 1998: 42).

Developing this trust depends on team members' capacity to communicate well with each other. As Cowley (1995) suggests:

> ... talking with other people is a complex task combining the giving and receiving of a range of messages, values and attitudes, not only through words but also through the looks, the gestures and the tones we use. We all communicate in different ways when we are with people, and it is important for us to have some awareness of the ways in which we communicate and how that feels to others, so that we are better and more clearly understood.
>
> (Cowley 1995: 42)

In our everyday lives we tend to think of communicating as natural and instinctive, and something we do not need to work at, but the reality is – we do.

## Activity 2.2 *Effective communication*

How often do you think about the effectiveness of your communication skills? Are you aware of times when you have not communicated effectively?

Think about a recent occasion in your setting, in carrying out your work or team role, when you were part of an effective communication. Think about the context, the dialogue, the body language and the outcome. Make a list of the points that made the communication effective.

Now think about a recent occasion – again, in your work or team role – when you were part of a communication that was less effective. Think about this in as much detail as you can. What contributed towards its ineffectiveness?

Good communication skills – expressing what you want to say, and how you interact and say it – are central to effective working. These include:

- listening to exactly what is being said, and not what you think was being said or what you wanted to hear;
- being able to express yourself well;
- engaging positively with your audience;
- maintaining eye contact and providing positive feedback (verbal and/or non-verbal).

Some of the barriers to effective communication are:

- not listening;
- failing to show that you are listening;
- inappropriate body responses;
- no feedback system (e.g. nodding, agreeing);
- talking too quickly;
- giving too much information too quickly;
- not offering information in a logical or sequential manner;
- not ensuring understanding;
- failing to eliminate distractions, e.g. the television;
- lack of clarity in speech, e.g. mumbling;
- using jargon and inappropriate language.

## Effective listening

Understanding ourselves as listeners is crucial to our role as effective early years practitioners, and considering the points listed above (and the opposites of each statement) provides a useful basis from which to consider how good we are at listening.

> In interpersonal interaction the process of listening is of crucial importance. For communication to occur between individuals there must be both the sending (encoding) and the receiving (decoding) of signals from one person to another. . . . In order to respond appropriately to others, it is necessary to pay attention to the messages which they are sending and relate future responses to these messages.
>
> (Hargie et al. 1994: 194)

**Activity 2.3 How do I listen?**

Listening implies that you respond and act upon what you hear as you listen. It goes beyond just hearing, and necessitates action. You must have been involved in conversations when you were aware that the other person was not listening to what you were saying.

■ How did that make you feel?

■ How did you know they were not listening?

■ What is the difference between simply hearing what has been said to you and listening to the other person with the intention of fully understanding the feelings behind what is being said?

■ How do you check that what you are hearing is really what the other person is intending you to hear, and vice versa?

■ How do you demonstrate to the other person that you are really listening to what he or she is saying?

An important aspect of being a good listener is understanding what an active process listening is and how much effort is involved. People often assume that listening is a passive task, but in fact it requires that you search for clues from the speaker through their body language and intonation as well as listening to what is being said. Being insensitive to others, and not really listening to them with an open mind, can lead to conflict and tension that militate against effective practice. Tensions within a team are easily passed on to others, and can cause serious problems if allowed to fester. It is essential that a setting is a place in which team members are able to share ideas in a non-threatening environment. Developing a positive ethos in which this can happen, and which allows conflicting ideas to be aired, will enable thinking and practice to grow.

## Developing a positive ethos

Valuing individuals' contributions, and nurturing respectful relationships between colleagues, are important factors in developing a spirit of mutual regard in an early years setting. They are also fundamental to good practice, and placing people at the heart of your setting will enhance not only outcomes but processes, too.

A setting has achieved a positive ethos when:

- team members are able to work well with and alongside colleagues, parents and carers;
- there is an open and honest sharing of information;
- there are clear lines of communication;
- individuals are confident that their voice will be heard.

A positive ethos fosters equality and empowers the people who work there and reflects the distinctive beliefs and understandings that underpin practice, fuel ideas and direct the ways in which individuals interact with others. Developing an effective and distinctive ethos in your setting will not happen overnight and depends on:

- good staff relationships;
- shared philosophy about working with children in the early years;
- respect for each individual, whether child, parent or colleague;
- clear guidelines and policies;
- a clear staff-development policy.

---

### Activity 2.4  Your setting's ethos

What kind of ethos do you think exists in your setting? Note your responses to the following questions:

What do you think are the values that underpin your setting?

Does the ethos of your setting reflect the community and location in which it is placed? How do you know this?

Whose values inform that ethos?

How do you ensure that the ethos reflects *all* values and beliefs within your team, setting and community?

What family or community participation systems do you have in place?

How do these relate to the ethos of your setting?

---

All practitioners in a setting need to develop a set of core values within which they can engage honestly with the everyday experiences of those they work with. Jeffs and Smith (1999: 81) have identified the following core values:

*Respect for persons* – recognising the dignity and uniqueness of every human being, and behaving in ways that convey that respect.

*The promotion of well-being* – working for the welfare of all and seeking to further human flourishing.

*Truth* – having a commitment to teach and embrace truthfulness; being open, in dialogue, to what others have to say; and confronting falsehood wherever it is found.

*Democracy* – believing that all human beings should enjoy the chance of self-government, or autonomy; and seeking within practice to offer opportunities for people to enjoy and exercise democratic rights.

*Fairness and equality* – working towards relationships that are characterised by fairness; confronting discrimination in the pursuit of promoting equality; and evaluating actions with regard to the way people are treated, the opportunities that are open to them and the rewards they receive.

It is important to recognise that your setting's ethos will evolve and change to reflect changing circumstances. Your beliefs about childcare and education may change over time, as you interact with others who have different viewpoints and as you learn more about how children learn. Your practice may change as a response to the cultural diversity of the children in your setting and society, or in response to legislation on inclusion such as the Special Educational Needs and Disability Act (SENDA) 2001. Developing a climate that is safe for all to participate in and to share ideas is an important factor in bringing about changes in thinking. So how do we create an environment that can support this kind of change?

## Environment

The environment of a setting reflects its ethos. The word 'environment' can describe a setting's physical, social, emotional or political context. It is important that we attend to every aspect, as each impacts upon the other: the physical environment will influence the way we feel and think about the activities we are engaged in; this in turn affects our social relationships which, in turn, affect the way we view and implement our practice. As we discuss in Chapter 4, a setting that cares about the expectations of the children, parents and carers, visitors and outside agencies it caters for will use its environment to celebrate the successes and progress of the children, communicate pride in what it does, and disseminate useful, clear information. The way we move around our setting reflects our thinking about the way we work and how children learn best. Giving consideration to developing a healthy ethos can avoid the build-up of tension.

## Equality

Ensuring equality involves the provision of equality of opportunity and access and involves combating discrimination on the grounds of class, culture, race, religion, gender, sexuality, physical and mental disabilities, and age. Discrimination creates inequalities in society, through a process which allows prejudical attitudes, including stereotyping and devaluing people because of their perceived differences, to operate unchallenged – a process that serves to take away people's rights and 'legitimise' unequal treatment. Can you think of an instance in your own life where you experienced discrimination? How did it make you feel?

In any early years setting, there will be diversity among staff and children. Our individual and collective responses to such diversity will depend on our perceptions of ourselves and of others, based on our view of the world. This is often the result of early experiences we have had or the opinions of others taken on board without analysis. Sometimes stereotypical views contain an element of truth, but this may have been distorted or buried under a layer of unthinking assumptions. They may also be 'self-fulfilling prophecies' in which we select the facts that support our idea of things and ignore those that contradict it. They can hide the real individual from our view. These views can create barriers, excluding and disempowering people because of who *we think* they are rather than who they really are.

## Empowerment

Empowerment involves the distribution of power so that people are able to take control of their lives. Having power is about having the ability to make choices. A setting which wants to empower people, staff, parents and children will recognise the need to share and even cede power to others, enabling them to make choices and informed decisions with respect to the setting. Penn says:

> . . . where hierarchical systems exist and so much power is invested in individual managers, then the quality of the management is important. A good manager, who works democratically with her staff and is an experienced practitioner, can influence the practice in the nursery. A poor manager, by the same token, has an adverse effect.
>
> (Penn 1998: 36)

Even in a home environment, where you may work as a childminder or nanny, there will be elements of power relations that affect the parents, carers and children with whom you interact. How decisions are made and communicated to those they affect is important in developing an open and positive ethos.

There is evidence that the high expectations that are now placed on all may have given rise to an increase in harrying management styles, and even bullying approaches, within institutions and teams (Scase 2002). There is a delicate balance between expecting a lot from people and expecting too much. The latter can lead to feelings of inadequacy and a reduction in confidence. You may have had personal experience of workplaces and work teams that enable or restrain the way you prefer to carry out your role.

The strengths in your setting should be celebrated; the weak areas need thought and action. The way people are managed reflects the values and ethos that management holds. If people are respected, the experience will empower them. On the other hand, if people are dealt with harshly or unfairly, then respect will probably not develop, making for an unhappy workforce and a strained environment which children will easily sense. Managing conflict sensitively enables issues to be resolved so that people are not damaged and communication lines are kept open.

As people come and go, and as children grow and change, so the dynamics of a setting are constantly changing. It is important to avoid complacency. A strength of any secure and dynamic setting is that it is always revisiting and reflecting on its practices, management, policies, provision and the ethos it supports.

## Review

In this chapter we have explored some of the important dimensions that need to be acknowledged and understood about working with other professionals. Effective communication, the development of shared understandings about young children and the importance of your own skills in creating a positive ethos and environment have all been a focus of this chapter. Regular review and reflection on the effectiveness of your provision and ways of working will ensure that practice does not stultify and that disquiet does not fester. Celebrating successes and embracing diversity and inclusion will greatly enhance the children's experiences and the quality of your experience as an early years practitioner.

## Questions for reflection

1 How does your role and the manner in which you carry it out contribute to your setting and enhance its effectiveness?

2 How good a communicator are you?

3 How are new people and families introduced to your setting and its ethos?

4 What areas do you think your setting does best and what areas are there for development?

## References

Brown, S.A. and McIntyre, D. (1993) *Making Sense of Teaching*, Buckingham: Open University Press.

Cowley, L. (1995) *Managing to Change*, Training materials for staff in day-care centres for young children, Module 3, Partnership with Parents, London: National Children's Bureau.

Department for Education and Skills (DfES) (2003) *Every Child Matters*, London: DfES.

Hargie, O., Saunders, C. and Dickson, D. (1994) *Social Skills in Interpersonal Communication*, 3rd edn, London: Routledge.

Jeffs, T. and Smith, M. (1999) *Informal Education*, 2nd edn, Education Now Publishing Co-operative.

Moyles, J. (2001) 'Passion, paradox and professionalism in early years education', *Early Years*, **21** (2), 81–95.

Penn, H. (1998) 'Facing some difficulties', in Abbott, L. and Pugh, G. (eds) *Training to Work in the Early Years: Developing the climbing frame*, Buckingham: Open University Press.

Rodd, J. (1998) *Leadership in Early Childhood: The pathway to professionalism*, 2nd edn, Buckingham: Open University Press.

Scase, R. (2002) 'Bullies who let Britain down', *The Observer*, 2 June, p. 8.

## Further reading

Anning, A. and Edwards, A. (2004) 'Creating contexts for professional development in educare', in Miller, L. and Devereux, J. (eds) *Supporting children's learning in the early years*, London: David Fulton Publishers.

Read, M. and Rees, M. (2003) 'Working in teams in early years settings', in Devereux, J. and Miller, L. (eds) *Working with children in the early years*, London: David Fulton Publishers.

Smith, A. and Langston, A. (1999) *Managing Staff in Early Years Settings*, London: Routledge.

## Useful websites

www.early-years-nto.org.uk/ – links to different career pathways and courses for professional development (accessed April 2005).

www.dfes.gov.uk – links to *Every Child Matters* and ideas of multi-professional work (accessed April 2005).

www.surestart.gov.uk – links to Early Years Sector-Endorsed Foundation Degrees, and professional development (accessed April 2005).

# **3** Partnership with Parents

## By the end of this chapter you will have:

- developed your understanding of the importance of children's early learning in the home and how practitioners can draw on this information to support children's learning and development in their settings;

- explored practices that foster parental partnership and identified the benefits for children, parents and practitioners;

- recognised the consequences for practice of change, and particularly transitions, in children's lives;

- examined different types of partnership and related these to your own practice in your setting.

## Introduction

'Partnership with parents' is a familiar phrase in care and education and all early years settings wish for a close, two-way relationship with children's parents and carers. However, the way in which a partnership is conceptualised and made workable varies considerably: what is deemed appropriate in one area of the UK may not be considered suitable in another; and what is seen as innovative practice in one setting may be seen as commonplace elsewhere. This chapter aims to develop your understanding of what partnership might mean, how it can be interpreted, and how it might be put into practice. It provides examples of partnership in action, and offers a framework for understanding the range of partnership practices that can be found in today's early years settings.

# Early learning

Young children learn a great deal before they attend early years settings or begin formal schooling: they learn from the many adults and children with whom they come into contact, and from observing the stream of life around them. Indeed, there is much in the home, the community and the world at large that feeds a baby's sensory learning long before the baby can crawl and speak. Once babies can move about with some independence and interact spontaneously with objects and people, the opportunities for learning are further increased. The experiences and opportunities for learning that are available to an individual child vary considerably, and are influenced by a family's social background, economic resources, and cultural and religious affiliations.

Education has traditionally been seen as the preserve of those who have been trained to work with children – particularly teachers in schools. Indeed, many parents still do not think of themselves as 'educators'. However, parents, as well as siblings and other family members, are responsible for teaching children essential skills such as eating, washing, going to the toilet, talking and walking. Irrespective of a family's social, economic, religious or cultural background, they will also support children's intellectual and social development. Parents and families teach by example and through their attitudes: how to express emotion; how to respond to other people; how to behave 'appropriately' as a boy or a girl; how to love and care for others; and how to make sense of the world. A family's values, beliefs, fears and prejudices will, at least initially, be passed on to children.

# Parents' wishes

Some parents spend a considerable amount of time carefully considering who should look after their child and which early years setting or school the child should attend. For other parents, their income, location or personal circumstances may mean they have little or no choice.

Researchers at the University of Strathclyde carried out a survey of 91 parents in Glasgow to find out their preferences, beliefs, knowledge and expectations when choosing suitable early years provision (Foot *et al.* 2000). The considerations that parents regarded as the most important were the happiness of a child and safety and security, followed by the quality of care and the attitudes of staff. The researchers found that parents prioritised similar considerations irrespective of socio-economic status and where they lived. They also found that preferences changed as children grew older and approached formal schooling, when concern about educational progress increased.

Some parents may have definite expectations based on information provided by religious or community groups, the media, relatives and, perhaps most significantly, friends. Indeed, the research by the University of Strathclyde highlighted that parents rely heavily on information provided by friends in forming their opinions and making their decisions – this will be especially so if other sources of information are not easily accessible. Expectations may be based on their own educational experiences or may be influenced by the recent focus on literacy and numeracy in schools, and do not necessarily accord with what settings *actually* provide.

---

### Activity 3.1 Choosing a setting

How do parents make decisions with regard to your setting? What do they consider to be important for them and for their child? If possible during your working day, ask these questions of one or two parents, and make a note of their answers.

---

Although 'happiness of a child' and 'safety and security' feature highly in most parents' reasons for choice, some parents may assume that these are 'givens' and instead focus on other reasons for their choice of setting. Were you surprised by the answers the parents you asked gave you? Perhaps you feel you need to review how you provide information for parents and the kinds of information you provide.

## Facilitating change and transitions

Practitioners can help parents to make informed choices by providing them with relevant information. Most practitioners now prepare a range of printed material in different formats that provide information for parents about the setting, the staff, the routines, the curriculum and expectations. These are often translated into the languages spoken in the local community. In addition, parents are often sent letters telling them when a place is available and invited to visit on an informal basis to see for themselves what the setting will provide. Face-to-face contact and exchange are important as a means of backing up written information – particularly when parents are encouraged to ask their own questions.

Home visits by practitioners to meet children and their parents 'on their own territory' have become commonplace and enable practitioners to gather information about the child and their family backgrounds and circumstances. For parents, they can provide the opportunity to ask questions in an informal and relaxed atmosphere, and to receive reassurance that their concerns and the needs of their children will be taken into account. Where financial constraints mean that home visiting is not a viable option or where parents are reluctant to accept a visit from a practitioner because it is perceived as prying into home circumstances, some settings choose to run induction days or use videos to provide information for parents and children and support the process of transition.

Gathering information about children before they attend on a regular basis helps practitioners prepare for and facilitate children's transition to their new setting. Such information can include details about their background and learning and language experiences, as well as basic information about their habits, including sleeping patterns and practices, eating, toileting, dressing, and conventions relating to touch and contact. Initially children may become distressed or embarrassed if they are asked to do things very differently from the way they do them at home. Gregory (1996) argues that it is important for practitioners to recognise the discontinuities as well as the continuities between home and setting so that they can plan, prepare for and support children's learning and development. For children with a learning difficulty or disability, sharing information is also of paramount importance.

## Activity 3.2 Working together

Read the following case study, in which Mark's mother reflects on her son's experience of starting at a local pre-school playgroup. As you read, consider the following questions:

How was Mark supported in the pre-school playgroup?

What were the professionals' attitudes towards his difficulty?

How was his assessment useful?

What were his needs?

How was his communication facilitated?

How did his mother value her communication with the professionals?

## Case Study: Mark at pre-school playgroup

It was obvious when Mark started playgroup that there were going to be some difficulties. We had noticed, just after his second birthday, that his language perhaps wasn't as developed as it should have been . . . he certainly didn't seem to be communicating very well. He didn't have any way of showing us what he needed, what he required, what he wanted, and he was very frustrated. He had an assessment from the health visitor, who thought that perhaps he was autistic to some degree. He was seen then by a speech therapist, who decided that he wasn't autistic but he obviously did have a speech and language problem.

So when he started playgroup it was obvious that the staff would have a little bit more difficulty with him perhaps than the 'average child' that went to the playgroup. They were very supportive. They knew of his problems before he started, in the sense that I'd shared all the information that I knew. The speech therapist had been to see the playgroup staff, and gave them some work to do with him. I had copies of this work as well at home. They knew what I was doing with Mark at home, and I knew what they were doing with him in playgroup. It was difficult for him to communicate with them as to what he wanted. For example, if he needed to go to the toilet at home, he could just go. But at playgroup it wasn't that easy. He had to go through a door and down some stairs. So, he had to be able to tell them, in a sociably acceptable way, that he needed the toilet.

The speech therapist had an idea that perhaps we could go and learn a sign language called Makaton, and the playgroup set up for me and three playgroup leaders to go to some evening classes to learn it. It was of great benefit to Mark. He could tell them that he wanted a drink, and that he needed to go to the toilet. He could tell them whether he was happy or whether he was sad. There was so much more he could do. It was hard for him to learn, but he was patient, and they were very patient with him. They'd let him know if he'd learnt new words, and I'd let them know if he knew a new sign on how to get things. He still had quite a lot of difficulties, and they would communicate with me mostly on a day-to-day basis about how they'd got on with him.

Mark's successful transition and inclusion required professionals to collaborate with his mother as well as with each other, and they developed a 'partnership' relationship. They were all involved in supporting his smooth transition and removing his barriers to learning within the playgroup. Mark's mother had knowledge about him, which she was able to share and which the practitioners valued because it enabled them to support him effectively within the playgroup. There was a team approach to overcoming his barriers to participation and learning.

Meetings and discussions, either in the children's homes or at the setting, are good ways of gathering this important information. Some practitioners ask parents to help them compile a notebook, which includes information on the background and learning experiences of their children. This notebook is then added to, both by the children and the practitioners, and provides an ongoing record and celebration of the children's achievements. The notebook is an open record, and does not contain confidential or sensitive information that would need to be kept in a secure place.

The 'key-worker approach' used by many early years settings allows parents to feel that they are confiding in a trusted practitioner who is taking a special interest in their child. The practitioner holds group sessions with parents, which explore parents' understanding and expectations of, for example, play or behaviour, and provides opportunities for both practitioners and parents to exchange views.

## Making the transition to school

Working productively with others is crucial to the role of an early years practitioner. The relationships that practitioners form with children and their parents are vital in enabling children to learn and to be happy and to make successful transitions. Many children find the transition from home or an early years setting to school especially difficult. Children who are familiar with pre-school playgroups, day-care, childminders or nursery will gain some understanding of 'institutional life' and the routines that are associated with it, but this will not necessarily prepare them for the routines and structures of school. For some children, it will be their first experience of a substantial time away from home. For children whose families travel or move home frequently, starting at a new setting or school happens often and it doesn't necessarily get easier each time – this can be the experience of children whose parents are refugees or asylum seekers, travellers or living in temporary accommodation, or in the armed forces. Most settings and schools strive instinctively to help children feel valued; ensuring this happens is not straightforward.

> ### Activity 3.3 First time in school
>
> What aspects of school life do you think children find difficult to cope with when they start school? Make a list under the headings of 'setting', 'curriculum' and 'people'. What is the essential difference between an early years setting and a school setting?

Cleve *et al.* (1982) carried out a study of the transition from 'pre-school' to infant school in the 1980s which is still of relevance today. Their findings were based on visits to over 60 infant and first school classes, and a large number of early years providers. They interviewed teachers, head teachers, supervisors, pre-school playgroup leaders, childminders and parents and observed a

sample of children before and after starting school. They were especially interested in experiences that cause children to become distressed, withdrawn, irri-
table, aggressive or bewildered – all indications of children struggling to adjust
to an unfamiliar environment. The study found that children could be upset by
factors related to the setting: the size of the building; having too much room, or
too little room to move around in; being a long way from the toilets; having
new constraints imposed on their movement; and having to move in new
ways, such as lining up. Children could also be distressed by the curriculum:
the introduction of unfamiliar activities and the loss of familiar ones; a longer
day away from home; a day divided up into sessions; a loss of large-scale
movement activities; having new materials to handle; reduced freedom of
choice; time pressures and constraints, for example the risk of being 'the last
one' at getting dressed; and playtimes or lunchtimes. Children could be upset
by the people: much larger numbers of children around them, with many of
them bigger and older; unfamiliar adults; having less adult attention; being
treated as part of a group; and having fewer opportunities to interact with other
children (Cleve *et al.* 1982: 195–202).

## Working in partnership to support children's learning and development

Two-way communication between practitioners and parents is crucial to a
child's progress because it enables:

- seeing from different perspectives – the more objective view of the practitioner and the more subjective view of the parents and family can offer the
  child a balanced view of their own learning;

- making connections between the home and setting – enabling children to
  make links between their learning in both situations will help to stimulate
  enquiry and talk;

- drawing on parents' knowledge of their children – enables practitioners to
  make an informed and sensitive response to children's needs and interests;

- informing parents about what their children are doing and learning – when
  parents know and understand what their children have been doing, they are
  in a better position to support their learning;

- instilling confidence in both parents and practitioners – especially important where there might be a mismatch between parents' and practitioners'
  views or knowledge, for example of mathematics or information communication technology. Children will become confused if they receive very
  different messages from different adults.

Developing confidence is perhaps one of the most important steps towards developing successful partnerships. When we feel confident about what we are doing, we feel better able to communicate our understanding, answer questions and calm anxieties. We can also encourage parents to undertake activities at home that will support their children's learning and encourage parents and children to share home learning, including bringing in booklets, posters, artefacts, photographs and videos which can form the basis for discussion and activities. Lending materials such as 'toy libraries' and 'story sacks', which are themed to support different areas of the curriculum, can form bridges between learning in the home and the setting. Sessions in which parents are involved in making story sacks that reflect the interests and enthusiasms of their children will also support involvement in the setting and provide informal opportunities for discussion. The Basic Skills Agency (BSA 2003) undertakes a range of activities for adults in relation to mathematics, literacy and the use of ICT. Many of the BSA's initiatives focus on raising adults' achievements as well as encouraging parents to work with their children.

An ongoing dialogue and exchange about what children are doing and learning will also cement respect and trust. Some settings use a book that goes backwards and forwards between the home and a child's setting in which parents and practitioners briefly note the important things that happen that they feel the other should know about. This can help to avoid rushed or superficial exchanges at the beginning or end of the day. One father's comments on the process in his child's nursery are given in the following case study.

## Case Study: Lucy's day

What I really like are the comments in Lucy's 'take home book'. They help me make sense of Lucy's day. They help fill in the gaps – I know when she can't quite make things clear. They help me understand what she is trying to tell me and then I can talk to her properly. They're really practical too – for example, they mean I don't give her the same things to eat again, or we might play a game or sing a song that I know she has enjoyed. Sometimes, there are fantastic stories. We really love these, like Lucy being entranced watching the leaves fall.

Another important aspect of partnership is supporting parents in developing their understanding of the aims and ethos of a setting. Many settings provide workshop sessions for parents and encourage parents to work alongside their own and other children, to share their expertise or skills and to join in outings and visits. In describing the work at the Thomas Coram Centre, Duffy and Stillaway (2004) highlight the need for a respectful and ongoing dialogue with parents, especially when introducing new initiatives, and the delicate balance between changing a family's conceptions of what early education is about and respecting cultural difference.

Dowling (1995) has outlined seven recommended practices that are important in developing partnerships and enabling successful transitions between settings:

For all parents—
- to become more aware of the educational value of life in the home;
- to understand the significance of the playgroup, nursery and reception curriculum and how each contributes to their child's subsequent well-being and achievement.

For early years practitioners—
- to become familiar with the curriculum and organisation offered, and the expectations of children in reception classes;
- to identify sources of match and mismatch with their own provision.

For practitioners working in schools—
- to gain as full a picture as possible of each child's past experiences, interests and achievements prior to starting school;
- to recognise, respect and support the vital role that parents and carers play in their child's progress and development.

And for all parties—
- to recognise the value of working in harmony to support the child.

(Adapted from Dowling 1995: 19–20)

## Types of partnership

Over the years, writers have put forward models, frameworks and typologies for understanding the theoretical and practical dimensions of partnership. The curriculum guidance documents produced respectively for England, Northern Ireland, Scotland and Wales each contain guidance on how best to achieve a partnership with parents through practical means. It is also important to have a wider sense of the scope of partnership and the many different ways in which it can be expressed. Partnership practice tends to be formulated by professionals – by policy writers, early years specialists, educational theorists and practitioners – but rarely by parents themselves. Achieving effective partnership with parents is a challenge for all early years practitioners, and for many parents the partnership can be seen as one-sided – parents and children are expected to meet the expectations of the setting – but little account is taken of parents' views or preferences. So it is important to have a conception of partnership that goes beyond what professionals might feel is appropriate; a vision that leaves some space for creative and unexpected ideas from parents and children.

Pugh and De'Ath (1989) studied 130 nurseries, early years groups and centres. They developed a framework to help practitioners and parents think widely about partnership. They identified the five dimensions to parental involvement listed in Table 3.1.

**Table 3.1** Five dimensions to parental involvement

| Type of involvement | Characteristics |
| --- | --- |
| 1 Non-participation | Parents are not involved in their children's learning |
| *Active* | These parents are 'active' non-participants who decide not to be involved. They may be happy with what's on offer, or very busy at work, or want time away from their children. |
| *Passive* | These parents are 'passive' non-participants who would like to be involved, but may lack the confidence to do this, or may be unhappy with the form of partnership offered. |
| 2 Support | Parents support a setting 'from the outside' |
| | These parents become involved but only when invited, e.g. by attending events or providing money for learning resources. |
| 3 Participation | Parents participate in a setting 'from within' |
| *Parents as helpers* | These parents help in ways such as providing assistance on outings, supporting children's learning in the setting, or running a toy library. |
| *Parents as learners* | These parents attend workshops and parent education sessions. |
| 4 Partnership | Parents are involved in a working relationship with practitioners |
| | These parents' involvement is characterised by a shared sense of purpose and mutual respect. For example: |
| | Parents have equal access to information and records; |
| | Parents share in the diagnosis and assessment of their children; |
| | Parents share in the selection of practitioners; |
| | Parents are encouraged to become practitioners. |
| 5 Control | Parents determine and implement decisions |
| | These parents are ultimately responsible and accountable for the provision of the setting. |

In some early years settings it might not be considered appropriate to establish a form of partnership whereby parents are equal partners in the way that type 4 in the table defines, or for parents to assume control, as in type 5. Parents who are working or have other responsibilities may choose non-participation, but practitioners should be wary of equating this with a lack of interest in the setting or their children's learning. In defining the kinds of partnership that should be associated with any one particular early years setting, it is important for practitioners to have a good sense of parents' capacity and desire to enter into such partnerships. Practitioners also need to be realistic about the time and resources available to them. Parents will be disappointed if professionals make promises that they are unable to fulfil.

## Review

In this chapter we have outlined some of the ways in which settings can establish and maintain dialogue and collaboration with parents to support children's successful transitions and their learning and development. Ball (1994) considers partnership to be about 'balance', which draws attention to the ways in which the needs, ideas and limitations of parents, children and practitioners must be considered. Practitioners in different settings will have strong feelings about the kinds of partnership that are most supportive of their work, and there are considerable variations in the ways in which early years settings interpret the notion of partnership. The form that partnerships take requires complex professional decisions to be made, including what is feasible, given the nature of a parent body, and what is most appropriate for children's needs. As with all aspects of organisation and provision, ways of working with parents need to be part of an ongoing review process and open to question and innovation. The central question that should be asked of any partnership arrangement is – to what extent is it directly or indirectly benefiting the children?

## Questions for reflection

1 What do you know about children's home backgrounds and experiences and how do you utilise this knowledge in planning for children's transition to your setting and their learning and development?

2 What do parents feel about your practices? How do you know and how could you find out?

3 What would be the benefits and constraints for you and your setting, the children and parents of developing your practice in this area?

## References

Ball, C. (1994) *Start Right: The importance of early learning*, London: Royal Society of Arts.

Cleve, S., Jowett, S. and Bate, M. (1982) *And So to School: A study of continuity from pre-school to infant school*, Windsor: NFER-Nelson.

Dowling, M. (1995) *Starting School at Four: A joint endeavour*, London: Paul Chapman.

Duffy, B. and Stillaway, J. (2004) 'Creativity: working in partnership with parents', in Miller, L. and Devereux, J. (eds) *Supporting children's learning in the early years*, London: David Fulton Publishers.

Foot, H., Howe, C., Cheyne, B., Terras, M. and Rattray, C. (2000) 'Pre-school education: parents' preferences, knowledge and expectations', *International Journal of Early Years Education*, 8 (3), 189–204.

Gregory, E. (1996) *Making Sense of a New World: Learning to read in a second language*, London: Paul Chapman.

Pugh, G. and De'Ath, E. (1989) *Working Towards Partnership in the Early Years*, London: National Children's Bureau.

The Basic Skills Agency (2003) *The Basic Skills Agency: Making a Difference* [online], http://www.basic-skills.co.uk/ (accessed April 2005).

## Further reading

Bastiani, J. and Wolfendale, S. (eds) (1996) *Home–School Work in Britain: Review, reflection and development*, London: David Fulton Publishers.

Fabian, H. and Dunlop, A.W. (2002) *Transitions in the early years; debating continuity and progression for children in early education*, London: RoutledgeFalmer.

Vincent, C. (1996) *Parents and Teachers: Power and participation*, London: Falmer Press.

Walley, M. (2001) *Involving Parents in their Children's Learning*, London: Paul Chapman.

## Useful websites

Department for Education and Skills (DfES) (2002) 'Parents' Gateway' [online resource], http://www.dfes.gov.uk/parentsgateway/index.shtml (accessed April 2005).

Scottish Executive (2002) 'Home Reading Initiative' [online], http://www.scotland.gov.uk/pages/news/2002/08/SEED075.aspx (accessed April 2005).

# 4 Positive Learning Environments: Listening to and Protecting Children

## By the end of this chapter you will have:

- considered the practitioner's role in creating a positive learning environment for children and adults;
- identified different ways of listening to children in order to help them express themselves and develop self-esteem;
- considered policies and practice relating to the health, safety and well-being of the children in your setting, and how you can inform parents about these.

## Introduction

This chapter focuses on how early years practitioners can develop positive learning environments. The arrangement of settings, the relationships among adults and children, and practice all have a profound effect on the care, learning and teaching provided. We explore the qualities required of an environment for it to nurture children's self-esteem, self-expression and enable all children to feel safe and secure, and include parents.

## Creating a positive environment for learning and developing

No environment is neutral. When you enter a place you react to it physically and emotionally. You see, you hear, you smell, you make judgements even before you make contact with the people in it. Children entering a setting for the first time will decide whether or not it is a friendly, familiar, overwhelming or peaceful place and will sense whether or not they feel safe and secure. Parents will recognise if they are really welcome or listened to. Practitioners will know if colleagues will be encouraging whenever they take the initiative or introduce new ideas.

Each early years setting has its own ethos which develops out of the beliefs, understanding and values that underpin practice. This ethos is evident in the way that practitioners work together and care for children, and the opportunities there are for learning. It reflects the way that the children and adults 'live' in the space. Children will sense which ways of behaving are more acceptable than others, and they will begin to pick up what is considered 'best' (e.g. adult-directed pictures or their own) or they will notice which activities adults value and what they 'like' children to play with. A setting that is 'open' enables people to ask questions, discuss ideas, develop materials, feel confident to try things out and make mistakes; while one that is 'closed' is controlled by time and 'rules', and focuses on specifically acquired knowledge.

## Activity 4.1 What children see

Put yourself in a child's 'shoes' and take a look round your setting. In particular, try to see it from the height and perspective of the children you work with. What messages do you think your setting gives to the children? How do they pick up those messages?

You may find the following questions helpful:

- What things in the room are familiar to me from the other places I 'live' in, my home or my neighbourhood?
- Is there anyone who looks or dresses like my mum or dad or my carer? If not, can I find them in books or pictures?
- How easy is it for me to move around?
- How do I know what to do and when to do it?
- How easy is it to talk to the adults?

In any setting, the surroundings and people have an enormous impact on how children feel about themselves and the way they learn. Children need significant relationships, but self-identity is also rooted in the child's experience with rooms, clothes, playthings, objects and spaces (Proshansky and Fabian 1987). Children need opportunities and encouragement to change their environment, e.g. one day the blocks are a castle, the next a train. Your role is to facilitate their play, to offer suggestions or ask questions and to follow up their chosen theme by providing additional resources.

## Case Study: Adapting and developing materials

Myrtle works with three- and four-year-olds in an early years centre. She set up two water trays outside and added guttering that led into the drainpipes. Myrtle wanted the children to look at how the water moved down the guttering and how it could move objects. She put some boats into the water trays, and the children began their investigation.

Boats seemed the obvious choice but the children didn't see it like that. Why boats? Why not cars? And they fetched these.

They began to ask questions. How did the water push the cars along? Myrtle encouraged them to watch what was happening, and they tried out different-sized cars. But it didn't stop there. They also wanted to know where the water went out of the guttering.

They had a discussion about pipes and their purpose. Having watched where the water went, they saw that there were other drainpipes. They moved on to talk about drainage and where the pipes would finally come out.

Myrtle had only slightly changed the arrangement of the water trays. However, the materials she had provided and her presence enabled discussion and questioning. Although the learning included her original plans, Myrtle allowed the children to develop these and gave them time to explore their own ideas.

## Creating a listening environment

Children communicate from the moment they are born. Babies express their actions and reactions through facial expressions, movements and cries. Parents communicate through body language, and babies notice their parents' feelings and responses. When very young children are trying out language, it is important that their efforts are taken seriously and that they are encouraged to express themselves, while older children need opportunities to describe what they are doing and give their opinions. Children need time to examine ideas without being directed down a particular route or cut off by 'closed' questions that ask for specific, adult-orientated answers.

There is a difference between allowing children to 'create worlds' and allowing them to 'shunt information' (Smith 1983). *Creating worlds* is about how children see their environment (e.g. that there are colours in it); *shunting information* is about their knowing facts about that environment (e.g. the names of those colours). As children get older, the demands on them to prove they have knowledge increase, as they are observed and tested to find out if they know what they 'ought' to know. Cousins (1999) gives the example of a traveller child whose teacher asked him to name the colours of objects. He asked why she wanted to know since she already knew the answer was 'red'. Simply asking and answering questions is not the same as having a conversation. This child wanted to explore what he knew further but his teacher was not enabling him to do so.

The Coram Family's 'Listening to Young Children' project (Clark and Moss 2001) was based on the premise that children are experts in their own learning and draw on their own interpretations to make meaning. The project identified many different ways to listen to children related to how they express themselves. These included words, play, movement, symbols, drawing and writing, facial expressions, noises, and interactions and reactions to things and to people. They called this 'the Mosaic approach'.

Much of our understanding about how children feel comes from observing what they do. If you work as a teaching assistant, you may be aware of children using body language to seek or avoid attention; or, if you work with babies, you may have noticed them communicating with smiles or movements during nappy changes. It is possible to take account of children's views right from birth simply by observing their actions and reactions (Pugh and Selleck 1996) and, as they get older, through observing their actions, reactions and body language during play and when changing from one activity to another. You may need to explore additional ways of listening to children with special needs, such as by using sign language, or, for those learning English as an additional language, by involving an interpreter if you don't share the child's home language.

## Activity 4.2 Learning through looking

Observe a child or children in your setting engaged in an activity. The following checklist may be helpful. Note the context in which you are observing.

- What feelings is the child expressing?
- What does the child's body language tell you?
- What noises (but not words) does the child make?
- How does the child make contact with others?

Note what you have learnt about this child during this observation. Remember that this is only a small snapshot of one child at one particular moment.

Observation is an extremely useful way to get to know children, but it presents only an adult perspective. Another way to build up a picture is to ask children about their opinions. Child-conferencing is another feature of the Mosaic approach. The Coram Centre devised fourteen questions to use in discovering children's views on why they come to nursery, including: who their favourite people are, who they like, what they like doing and how they see the adults in the nursery (Clark and Moss 2001). These questions may seem obvious and straightforward; however, the Coram researchers discovered that where and how the questioning took place was key to the way that children responded. Some children enjoyed being asked to the head's office to talk, as this gave the discussion an air of importance. Others preferred talking as they walked around, pointing out whatever was significant to them. To listen fully to children, we have to be alert to how they are telling us things, and to recognise that different occasions may bring different responses.

## Listening to children

The 1989 United Nations Convention on the Rights of the Child (UNCRC) states that the best interest of the child must be a primary consideration. Adults can only do this if they develop ways to find out what children really think so that they act as a source of expertise, skill and information for adults and contribute towards meeting their own needs. Listening to children has been likened to 'pulling up another chair alongside those already present within these processes [i.e. the adults] so that the *voices* of young children are also heard' (Lansdown and Lancaster 2004:19). Listening intently to children means showing genuine interest, respecting their rights, not pressing if they are not ready or able to express their feelings verbally, and allowing them some control so that they can stop the discussion if they want to.

Other ways in which children can express themselves are through pictures and writing. Talking with children about what they have drawn can reveal a lot: how they feel about themselves, their families, friends, their environment or, indeed, you. Giving children cameras and asking them to take photographs provides another snapshot of what they consider important. This 'mosaic' of ways of listening helps children to express themselves, thereby bringing to light any problems they may be experiencing and giving practitioners a deeper understanding of their personal, social and emotional development. Practitioners need to create opportunities for children to talk, often informally, about what they feel and how they see things.

Staff in schools are increasingly using 'circle time' as a way of involving children (Mosley 1996). Carefully facilitated, circle time can encourage children to develop trust among their peers and to discuss such issues as bullying and supporting each other. Having the confidence to talk openly in a group will often give children the confidence to talk more intimately on a one-to-one basis.

## Case Study: Woodlands Park Nursery

Woodlands Park Nursery has an after-school club for Reception and Year 1 children. The staff followed the Mosaic approach and consulted the children about what they wanted from the club through interviews, questionnaires and taking photographs. They discovered the children wanted to paint the room, so the staff compromised and let them paint the display boards. They all discussed the colours they would like and some children and staff went shopping for the paint. As the children became used to being consulted and listened to, the practitioners at the club found that they were disclosing more. One boy told them that he found it upsetting when other children 'said something bad'. A girl disclosed that she was being bullied by children at school and in the club – something that staff felt she would not have done before they decided to consult on children's views.

# Child protection

Social workers have a statutory responsibility to offer protection to children, but they can only work effectively as part of a whole team. They have to receive a referral before they know that a child is at risk. The referral may come from a practitioner, a health visitor, a general practitioner, a school nurse or teacher, a police officer, or a neighbour. The types of abuse (Department of Health *et al.* 2000) that a child may suffer include:

- physical abuse – includes causing physical harm to the child;
- emotional abuse – includes adverse effects on the emotional development, such as making the child feel worthless or unloved. All child abuse involves some element of emotional abuse;
- sexual abuse – includes actual or likely sexual abuse or exploitation of the child;
- neglect – includes persistent failure to meet the child's basic needs or protect him or her from danger.

The act of children 'disclosing' can be very painful for adults. They may not want to believe what the child is intimating or they may feel powerless to help. The government's Green Paper, *Every Child Matters* (DfES 2003), highlights the failure of adults to protect children and notes that early intervention is key to effective protection. It recommends a universal service for children, with a Director of Children's Services who is accountable for local education and social services. The document cites poor coordination of services as the main reason for failure to identify vulnerable children early enough, and calls for services to work in an integrated way.

Early years practitioners have a vital part to play by being alert to children at risk. It is crucial that you read the child protection policy and procedures for your setting, and that you discuss them with other staff, or, if you are a childminder, with network advisers. You should know who holds the responsibility for child protection, and you should inform them immediately you have concerns.

## Activity 4.3 Sylvie

Consider the following case study.

### Case Study: Sylvie

Betty is a nursery nurse in a village infants' school. She was on playground duty when she heard two seven-year-old girls talking. Sylvie told Melissa that her daddy had been angry last night and had hit her mummy. Sylvie and her little brother had been scared and they did not want to make a noise in case Daddy got more cross. Sylvie said she thought Mummy was dead, but then she got up and told Sylvie to go back to bed as Daddy was only playing about. Sylvie started to cry and she told Melissa that she was very frightened that Daddy would kill Mummy.

Betty spoke to the class teacher, who called the deputy head, who was the designated teacher for child protection. Betty wrote everything down as accurately as she could while the deputy head rang the social services department. Alison, a social worker from children's services, managed to get to the school and speak to Betty and the teacher before the parents arrived. When Sylvie's mother, Sue, arrived, the teacher asked if she could have a word privately in the office. Alison sensitively explained to Sue why she had been called and the reason why it was important for Sylvie. At first, Sue said that Sylvie was imagining things, but then she burst into tears and said she was frightened because she thought the kids might be 'taken off her'. Alison reassured Sue that she would help, but that she had to ensure that the children were safe.

Betty did the right thing by reporting what she had heard quickly, but consider the following:

- Why might it have been dangerous to delay?
- Why was Sylvie at risk?
- Consider the child protection policy in your setting. Explain why you think it is effective or not.
- Consider confidentiality requirements in relation to supporting Melissa.

The social worker subsequently visited Sylvie's family so that she could make a professional decision about whether the children were at risk and to offer appropriate support to the family. There are many areas to consider, including the emotional abuse of children witnessing violence. Local authorities have a legal responsibility to safeguard and to promote the welfare of vulnerable children. There are several key principles in the Children Act 1989 which are relevant to child protection issues, including:

■ whenever possible, it is in the child's best interests to be brought up within their own families;

■ parents may need assistance from time to time with their child-rearing responsibilities.

If the child is thought to be at risk, a detailed assessment may be carried out which considers the following three areas:

■ the child's developmental needs;

■ family and environmental factors;

■ parenting capacity.

Look at the assessment framework in Figure 4.1 to see how many factors are considered in each of the three areas. The framework has been developed so that there is a systematic method for understanding and analysing what is happening to children in the context of their families and communities. Note that safeguarding and promoting the welfare of the child is at the centre of the framework. The aim is to build on strengths in the family as well as identifying difficulties. It is important that staff are involved in the assessment, so that all relevant information is considered, and that the decision reached is best for the child's health and emotional well-being.

Dowling (2004) reminds us that while it is difficult for us to be articulate when we are feeling angry or anxious, it is the same for very young children. Being in a positive listening environment will encourage them to express their feelings safely. They can develop self-esteem knowing that they have the right to voice their opinions, question what is happening to them and be included in decisions that affect them.

## Involving parents

Developing a positive learning environment for children goes hand in hand with developing an environment in which parents feel welcome and able to share their ideas and confide in staff. If you are working with parents from different ethnic groups, there may be different cultural expectations and beliefs

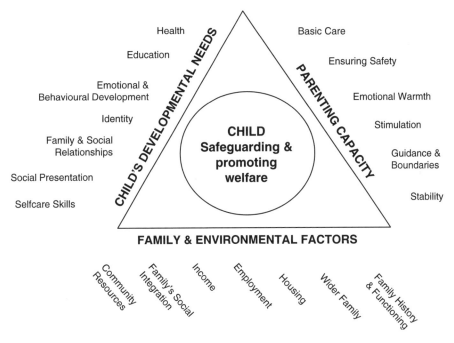

**Figure 4.1**   Assessment framework
*Source:* DoH *et al.* 2000: 17

to consider even if you share the same language. Research in Southwark has shown that when social workers from different ethnic groups are employed, this can have a positive impact on the take-up of services by members of the same ethnic groups (Wheal 2000). Social class can also play a part in how parents relate to practitioners. However, practitioners cannot make assumptions about any parent. It is relatively easy to develop informal communication with parents and carers – for example, by greeting them when they come or by exchanging information each day. But if practitioners want truly to involve parents in their children's learning, there will be times when difficult issues or differences have to be discussed and dealt with.

One area in which opinions can be sharply divided is that of discipline and managing behaviour, including smacking. Both practitioners and parents may have strong views and, within a group of parents, there will be differing views on what constitutes smacking and whether or not it is acceptable. You need to make it clear to parents that smacking is not permitted in early years settings. In 2003 it became illegal for childminders to smack children in their care, a ruling that brought them into line with other early years workers. Communicating well with parents involves respecting their views and listening to their ideas. Where these ideas are different from yours, explaining your practice knowledgeably and sensitively will help parents to have confidence in you.

# Keeping children safe: policies and procedures

The Children Act 1989 states that local authorities are responsible for maintaining standards of childminding and day care, and for ensuring that any practitioner is a 'fit person' to care for children. National Care Standards have been established in all UK countries and practitioners should ensure they are familiar with these. Parents will want to know about the people working with their children. Part of your role is to inform them of the legal protection available for their children and the steps you will take to look after them. You need to be aware of policies and procedures for health, safety and child protection, and how they relate to your setting, and allow parents access to them. You should also be able to refer them to the care standards adopted by your setting. Some early years settings display their policies for parents to see, or refer to them in their booklets. If, for example, you are taking children on an outing, parents will want to know what you are doing to prevent accidents. You will also need to explain how you make your risk assessments and what measures you are taking to keep your setting safe. When a child first enters your setting, it is important that the following information is shared and discussed:

- allergies or health problems;
- who is responsible for bringing and collecting children;
- particular issues relating to individual children, e.g. a communication difficulty;
- fears or emotional difficulties children may be experiencing, such as the death of a much-loved pet or changes in the family;
- procedures if there is an accident, and how parents are informed.

## Activity 4.4 Reviewing policy and practice

Review the documents mentioned above and the guidance and information you provide for parents, and consider:

- how current they are;
- when they were last updated;
- the types of information you share with parents;
- whether you are meeting statutory requirements.

Make a note of any changes you need to make.

# Risk and resilience

Clearly it is crucial to keep children safe, but they also need an environment in which they can try out new things. Lindon (1999) has expressed unease about the growing focus on the dangers facing children, which may stop parents and practitioners allowing them to explore or take some risk. Being overprotective leaves children few chances to develop new skills intellectually or physically, or to learn strategies for making their own risk assessments. It is possible for adults to show children new skills, and encourage ways of becoming more competent and confident, without always telling them directly what to do and how to do it. Lindon suggests the practitioner's role involves helping children to be active rather than passive recipients of knowledge, and to learn life skills for approaching problems. Her emphasis is on children learning to 'master' a situation rather than feeling 'helpless' when faced with something new. By drawing on their own experience, adults can help children think through what they might do, what happens when things go wrong, how they might negotiate and when they need to ask for help. Children also need opportunities to reflect on what they have done. Then, when they are faced with new situations, they can use past experience and adapt strategies they have already learned.

# Review

In a positive learning environment, children are listened to and their rights are respected; they feel safe and secure, and are able to explore and take risks physically, emotionally and intellectually. The physical environment does not constrain the children and practitioners do not impose unnecessary restrictions, but enable them to learn and develop. Parents are made to feel they can make an important contribution, because they are able to discuss issues and concerns with you and make suggestions. As an early years practitioner, you have a responsibility to create an ethos and environment where both children and adults can learn and develop together.

## Questions for reflection

1 How could you enhance your physical environment to make it more welcoming for children and parents and ensure it reflects and builds on children's experiences and backgrounds?

2 What steps can you take to provide a listening environment in your setting?

3 What information do parents need to have if their children are going to be safe and secure in your setting?

# References

Clark, A. and Moss, P. (2001) *Listening to Young Children: The Mosaic approach*, London: National Children's Bureau.

Cousins, J. (1999) *Listening to Four Year Olds: How they can help us plan their education and care*, London: National Early Years Network.

Department for Education and Skills (DfES) (2003) *Every Child Matters*, London: The Stationery Office.

Department of Health (DoH), Department for Education and Employment (DfEE) and Home Office (HO) (2000) *Framework for the Assessment of Children in Need and their Families* (Quality Protects), London: The Stationery Office.

Dowling, M. (2004) 'Emotional wellbeing', in Miller, L. and Devereux, J. (eds) *Supporting Children's Learning in the Early Years*, London: David Fulton Publishers.

Lansdown, G. and Lancaster, Y.P. (2004) 'Promoting children's welfare by respecting their rights', in Miller, L. and Devereux, J. (eds) *Supporting Children's Learning in the Early Years*, London: David Fulton Publishers.

Lindon, J. (1999) *Too Safe for Their Own Good: Helping children learn about risk and lifeskills*, London: National Early Years Network.

Mosley, J. (1996) *Quality Circle Time in the Primary Classroom*, Wisbech: Learning Development Aids.

Proshansky, H.M. and Fabian, A.K. (1987) 'The development of place identity in the child', in Weinstein, C.S. and David, T.G. (eds) *Spaces for Children: The built environment and child development*, New York: Plenum Press.

Pugh, G. and Selleck, D. (1996) 'Listening to and communicating with young children' in Davie, R., Upton, G. and Varma, V.P. (eds) *The Voice of the Child: A handbook for professionals*, London: Falmer Press.

Smith, F. (1983) *Essays into Literacy: Selected papers and some afterthoughts*, Exeter, NH: Heineman Educational.

Wheal, A. (ed.) (2000) *Working with Parents: Learning from other people's experience*, Lyme Regis: Russell House.

# Further reading

Coles, M. (1996) 'The magnifying glass: what we know of classroom talk in the early years', in Hall, N. and Martello, J. (eds) *Listening to Children Think: Exploring talk in the early years*, London: Hodder and Stoughton.

EPPE Research Team (2003) 'The Effective Provision of Pre-School Education (EPPE) Project', *NSIN Research Matters No. 21*, National School Improvement Network Bulletin, Autumn 2003, London: Institute of Education, University of London.

Humphreys, C. (2001) 'The impact of domestic violence on children', in Foley, P., Roche, J. and Tucker, S. (eds) *Children in Society: Contemporary theory, policy and practice*, Hampshire: Palgrave/The Open University.

Whalley, M. (1994) *Learning to be Strong*, London: Hodder and Stoughton.

# Useful websites

National Childminding Association (NCMA) (2004) *Quality First* [online], http://www.ncmaqualityfirst.co.uk/ (accessed April 2005).

National Day Nurseries Association (NDNA) (2004) *Quality Counts* [online], http://www.ndna.org.uk/document_tree/ViewACategory.asp?CategoryID=5 (accessed April 2005).

Sure Start Unit (2004) *Investors in Children* (IiC) [online], http://www.surestart.gov.uk/ensuringquality/investorsinchildren/ (accessed April 2005).

# 5 Reflection in Practice

## By the end of this chapter you will have:

- considered how your own learning and experience of working with young children provides the basis for future professional development;

- explored ways of collecting and interpreting evidence of your learning and professional development;

- understood why 'knowledge-in-action' and 'reflection-in-action' are important;

- developed a deeper understanding of your own professional practice and considered your future professional development.

## Introduction

Early years practitioners undertake one of the most important jobs imaginable, supporting the learning and development of young children, hence the drive of government and authorities to improve the qualifications and status of this workforce. Progression routes are opening up that have previously been unavailable to the majority of early years practitioners (Abbott and Hevey 2001; DfES 2001). These developments will be an important step in providing the knowledge and skills needed for working with young children and their families in a rapidly changing political and educational climate as outlined in Chapter 1.

In this chapter we invite you to explore and reflect upon your role as an early years practitioner, how it came about and how it has changed. We go on to discuss the role of knowledge in professional development and what we mean by evidence of learning. Finally, we move on to evaluating your own learning, exploring implications for you and also for your workplace, and encouraging you to put in place an action plan and to set goals for your future professional development.

# Your own learning and development

Practitioners working with young children need to take a critical look at both theory and their practice. This poses a challenge for many early years practitioners, who may be undertaking further professional development, which builds on years of valuable practical experience. In this chapter this experience is acknowledged, but we also ask you to analyse it, to step back and to develop a reflective stance in relation to your practice. In so doing you will learn to see familiar practices with a new and professional eye.

As Annings and Edwards (1999) note in a discussion of 'communities of practice', newcomers are introduced to ways of working through participating in the routines and practices of the workplace, so traditional practices may be passed on without questioning or scrutiny. That is not to say we should throw the baby out with the bathwater; some of the best traditions may be retained, but all need to be scrutinised to see whether they are still appropriate or relevant in the light of new knowledge and developments. Annings and Edwards highlight the need to be forward-looking in passing on the traditional ways of working, so that 'best practice' is developed and evolves appropriately for tomorrow's world.

In the first activity in this chapter we ask you to look back on your experience and consider how this has impacted on your learning and your practice. We also ask you to think about the evidence you can provide to support what you say.

## Activity 5.1 My learning and practice

**Table 5.1**   My learning and practice

| My learning | Evidence from practice |
|---|---|
| Children learning | |
| The role of the adult | |
| Inclusive provision | |
| The curriculum | |
| Positive environments for learning | |
| Relationships and partnerships | |

In Table 5.1 we offer some headings, which summarise some key aspects of learning and practice in early years education and care. Use the headings presented in the boxes to summarise your own learning. You may wish to photocopy and enlarge this grid. Under each heading provide an example of your learning. In the box next to this summarise the evidence you can offer of this learning and note how it has impacted on your practice or your setting. Use the questions below to help you to work through the activity.

What did you do?

What did the children learn?

How do you know this?

What is your evidence?

How will you extend the children's learning?

What would you do differently next time?

This cycle of looking at what you did, why you did it, what your evidence is for, what you or the children learnt and what you might do next is an important part of reflecting on practice.

Table 5.2 shows a completed grid.

These responses will of course not be the same as yours. Each individual will have learnt something different and will use that learning in different ways. Sometimes courses of study or reading books do no more than confirm your existing knowledge and verify your current practice. Some may have provoked you to think and work in new and different ways. Others may have whetted your appetite and left you wanting to know more. This process of looking back on your learning and your developing practice form the basis for reflecting and reviewing how you put your new knowledge into action.

## The nature of evidence and 'knowledge-in-action'

On a daily basis we are often too busy to stop and think about what we do, to write about it or articulate it to others. We rely on our intuition to put our knowledge into action in the workplace. Claxton (2003) argues the case for intuition as a 'different way of knowing' and that in using intuition we are often drawing upon a tacit database of first-hand experience. He also argues that to use conscious reasoning, or to constantly 'stop and think', in our daily practice can interfere with the skilled performance that stems from underlying expertise. For example, in making a decision about a particular child, it is

**Table 5.2** Completed example of my learning and practice

| My learning | Evidence from practice |
|---|---|
| *Children learning*<br>That children need a stimulating environment with a variety of activities, but also time to 'relax'. | I am now more aware of displaying activities to look more 'inviting'. The children now go to all activities, not just the more 'interesting' ones. We have placed more cushions and rugs around the setting so that children can 'flop'. |
| *The role of the adult*<br>To provide experiences for children to learn and enjoy, but not to 'take over' or direct activities too much. Let children lead. | The children are now using activities in a more spontaneous way, role-playing from their own experiences. |
| *Inclusive provision*<br>To think carefully of the needs of all the children in the group, so all have access to the activities. | Child with visual impairment sits at front of group for story time. We now have a picture timetable for children, especially those with communication problems. |
| *The curriculum*<br>Should be broad, and topics should be expanded to include all development areas. Children should be consulted on what they want. | More staff meetings focused on the curriculum. Children discuss in 'circle' time, so that we can find out their interests and ideas. |
| *Positive environments for learning*<br>Bright, cheerful surroundings important, multicultural activities, not stereotypical images. | We now have more pictures and posters in the setting that reflect the experiences and backgrounds of the children. We have painted some display areas. |
| *Relationships and partnerships*<br>This area still has to be worked at. I need to make more time to talk with parents. | I am making more effort to be available at the start and end of sessions to talk with parents. |

likely we are drawing on a huge database of largely unarticulated impressions and information. However, as professionals, we must learn to challenge the basis of our practice. This will come from thinking about and reflecting on what we do. Schön's (1983) book *The Reflective Practitioner* has had a significant influence on how professionals reflect on their work. He suggested that professional development, through reflecting whilst undertaking the work itself – what he called 'reflecting-in-action' – is essential. This is because the world in which we work and live is increasingly complex, such that each situation demands not a generalised response, but one that is relevant to the particulars of that particular moment.

'Reflecting-in-action' means deliberating about the decisions you make in relation to children in your setting. It means generating ideas about why you think a child, a colleague or a parent or carer may be responding in a certain way, so that your own response is thoughtfully tailored to the particular moment. Schön suggests that the often unspoken and non-explicit knowledge of our own practices that we demonstrate intuitively can become routine and even inappropriate. If we reflect on what we are doing, we can consider why we are doing things in the way that we are, and perhaps understand what we are assuming when we behave in certain ways. 'Reflecting-in-action', he suggests, is something we do in the moment, during our working interactions, hence the 'in-action' part.

Schön suggests that 'reflecting-in-action' is often prompted by surprise in our daily routine; this would include those surprises that are pleasing as well those that are unwanted. It can help us make sense of these surprises and give us insight into a situation. It can help us to 're-frame', or look differently at our knowledge in action, leading to a greater understanding or maybe change.

Schön called this underlying knowledge, which we learn and build up in great part through experience, 'knowledge-in-action', suggesting that when professionals 'go about the spontaneous intuitive performances of everyday life, we show ourselves to be knowledgeable in a special way' (1983: 19). This 'knowledge-in-action', then, is knowledge that we use, and which we may feel we 'know' without being able to say why we do and without having a 'theory' of knowledge.

## Case Study: Alsana – a childminder

Alsana, a childminder, was asked by the parent of a new child, who had moved to the area from Sweden, why the children in settings in England had such limited access to the outdoor area. She explained that in Sweden the children went outdoors in all weathers, providing they wore appropriate clothing, and for much longer periods of time. This made Alsana realise that although she understood the importance of outdoor play, she had not reflected on her routine practice of planning for just one or two outdoor periods a day. She realised she had no clear rationale for her approach and she decided to think about how she could be more flexible in the future.

Select a recent surprise, a 'blip' that you have had in your work that has caused you to consider or reflect on your routine practice. Note down what 'knowledge-in-action' was challenged by this surprise and what understanding you gained from your reflection. How has this affected your practice?

A group of practitioners who had been working in the same day nursery for a number of years were brought together by a new manager to discuss the daily routine, which included children having afternoon sleeps. This practice was based on the knowledge that young children need periods of rest. During the discussion it was found that most of the practitioners strongly disapproved of the routine aspect of this practice but had not discussed it or reflected on it together and therefore had not challenged it. As a result of collectively reflecting on the practice, they agreed they would think about how the routine might be changed so that children could have more 'say' about their rest times. It took someone who was new to the nursery to encourage the team to look at their existing practice with a new eye, to question the reasons for the practice and so to bring about change.

## Interpreting 'knowledge-in-action'

The term 'knowledge-in-action' is knowledge we use intuitively in our work. It is embedded in what we do every day. However, in order to move on in our learning, we need to become more conscious of this underlying knowledge. We have to move from intuitive knowledge to a conscious awareness of why we do what we do, to be more aware of the links between theory and practice. Anning and Edwards (1999) describe a project in which a group of practitioners benefited from help and support in articulating their 'knowledge-in-action' and in understanding and developing their practice. The idea behind the project is that professional communities contain shared but often unspoken knowledge and practices (i.e. 'knowledge-in-action'). In the 'community of practice' that they developed in their project, they aimed to encourage the explicit sharing of knowledge and practices between education and care contexts. They introduced the notion of guided participation, as a way of the practitioner helping to evolve the practices of a workplace. Practitioners engaged in working with someone modelling good practice; discussing; planning and reviewing children's learning. They also became involved in collaborative practice-focused research with external agencies, in this case comprising the local university and the LEA, collecting and analysing data.

If you work in a home-based setting, this sort of collaboration may not be possible. Similarly, if you work in a supporting role, you may feel powerless to bring about change in your practice at this stage in your professional development. However, in reflecting on your practice, you may like to think about how the five areas of institutional development listed below play a role in the development of your own setting. These five areas are:

- a shared sense of purpose;

- a collective focus on learners;

- collaborative staff activity;

- making professional activity visible;

- reflective dialogue (finding time to discuss evidence from your setting with colleagues).

(Anning and Edwards 1999: 149)

However, in today's world, to reflect upon and develop 'best practice' is not sufficient; we need to collect evidence of different kinds about different aspects of our practice. We discuss the nature of evidence and why we need it in the next section.

## What is evidence and why do you need it?

As practitioners in early years settings, we increasingly need to collect different types of evidence of our practice for a variety of reasons. These include collating examples of children's 'work' to show what they have learnt or achieved or evidence to demonstrate that we are competent in the work that we do. Sometimes this evidence is demanded by an external agency, such as an examination and assessment framework, or our employer, or an inspection team. You may have had experience of all or some of these. Depending on your role, the evidence that you are asked to provide may include:

- planning notes and progress records on children's learning;

- attendance records (yourself and children);

- observations of children;

- evidence of children's learning;

- records and reports to parents;

- policy documents;

- health and safety records;

■ appraisal records;

■ risk assessments.

So there are many reasons why evidence may be asked for. In this chapter we focus on evidence relating to your personal/professional development. In later chapters we discuss the importance of child-focused evidence in supporting children's development and learning. What counts as evidence will depend on what you need it for and how you collect and interpret it.

## Personal/professional evidence

Personal/professional evidence would include the sorts of records which you are required to keep by people or organisations that are responsible for assuring the quality of your provision. Who these bodies are will depend on the setting and the country you work in, but they may include the governing body or organising committee, the local authority, the parents who employ you, the inspectorate, or your own examining body if you are training or studying. The records that you keep enable the accrediting or inspecting organisation to be clear that you are appropriately fulfilling the requirements of your job. You may also choose to keep evidence for accountability purposes; for example, as a nanny you might keep a daily diary of the children's activities.

It is important to be clear about the purposes for collecting the evidence. Purposes might include:

■ to improve professional practices;

■ to provide information for policy, planning, decision making;

■ for exploration, to further understanding;

■ to provide accountability;

■ evidence of practice to contribute to a qualification;

■ for accreditation for a quality assurance scheme or 'kitemark'.

Collecting evidence involves studying the activities of others in one way or another, for example undertaking research work, which includes gathering evidence about the participants. Many professionals work within an *ethical code* which provides guidelines relating to, for example, consent to participate, confidentiality of the information obtained, protection of the participants from physical or mental harm and not infringing privacy. As an early years practitioner undertaking this aspect of your role you must take responsibility for the well-being of those involved.

## Activity 5.3 Identifying and using evidence

We would now like you to think about and make a note of the kinds of evidence you might need to produce in your setting.

The evidence you collect will depend on the purpose for which it is to be used. An aspect of collecting evidence of learning and professional practices is, of course, being clear about your audience. Depending on the purpose, this might include:

- yourself;
- your colleagues and other professionals both within and beyond the setting;
- parents and carers;
- the children themselves;
- the Local Authority or Local Education Authority;
- your assessor;
- management within your setting
- OFSTED or other inspectorate bodies.

We have said that how you go about collecting evidence will depend on its purpose and audience, and that this will influence what you collect and why. A playgroup leader made the following list.

*For myself*: photographs as evidence of me working with the children, collecting work the children have done, obtaining witness statements to present to my assessor.

*For my colleagues and other professionals*: child observations – to monitor development or linked to child protection.

*For parents/carers*: progress reports on their child, general records which are shared with parents at regular intervals.

## Case Study: Leon – a 'portfolio worker'

Leon lives and works within community services on a large housing estate in Newport, South Wales and has a wider role in relation to collecting evidence. In the mornings, he works in a crèche adjacent to the local primary school, and from 3.30 p.m. he is involved in a leadership role in out-of-school care, based in the primary school. His team is currently working towards an inspection carried out by the Welsh Care Standards Inspectorate and he needs to make sure that his team has the evidence to meet the criteria set out in the national standards (Welsh

Assembly Government 2002). For example, in relation to Standard 7 Behaviour, he knows that the inspector will be looking for records of significant incidents, such as bullying, and that they will wish to see a written policy statement on how behaviour is managed in the setting. He will also need to ensure that staff are able to articulate the strategies they use for dealing with behaviour and so provide oral evidence, a process which will contribute towards their professional development. He is particularly proud of the work he and his team have been doing with parents (Standard 4: Working in partnership with parents). As evidence of this work, he is including the information about the policies and procedures he has given to parents, copies of the children's records and the arrangements for children arriving and departing.

As a 'portfolio worker' who works in more than one setting, Leon is aware of the different types of evidence needed across the two settings and the different purposes for which they might be needed. In the example above, Leon collects evidence for professional development and for accountability purposes. Leon's multiple work roles are an example of the changing nature of work in the field of early years education, care and playwork.

## Your professional development: moving on

Throughout this chapter, you have been encouraged to reflect on your professional practice and on how to improve this. It is tempting to think of professional development as occurring only through undertaking courses. But professional development often involves a mix of learning, developing relationships and formal training. This is about doing the job professionally. In thinking about your own professional development experiences, you have probably undertaken different types of professional learning for different purposes. There is a wide range of professional learning available to you as an early years practitioner. This includes:

- self-directed study linked to awards;
- practitioner research;
- work-based learning;
- receiving or giving on-the-job coaching, mentoring or tutoring;
- settings-based and off-site courses of different lengths;
- job shadowing and rotation;
- peer networks;

- cluster projects involving collaboration, development and the sharing of experience/ideas;

- learning mediated through information and communication technologies (ICT);

- self-assessment and reflection on your own knowledge in action.

These categories overlap and frequently occur alongside one another.

## Where next? Action planning and goal setting

In the final section of this chapter we enable you to:

- establish and implement procedures to review and update your current knowledge and practice;

- integrate outcomes from this review into your own practice;

- identify possible next steps in your professional development.

We focus on your future learning and professional development in relation to short-, medium- and long-term goals – that is, what you would like to be doing in six months', two years' and five years' time. As we have noted, professional learning can take many forms. We assume that many readers of this book will be studying for a Foundation Degree in Early Years. Some of you may be considering working towards Qualified Teacher Status or making a career change within the sector or across sectors. Whatever your plans, it is advisable to devise an action plan for the future.

### Activity 5.4 Looking ahead

To help you to begin to identify some short-, medium- and long-term goals for your professional development, we would like you to think about where you are at the moment in relation to your own knowledge and practice. To help you to do this, we have outlined below some key areas of learning and practice for Senior Practitioners taken from the Statement of Requirement (DfES 2001: 34 and 35). These may help you to identify some goals relating to your own knowledge and practice. They include the ability to:

- contribute to the protection of children from abuse;

- work with other professionals;

- develop, implement and evaluate specific plans and activities to meet individual needs of children;

- assess and enhance the cognitive and intellectual development of children;

- assess and enhance the personal, social and emotional development of children;
- work with parents to enhance their children's learning and development;
- develop your own resources;
- enable children to participate confidently and effectively in activities;
- evaluate and use ICT to support children's learning;
- manage sessions with groups of children.

Note briefly how you do each, how well you do it and what your evidence is for this. Refer back to the evidence section of this chapter to help you decide what evidence you might use.

Highlight those aspects that you feel you do well. Then identify those that you feel you need to improve on. Consider how you would go about achieving this. Consider also how your plans fit into the overall aims and targets for your setting.

The following questions may help you to make notes.

What are your long-, medium- and short-term goals?

How do these fit in with the plans and targets for your setting?

What is the timescale involved?

How will you find out the information you need?

What cost will be involved?

How will you meet these costs?

What support, if any, is available to you?

What will your first step be?

How will these goals fit in with the rest of your life?

Now divide a large sheet of paper into six columns with six headings as in Table 5.3. Then follow the instructions below.

Table 5.3 Goals for my professional development

| Short-term goals | How I will achieve them? | Medium-term goals | How I will achieve them? | Long-term goals | How I will achieve them? |
|---|---|---|---|---|---|
|  |  |  |  |  |  |

- *Short-term goals*: In the first column identify one or more short-term goals. You may have already thought about these and know what they are. In column 2 make brief notes about how you would go about achieving the goals you have identified.

■ *Medium-term goals*: Now repeat the activity for your medium-term goals. From the above activity, you should be able to identify those goals which will take longer than a few months to achieve. These are your medium-term goals. Add these to your diagram and note down how you might achieve these.

■ *Long-term goals*: Having identified those areas that you want to develop further in the short- and medium-term, now repeat the activity for your long-term goals.

When you have completed this activity, ask a colleague, or someone who knows your work well, to look at the goals you have identified. Do they agree that these are appropriate for you? Discuss with them your ideas for how you could achieve these. Consider also how your goals and plans fit into the overall aims and targets for your setting.

We hope this activity has helped you to think about your future and where you want to be in, say, five years' time. It should have helped you to think about the importance of having realistic deadlines and considering the means to achieve these, whether in terms of family support, financial support or possibly support from your employer. Individuals will progress at different rates and in different ways along their professional journey. The changing context for early years practitioners outlined in Chapter 1 means that you will need to keep up a continuous cycle of reflection on your professional development to meet the new opportunities and challenges that this changing scenario will present.

## Review

In this chapter we have argued that even very experienced early years practitioners need to review, challenge and reflect upon their 'knowledge-in-action' because of the significant changes that have been taking place within and around this occupational sector. We have emphasised the importance of developing new knowledge, of understanding and articulating 'knowledge-in-action' and of reflecting on practice. Practitioners working with young children and their families will need to be trained to high professional standards. This will require new forms of training and qualifications which bring together both practical and theoretical learning.

### Questions for reflection

1 How does the learning of individuals in a setting contribute to making the setting a 'learning organisation'?

2 How relevant is the 'community of practice' notion in your own work?

3 How might the notion of 'reflection in action' inform your practice?

# References

Abbott, L. and Hevey, D. (2001) 'Training to work in the early years: developing the climbing frame', in Pugh, G. (ed.) *Contemporary Issues in the Early Years: Working Collaboratively for Children*, 3rd edn, London: Paul Chapman Publishing, pp. 179–93.

Anning, A. and Edwards, A. (1999) 'Creating contexts for professional development in educare', in Anning and Edwards (1999) *Promoting Children's Learning from Birth to Five: developing the new early years professional*, Buckingham: Open University Press, pp. 144–59.

Claxton, G. (2003) 'The anatomy of intuition', in Claxton, G. and Atkinson, T. (eds) *The Intuitive Practitioner: on the value of not always knowing what one is doing*, Buckingham: Open University Press, pp. 32–53.

Department for Education and Skills (DfES) (2001) *Early Years Sector-Endorsed Foundation Degree: Statement of Requirement*, London: HMSO.

Schön, D. (1983) *The Reflective Practitioner*, London: Temple Smith.

Welsh Assembly Government (2002) *National Minimum Standards for: Childminders/Crèches/Full Day Care/Open Access Play/Out of School Care/ Sessional Care*, www.wales.gov.uk/subisocialpolicycarestandards/index.htm (accessed April 2005).

# Further reading

Atkinson, L. (2003) 'Trusting your own judgement (or allowing yourself to eat the pudding)', in Claxton, G. and Atkinson, T. (eds) *The Intuitive Practitioner: on the value of not always knowing what one is doing*, Buckingham: Open University Press, pp. 53–67.

Ellis, S. and Hancock, R. (2004) 'Developing the role of a senior practitioner: a personal perspective', in Miller, L. and Devereux, J. (eds) *Supporting Children's Learning in the Early Years*, London: David Fulton Publishers/ The Open University, pp. 230–239.

Karstadt, L., Lilley, T. and Miller, L. (2000) 'Professional roles in early childhood', in Drury, R., Miller, L. and Campbell, C. (eds) *Looking at Early Years Education and Care*, London: David Fulton Publishers, pp. 26–35.

## Useful websites

http://www.ncsl.org.uk – for information on National Professional Qualification in Integrated Centres Leadership Programme.

www.teachernet.gov.uk – for information relating to achieving Qualified Teacher Status.

www.dfes.gov.uk – links to *Every Child Matters*; 5 year strategy; and Children's Workforce Unit (commoncore).

www.surestart.gov.uk – links to Early Years Sector-Endorsed Foundation Degrees, Statement of Requirement and Senior Practitioner role.

# Part 2

# Ways of Learning

# Introduction to Part 2: Ways of Learning

Part 2 of this book focuses on young children as learners and the different factors that shape and have an impact on what and how they learn. The chapters draw on socio-cultural theory, which perceives children as active participants in their own learning, constantly struggling to make sense of their world through the many experiences and interactions in which they are involved on a day-to-day basis. Within this perspective, the role of others, both adults and children, the social nature of learning and the contexts in which learning takes place are significant factors for practitioners to consider in supporting and extending children's learning and development.

Chapter 6 explores the nature of play and its importance in young children's learning. Play performs an important function in young children's lives and enables them to experiment in a safe and secure environment and explore and develop their knowledge, understanding and skills. In this chapter we explore the different kinds of play children engage in and the implications for provision and practice. Through a case study approach, we encourage the reader to reflect on observations of children's play and what these can tell us about children's learning. Observation enables us to ascertain what children know, understand and can do and then use this information to ensure that provision builds on and extends children's learning and development.

Chapter 7 focuses on the learning of very young children from birth to three and considers what new research into the brain is telling us about what young children know and can do. Young babies are constantly exploring their world, stimulating connections and pathways within the brain that support learning. In this chapter we discuss the implications of this new knowledge and understanding for practitioners working with babies and young children. The role of play and adult roles in facilitating play for young children are explored, and we examine the role and value of 'key persons' in early years settings, in supporting parents and children's learning.

Chapter 8 continues our focus on how children learn and, in particular, on how children learn language. We consider the view of learning that has emerged from and been influenced by socio-cultural theory and the implications for practice in early years settings. We examine the role of language, and in particular talk, in children's learning and development. For most children, language provides the means through which they explore their experiences and represent their thinking, and practitioners have a key role to play in supporting children in developing their knowledge, understanding and skills in this area.

Chapter 9 examines inclusion and equal opportunities and considers the impact of discrimination on children's learning and lives. In this chapter we look at how early years practitioners can apply the values and principles underpinning inclusion, equal opportunities and anti-discrimination to their work with children and parents. We also examine the ways in which practitioners can support children's learning and the development of a strong sense of self-identity by acknowledging, understanding and building on their experiences and backgrounds and by challenging prejudice and discrimination.

Chapter 10, the final chapter in this part, focuses on assessment. Assessment is a key part of the teaching and learning cycle and informs everything we do. In this chapter we examine assessment *for* learning as well as assessment *of* learning. Information about what children know, understand and can do is vital if we are to provide appropriate resources and experiences to support children's learning. This chapter returns full circle to the importance of observing children and using our knowledge of how children learn and develop and our understanding of individuals to inform the way we interact with children and support their learning.

# 6 Learning through Play

**By the end of this chapter you will have developed your:**

- knowledge and understanding of how young children learn through play;
- understanding of your roles and responsibilities in providing contexts and support for play;
- skills in observing children play.

## Introduction

In this chapter we explore, through the use of case studies in particular, the importance of play in children's learning. We investigate the link between play and learning, explore different stages and types of play before considering our role as practitioners in supporting children learning through play.

## Learning and play

Play is the child's means of living and of understanding life.

(Isaacs 1954: 23)

Play is not only crucial to the way children become self aware and the way in which they learn the rules of social behaviour; it is also fundamental to intellectual development.

(ACCAC 1996: 3)

Children in the Foundation Stage learn best through play, experience and conversation.

(ECEF 1998: 52)

Most parents and early years practitioners would agree that young children learn best through play, regarding the links between the two as obvious. Young children learn more during the first five years of life than at any other age and we know now that children are learning from the moment they are born. They learn to talk, walk and feed themselves, and begin to explore the world around them. With the support of adults and siblings, they make discoveries about their physical, social and emotional enviornments. Children learn all this without formal teaching. They learn by copying their peers and adults as they seek to make sense of their world. However, this does not necessarily mean that there is no place for more formal teaching and learning.

Often play and learning are so closely intertwined it is impossible to distinguish between them. Children playing with construction bricks may be engaged in the fun activity of building a tall tower, but they are also learning about the properties of those bricks and how to place one on top of another in a way that reduces the likelihood of them toppling over. So what exactly is learning? What is the relationship between learning and play, and why is play so important in early years settings? An important first step in trying to answer these questions is to explore what *you* understand by learning, play, and learning through play.

## Activity 6.1  Learning and play

Complete the following sentences. Remember, this is about identifying your own opinions – there are no right answers. You don't need to spend a long time considering your response; the first thing that comes to mind when you read the first few words of each sentence will be fine.

Learning is . . . . . . . . . . . . . . . . . . . . . . . . . . . . . and happens when

. . . . . . . . . . . . . . . . . . . . . .

I think young children learn best when . . . . . . . . . . . . . . . . . . . . . . . . . . . . . . .

Play is . . . . . . . . . . . . . . . . and happens when . . . . . . . . . . . . . . . . . . . . . . .

Young children play best when . . . . . . . . . . . . . . . . . . . . . . .

Learning through play is . . . . . . . . . . . . . . . . . . . . . . .

(Adapted from Drummond *et al.* 1989: 19–20)

Here are some responses from practitioners. Michele, an assistant in a nursery, wrote:

Learning is important for life skills and it should be fun and stimulating. Young children learn best when they are actively involved and there is support that has meaning and purpose. They learn better when they are interested and see a purpose for the learning. Learning and play need to be in the learner's control and involvement is an important criterion for success.

The following comments were made during a training session in which practitioners listed what they thought about play:

play is child-initiated;

children make their own rules;

play is creative;

play is self-directed;

children use 'props' to help them in their play;

these props can be used to represent all manner of things in the play;

play can be individual or social;

play is a process;

play does not necessarily have an end product;

play is not the opposite of work;

play is dependent on context and content.

These responses view active involvement as crucial to play and learning, and assert that context and content must be meaningful to children. They note such things as the value of play, different types of play and the various stages of play. Also included are references to learning not always being easy, using all the senses, linking ideas together and changing ideas through experience.

Defining play and learning is not easy, but it is important to understand the nature of both and the way they support children's development in the early years.

## Play

Macintyre (2001: 2) suggests that play:

- is enjoyable, freely chosen by the player;
- can be abandoned without blame;
- has no preconceived outcome; the agenda can develop as the play goes on;
- gives pleasure and often counteracts stress;
- develops skills which are important in non-play, i.e. work situations.

Play makes a significant contribution towards the mental health and social well-being of the child. Children will have had different experiences of play and playing, depending on their home and cultural backgrounds. As a result some children, on entering new settings, may need support and guidance on how to play, how to access group play, and how to play together. In particular, those with learning difficulties and disabilities may need more specific and specialised help in playing and communicating with others. There is a place for 'scaffolding' children's understanding of and ability to play, just as there is for 'scaffolding' their learning, to take account of their diverse life experiences (Bruner 1972).

However, experience suggests that play will continue only as long as children find it interesting and want to participate. Learning and play need to be under the learner's control and their involvement is an important criterion for success.

## Types of play

Children can be seen playing in all kinds of different situations, but what they do when they play has many common features regardless of the context, materials and equipment available.

This section explores the common understandings behind several key terms that are often used to describe types of play that will help us to understand better what is going on when we observe children at play. Practitioners use a number of different terms to describe play – role-play, socio-dramatic play, imaginative play, symbolic play, constructive play, fantasy play, rough-and-tumble play, exploratory play, repetitive play, and games played with rules. Some may appear self-explanatory, but it is important that you understand what each involves, the relationships between them, and the value of their contribution to the child's growth and development both as an individual and as a learner. Table 6.1 provides an overview of key aspects of different types of play you may find useful in identifying what children are doing as you observe them playing.

**Table 6.1** Key aspects of play

| Type of play | What it is | Developmental aspects |
| --- | --- | --- |
| Symbolic play | Provides children with opportunities to explore and extend their world. Materials and objects are used to represent all kinds of things and people. Objects take on personalities and actions as well as functions. | Begins as children develop language skills and the ability to manipulate materials. They test and challenge their understanding of the world by trying out ideas with objects. |

| | | |
|---|---|---|
| Socio-dramatic play | Involves interaction and communication with others as children can act out stories on their own and with others. Allows them to explore the nature of a particular role, adapting and modifying it as a result of interacting with others. | Develops as child develops and has wider experiences. |
| Role-play | Children take specific roles, and explore and play with their ideas about the role and the context. They act out, on their own, their perceived understanding of a role. | Develops as child develops and has wider experiences. |
| Fantasy play | A form of role-play. Children create their own stories, and challenge accepted norms and expectations. Involves make-believe, where objects and people take on new, innovative functions and roles. | Develops as child develops and has wider experiences. |
| Practice play | Takes place in any context and may be found in all types of play. Involves practising new skills and roles. Can be repetitive. Will vary according to cultures. | Appears at all stages and in all kinds of play as children practise to refine their ideas and skills. Safe and reassuring to player. |
| Constructive play | A term used by practitioners to extend description of some symbolic play. Involves exploratory play with all kinds of materials, to construct and build artefacts. Provides opportunities to discover more about the properties of materials. | Is found at all stages of development. Shows perseverance. |
| Physical play | Rough-and-tumble. Fun, free-flowing and physical. Children can develop their physical abilities and refine their motor control. | Very common with young children. May overlap with constructive and symbolic play. |
| Games with rules | Children develop their skills at devising rules. Playing simple games with rules helps them to learn to take turns, think logically, work in teams, take chances and develop observation skills. | Develops as children acquire the skills of playing and working with and alongside others. The level of complexity will depend on child's age and experience. |

In real life it is often difficult to allocate children's play to just one of the descriptors above. Depending on their age and stage of development, you can watch children move from one kind of play to another and see little or no perceptible dividing line.

> In playing, [children] behave in different ways: sometimes their play will be boisterous, sometimes they will describe and discuss what they are doing, sometimes they will be quiet and reflective as they play.
>
> (QCA/DfEE 2000: 25)

The characteristics of play change as children pass through different stages of development. Nevertheless, observing children at play is an important way to begin to understand the interesting and complex nature of play and its vital role in children's learning. The next activity invites you to read about two children playing with large blocks, and to reflect on what is happening.

## Activity 6.2 Types of play

Read the transcript below of an exchange between two boys building a garage in the block corner of a nursery class in a primary school. As you read, try to identify the types of play the children are engaging in. The following questions may help you with your analysis:

How would you categorise what the children are doing?

What do you think the children might be learning as a consequence of their play?

How useful are the categories in thinking about the children's play?

How might you adapt the categories to make them more useful for you?

## Case Study: Building a garage

Two children – Sam (aged 3 years 9 months) and Nicholas (aged 4 years 2 months) – are building a garage, using large blocks and discussing what is to go where and how it will work. The short extract below shows the ways in which similarly shaped blocks can take on different forms and functions in children's imaginations as they play.

Nicholas: I'll get another block to go here. It is the petrol pump.
Sam: We need two pumps – one for unleaded.
Nicholas: No, we need three pumps 'cos we need diesel too. My dad's car's a diesel. I'll make another pump. You finish the mending bit.
Sam: OK.

They build quietly alongside each other for a few seconds.

Nicholas: I've finished that, but we need the tubes to go in the car.

Nicholas walks to a box of fabrics and searches through it, with little success. He goes to another box that has small skipping ropes and searches through this until he finds one rope with no wooden handles. He returns triumphant to Sam.

Nicholas: Look, I've got this – it could make one pump.
Sam: We need more.
Nicholas: There was only this in the box.
Sam: Could we cut it?
Nicholas: Should we ask first?
Sam: No, we can cut it with scissors.

Sam collects a small pair of cutting scissors and tries to cut, but realises this is not working and he needs bigger, stronger scissors. Nicholas tries to do the same but with the same result. They ask the nursery nurse nearby if she can help them.

Sam: Can you cut this rope up for us?
Practitioner: Why do you want to cut it?
Nicholas: We need three ropes for our petrol pumps.
Practitioner: Have you looked in that blue box over there? There's lots of bits of cord and rope you might use without cutting this long piece.

The boys go over to the box and spend several minutes picking out and selecting three different bits of rope which are then taped – both boys working together – to each pump with masking tape, and lots of it!

Analysing play is not easy and takes practice, involving you watching, observing, and being able to identify what you see. Observation is an important part of a practitioner's role in working with young children. Being able to describe what you actually see, and not what you think is happening, will help you gain a better understanding of children's current interests and dispositions.

In the case study above, the two boys built their garage using blocks and ropes to stand in for bricks and mortar and garage furniture. In doing this, they are engaging in *symbolic play* in which everyday objects take on different functions. The boys explore ways of stacking blocks, and make discoveries about the properties of the rope and the masking tape as they fix up the petrol pumps. At times, they play together, discussing ideas and negotiating roles; at other times, they play in parallel, each attending to his own area of interest.

*Role-play* is also a strong underpinning feature, although it may not be immediately obvious from this short extract. Each boy sees himself as a worker in the garage and is playing out his understanding of that role.

However, because the children are constantly interacting with each other to define their roles and responsibilities, we could more accurately describe this as *socio-dramatic play*. Based on their different experiences of garages – gained perhaps from a variety of sources, including stories, media and visits to garages with parents or carers – the boys are able to negotiate and redefine those experiences as they play. They organise and make their own rules within the fantasy. These rules will disappear when the game is finished or has to be put away, but they may be replayed on another day in a similar pattern or with minor modifications as the children practise and refine their play.

Sam and Nicholas can interact with each other because they have reached the developmental stage of associative play that is typical for children of their age. Stages and types of play are summarised in Table 6.2 but these should only be used a guide, as individual children's ability to engage in the different types of play will vary considerably depending on their age, context, experience and interests.

**Table 6.2**  Types and stages of play

| Type | Age | Characteristics |
|------|-----|-----------------|
| Solitary | 0–2 years | Play alone, with little interaction. |
| Spectator | 2–2.5 years | Watch others play, but tend not to join in. |
| Parallel | 2.5–3 years | Play alongside others, but not together. |
| Associative | 3–4 years | Begin to interact and, to some extent, cooperate with others. Develop friendships and preference for playing with certain, usually mixed-sex, groups. |
| Cooperative | 4+ years | Play together with shared goals. Play can be complex, and children support each other in their play. Divide into single-sex groups as they enter primary schooling. |

(Adapted from Tassoni and Hucker, 2000: 7–8)

As we can see from the table, initially young children play alone and there is little interaction with other children. However, as they develop and are supported in their play by adults and older children, they learn the skills required to play together. The more opportunities they have to play with other children of different ages, the wider will be their experience of the various stages of play described above. Children from large families are often able to play more cooperatively on first entering an early years setting, because they have already played alongside older siblings who have modelled other ways of playing.

The stages summarised in the table are not discrete; they are revisited throughout childhood, and continue to have meaning throughout an individual's adult life. As children grow and develop, and pass through the stages, they assemble a menu of ways of playing which they use as and when they choose. Many children, even when they grow older, enjoy playing on their own as much as they do playing with a friend or group of friends. Meanwhile, even very young children will engage in playful behaviour and respond to parents or carers. This is illustrated by a young mother who was sitting in church, with her eight week-old son in a pouch in front of her who was playfully responding to his mother's quiet whispers and smiling face with his own noises and smiles. At one point he was gurgling quite noisily and she 'ssshed' him. Here was a child who already knew some of the basics of communication, taking turns with his mum at making noises and smiling – playing at talking together. He was enjoying a playful encounter with another whilst also being introduced to some accepted conventions or rules.

In order for the children we work with to benefit fully from the opportunities that play offers, it is important that we understand, plan and support appropriately. From your experience of watching children play, and the two examples above, it is possible to see that there are three common features of play – that it involves children:

- choosing to engage in the experience,

- having control over it, and

- enjoying what they are doing.

Children seen running, jumping, climbing and involved in other movements could be playing chase or football, building a shelter, acting out a story or making up a game as they go along. Other play experiences include using construction kits, doing art and craft activities, model making, putting together structured toys such as jigsaws and other puzzles, playing with 'small world' toys such as dinosaur models or farm animals, making music, or playing computer and electronic games. Children play in a variety of settings – in school, at home, in the garden or street. They may play on their own or with their peers and/or elders. But does all play actually lead to learning? Whether or not we would want it to is not the question. What is essential is that we understand how children learn and the contribution and value of play to children's learning. This will enable us to assess when children are making progress in their learning and plan appropriate interventions.

## Free and structured play

As the English Foundation Stage (QCA/DfEE 2000) curriculum suggests, children can learn with challenge and enjoyment and this was certainly true of the two boys in the earlier example of play with building blocks. Through their play, they showed the breadth of knowledge they had about garages and their developing social skills of working cooperatively. This scenario was a clear example of free play, where the children set the agenda and pace of their play. Free play is where children set the scene, the pace, decide the context and lead and control the action.

Structured play is play that may have been initiated and planned by adults or children but which has significant interaction and support from others to extend the experience.

In the same nursery, on the same day as the garage scene, it was also possible to see examples of play where the adults were more directly involved.

## Case Study: Building a bridge

Outside, four girls were building a bridge across an enormous hole they had dug in the sandpit. The teacher, who had helped with the digging, was actively questioning the children to help them solve the problem of selecting an appropriate piece of wood for their bridge. There was much discussion about the width and length of the wood needed to span the hole, with significant use of words like 'longer', 'shorter', and 'wider'. The two younger children were not clear about the difference between the first two and appreciated the gentle support of the adult as they giggled and struggled to lift their piece of wood over the hole.

## Role of the practitioner in play

Play is so valuable that it is important to provide appropriate experiences, activities and resources that will help children to develop their ability to play and learn.

## Activity 6.3 Melinda's role

Read the case study below, which is an observation of the digging area in a nursery school. As you read, note the roles the practitioner takes as they play.

## Case Study: Melinda in the garden

Melinda, working with a group of three children, was digging with them and modelling some of her own and their reactions as they dug. She made the same grunting noises as the children as she lifted the spade, piled with soil, out of the ground and onto the growing pile at the side of the digging pit. She asked one of the children why they were picking out the hard lumps and putting them in a different pile and was informed they were potatoes. She asked how she would know if she was digging up potatoes. They said you had to look carefully as you dug and you would see the lumps in the soil and sometimes you would tip them on the wrong pile! One of the girls said she was always doing that and one of the boys said he did the same.

Melinda asked what they were going to do with the potatoes and why they were in the ground. Through discussion she found out that they knew potatoes grew in the ground, that you had to dig them up and wash them. After working with the children for some time, she left the children playing on their own, but as she walked away she reminded them that they needed to wash the potatoes before they could cook them. (As these were not real potatoes but lumps of hard soil or pebbles, when they were washed the children had fun watching the mud soften and the potatoes disintegrate.) Melinda watched from the sidelines.

Later Melinda commented that there was always digging available at all times of the year in the garden but the level of activity had declined recently. It was late October, the weather was colder and the ground harder, but recently two boys had teamed up and spent several sessions piling up hard lumps of soil, 'their potatoes'.

Amal had been digging up potatoes with his grandfather on his allotment and packing them into sacks for use through the winter. He was reliving this experience with his friend Sanjay. The practitioner saw this as an opportunity to try to encourage others to dig and be involved in outside play.

Having observed Amal and Sanjay over three days and noticed how two girls were interested but had not yet joined in the digging, Melinda went to the planning session with colleagues to discuss how to extend the children's play. Several ideas emerged, including providing some different tools such as trowels, sieves, buckets, wooden boxes and sacks in which to put the potatoes. They also found one or two story books and some reference books about growing vegetables, which were put into the book corner and read at story time over the next few days. Alongside this, different varieties of potato were buried in the digging area, by the staff, before the children arrived.

When the children began to find real potatoes, many other children came over to see what the excitement was. Some came to watch and others to dig. These potatoes were then washed and sorted into groups. The children decided there were three varieties of potato. One of the children asked if the red potatoes were red inside. Another child said, 'No it wasn't'. Melinda suggested that they take some potatoes inside and cut them up to see what they were like inside. Four children went in to do this.

Later in the week, the children, with another practitioner and careful supervision, were able to make and cook some chips and mashed potatoes that were shared amongst the group. This was well received by the children. Amal's grandfather came to talk with the diggers and a group visited his allotment and went to the local shops to buy different potatoes, including sweet potatoes and yams. These were all examined, cooked and eaten.

The digging continued for some days, with staff encouraging children to explore the contents of the soil and to extend their digging to clearing some of the flower beds. These were cleared and the children planted some different bulbs in their chosen areas. Labels were made which showed the children's developmental writing with the proper names alongside.

The digging as a regular activity has much to offer children, as do many regular experiences. However, here the practitioner felt there was a need to develop the use of the digging area. To do this it was important to watch the children at play and to explore their current understanding and interest in the digging. Providing meaningful contexts for play will enhance and deepen the learning. Hughes (1986) says that children can operate at much higher intellectual levels if they are working in a context that is meaningful to them. In this case, it would not have been appropriate to bury 'treasure' to dig up, as the children were very focused on the potatoes. Providing a wider range of digging implements and ways of sifting the soil away from the potatoes enticed more children into the digging pit. The practitioner noted that two girls involved in the digging had not been seen in this area before. If she had not provided a context that enticed these two to participate, she might never have learnt what competent diggers they were. These girls, she later learned, had also been involved in gardening activities at home with grandparents. By watching and then planning and implementing their plans, the practitioners helped more children to gain more from the activity. By introducing a wide range of vegetables at a later stage in their garden work, the practitioners also took account of children's different cultural experiences outside school.

Digging is one of many physical activities that children can undertake which enable them to explore their own physical capabilities and well-being, and to learn new skills and techniques with the help of more experienced others, such as older children or adults. The context in which the digging is placed will have a significant effect on which children participate.

## Activity 6.4 Your role in supporting children's play and learning

Think of one structured play activity that you undertake regularly with the children in your care. For this activity, list the preparations you usually make beforehand. Include the resources you have to collect/provide and any other organisational activities you have to undertake. Note your purpose in providing certain resources or for doing this activity with children. The following questions may help you to think about what you do and why.

What do you want them to gain from the experience?

Why do you do this regularly with children?

What changes do you make, if any, each time?

Why do you or do you not make changes?

What informs your decisions to change or leave things?

Do you keep a record of what you do with children and what they achieved?

What other matters do you have to consider?

You will, it is hoped, have been clear about what you wanted the children to learn through the chosen activity. It may have been extending their fine motor skills or extending their knowledge about materials, or how books work. To extend children's understanding of skills and knowledge, it is important to watch what is happening and use this to inform changes, as Melinda did in the earlier case study. She also used the expertise of colleagues to widen her understanding of the potential of developing the activities within such a meaningful context. Sometimes, simple things, like moving equipment and material around, can be a trigger for different play activities or scenarios to emerge that will extend learning. Having some wooden blocks or figures set up in an enticing layout on the carpet when children arrive can stimulate different play, especially if they are used to having all the toys packed away in boxes when they arrive. The reverse can also be true.

Painting, building, digging, water play and cooking are just some of the common or regular experiences children are provided with in different settings. But if these do not vary or take account of children's interests and abilities, the learning will not be as effective and could even deter some children from participating. Simple things, such as using different kinds of paints or brushes, are obvious starting points to developing variety in children's paintings. By supplementing the normal provision, the children in the earlier case study were enticed more and more into the digging area. They did not have to be coerced but were the ones who set the agenda and pace of their learning. The adults responded to their questions, interests and needs by providing a rich array of resources and some 'unexpected' finds.

This case study shows the dynamic and cyclic nature of working alongside children as they play.

The potato scenario highlights several roles the practitioner took on. These included observing, planning, resourcing, playing with, supporting, modelling and questioning what was happening. Being aware at all times of the wide range of roles is important if we are to support children to develop a love for learning. As the Northern Ireland Curriculum Guidance suggests, 'young children require adults who will treat them as individuals and sensitively participate in their play' (DENI 1997: 7)

## Review

In this chapter you have explored learning, your own experiences as a learner, your understanding of play and how it facilitates and supports learning. We have examined different types of play through the use of case studies and have shown the complex dimensions to play and how children move in and out of these many times in any play sequence.

Children's work is their play and the role of practitioners is to value this and understand the holistic way in which children play and learn. Play is a very important part of a child's world and our role as adults is to support and extend young children's experiences. A balanced curriculum and a rich, stimulating and supportive environment are crucial dimensions for learning through play.

### Questions for reflection

1 Which kinds of play does your setting support best?

2 Which areas of your provision best support free play in your setting?

3 Which areas need development?

## References

ACCAC (1996) *Desirable Outcomes for Children's Learning before Compulsory School Age*, Cardiff: ACCAC.

Bruner, J. (1972) *The Relevance of Education*, London: Allen and Unwin.

Department of Education Northern Ireland (DENI) (1997) *Curricular Guidance for Pre-School Education*, Belfast: CCEA.

Drummond, M.J., Lally, M. and Pugh, G. (1989) *Working with Children; Developing a Curriculum for Early Years*, London: National Children's Bureau/NES Arnold.

Early Childhood Education Forum (ECEF) (1998) *Quality in Diversity in Early Learning: A framework for early childhood practitioners*, London: National Children's Bureau.

Hughes, M. (1986) *Children and Number*, Oxford: Basil Blackwell.

Isaacs, S. (1954) *The Educational Value of the Nursery School*, London: BAECE.

Macintyre, C. (2001) *Enhancing Learning Through Play*, London: David Fulton Publishers.

Qualifications and Curriculum Authority (QCA)/Department for Education and Employment (DfEE) (2000) *Curriculum Guidance for the Foundation Stage*, London: QCA/DfEE.

Scottish Consultative Council on the Curriculum (SCCC) (1999) *A Curriculum Framework for Children 3–5*, Dundee: SCCC.

Tassoni, P. and Hucker, K. (2000) *Planning Play and the Early Years*, Oxford: Heinemann Educational Publishers.

## Further reading

Holland, R. (2003) 'What's it all about? – How introducing heuristic play has affected provision for the under threes in one day nursery', in Devereux, J. and Miller, L. (eds) *Working with Children in the Early Years*, London: David Fulton Publishers.

Miller, L. (2000) 'Play as a foundation for learning', in Drury, R., Miller, L. and Campbell, R. (eds) *Looking at Early Years Education and Care*, London David Fulton Publishers.

Tucker, K. (2005) *Mathematics Through Play in the Early Years*, London: Paul Chapman Publishing.

Wood, E. (2005) *Play Learning And The Early Childhood Curriculum*, London: Paul Chapman Publishers.

# 7 Learning and Developing from Birth to Three

## By the end of this chapter you will have:

- understood how babies and young children think and learn about their world and themselves;

- considered ways in which adults support early learning through specific approaches and practices;

- learnt about aspects of policy and provision for children up to age three years.

## Introduction

Scientists used to think that babies were born as 'tabulae rasae', or blank slates, that they made little response to their environment and thus warranted little attention other than to their basic care needs. Babies were defined by what they didn't know rather than what they did know. Now, we know a great deal more about children's minds and brains than a hundred years ago, and we have a greater understanding of how children come to learn about the world around them. Scientists and thinkers have begun to find answers to questions such as 'How do children do all the things they do?' and 'How do they know so much already?'

## Understanding how children learn

Two important ideas relate to children's early learning.

1 Babies and young children should be thought of in terms of what they know and can do.

2 They probably know more than we think they do.

These ideas show the importance of basing theory on close observation of children. Modern technologies now make it much easier for researchers and practitioners to observe, record and think about the behaviour of babies and young children.

## Babies as learning machines

Studies of brain activity in babies show that their brains are sensitive to everything that happens around them. Observation of electrical activity in the brain shows what happens when cells send messages to each other. Such studies show that everything we see, hear, touch, taste, think and feel causes a reaction in our brain. This knowledge adds to what we already know about the importance of early learning for children.

At birth, a baby has all the brain cells needed for life – over a billion! There are over 50 trillion connections between these cells, and each one can connect with up to 15,000 other cells (LiLI 2003). Connections are strengthened through everyday activities and experiences, such as hearing favourite nursery rhymes. Connections that are not used wither away, a process known as 'pruning'. By age ten, children's brains begin to dramatically prune extra connections, so providing young children with the right kind of experiences (discussed later in this chapter) at this critical stage is vital to their future learning. This does not mean that children's later learning is less important, just that it is different. Also, early experiences and relationships do not predetermine outcomes for children.

Gopnik *et al.* (1999) compare the 'finding out' methods of babies and those of scientists, and make the analogy that babies are like computers. The 'baby as computer' analogy has three key components:

- special inbuilt programs (for people, objects and language);
- learning mechanisms that allow them to revise, reshape and restructure their knowledge;
- the best technical support system in the world (i.e. parents, carers, other adults and siblings).

Most powerfully of all, Gopnik *et al.* suggest, these three components are held together by language and love. Babies love to learn and adults love to teach; this is an irresistible combination and the basis for a strong learning partnership (Gopnik *et al.* 1999).

## The importance of early relationships

Rich interactions between adults and children are important not only for children's language development (discussed in Chapter 8), but also for other aspects of their development and learning. Trevarthen (1977, 1993) shows that exchanges between mothers and babies are about mutual interactions, where sometimes babies take the lead. These interactions are the way in which babies and young children come to experience their world. Reciprocal and sensitive interactions require parents (or other adults) to understand and give careful attention to the emotional state of babies and young children. During this process, babies also have their attention drawn to aspects of the culture surrounding them. So, these early relationships, as well as being important for language learning and social and emotional development, are crucial for babies as they learn about the world they live in.

Babies, however, are not always smiley and happy and relationships then can seem more difficult. If a baby is upset and other children need supporting and you have tried everything possible to make the situation better, you may ask 'Why is this happening? Is it my fault?' As a practitioner or a parent, you may feel that you should be able to deal with every situation.

---

### Activity 7.1 Louisa and Pete

The following observation is taken from a three-year project carried out by Elfer and Selleck (2002), which studied group care for babies and children.

> Louisa has been crying inconsolably. Pete says 'It is a long day for you, isn't it?' . . . Pete tries to see [the situation] from Louisa's point of view as a six-month-old baby, and offers sympathy even though he is feeling rather worn down by her crying and has been wondering if it is his fault somehow.
>
> (Elfer and Selleck 2002 cited in Edwards 2002: 16)

Now think about a situation you have experienced where a child's behaviour was difficult for you. Write a short account of the way it made you feel. Note the actions you took. Did you try to look at the situation from the child's point of view? What feelings was the child displaying? Think about whether you find some children's feelings more difficult to accept than others.

---

In caring for a child, it can be hard to have your most caring efforts seemingly rejected. However, it is important that adults help children to feel that their negative and positive feelings are accepted. Children need to know they can express feelings within set boundaries and to learn acceptable ways to express themselves. Positive relationships develop and unfold in a secure and loving environment. When this happens, children are able to develop positive self-image and self-esteem, as we see in Chapters 4 and 11 of this book.

# Attachments

'Attachment theory' was formulated by Bowlby in 1969. He sees attachment as a device that:

- provides children with a sense of security;
- promotes communication and the expression of feelings;
- acts as a secure base for children to explore their world and to learn self-regulation and self-control;
- contributes to children's developing sense of self.

This early attachment is thought to be universal, although how it is expressed varies according to culture. At one time, it was believed that babies could only relate in this special way to their mothers (Bowlby 1982). We now know that babies between three and six months form preferential attachments to their primary carers, which may include attachments to older children. Attachment behaviour includes increased social smiling, face-to-face and eye contact, and attempts to win the attention of primary carers. If these attachments are carelessly disrupted, there can be serious consequences for children in building loving and trusting relationships with other people.

Babies who spend time away from their primary carers need to be provided with opportunities to form close links with another carer. Separation will then not be harmful as babies *are* able to develop relationships with other people they spend time with on a regular basis (Schaffer 1977; Rutter 1981). However, the quality of these relationships is important. The new adult needs to become a familiar figure and to get to know the child's special likes and dislikes, language and culture. Achieving this type of relationship in group care or home-based settings is challenging. Selleck (2001) acknowledges it is not always easy to look at things from the point of view of the child or the parent: 'Work with babies and toddlers is physically demanding, emotionally draining as well as intellectually challenging. It needs very observant and astute people to tune in to babies and their families' (2001: 84).

# Key persons: building relationships

Developing quality relationships between children and adults involves a series of finely tuned joint interactions. Through the key person approach, practitioners can build relationships with the children in their care, so that close attachments are formed. While the terms 'key person' and 'key worker' are often used interchangeably, Elfer *et al.* (2003) offer a useful distinction between the two roles. They suggest the key worker role is about liaising with different professionals or different disciplines, and ensuring coordination of services, whereas a key person role is:

> . . . a way of working in nurseries in which the whole focus and organisation is aimed at enabling and supporting close attachments between individual children and individual nursery staff. The key person approach is an involvement, an individual and reciprocal commitment between a member of staff and a family. It is an approach that has clear benefits for children, parents and the nursery.
>
> (Elfer et al. 2003: 20)

The benefits of a key person approach are summarised as:

- for the child, ensuring that each child feels individual and special while they are away from home;
- for the parents, offering a relationship with someone who is committed to their child;
- for the key person, feeling that they really matter to the child and his or her family;
- for the nursery, evidence suggests that this approach leads to better satisfied and engaged staff and parents, and that it can help to reduce staff sickness and absence.

Elfer *et al.* (2003)

It is important to recognise the *nature* of the key person approach rather than the *term* used to describe it. The key person approach prioritises the importance of close, loving relationships in both group and home-based settings. Dahlberg *et al.* (1999 cited in Elfer *et al.* 2003) suggest that early years settings should be an opportunity for children to experience *different* relationships with adults and children. However, practitioners should acknowledge the primacy of the family and strive for the best possible communication with home, and consider the best methods of establishing and sustaining the relationships that are essential to every child's identity, emotional well-being and cognitive development (Goldschmied and Jackson 1994; Elfer *et al.* 2003). Parents can find separation from their child hard, and practitioners acknowledge avoiding close relationships with children because of the emotional distress this can involve for themselves as practitioners (Hopkins 1988 cited in Elfer *et al.* 2003).

## 'Islands of intimacy'

In order to create time for developing close relationships, particularly in group settings, Goldschmied and Jackson (1994) suggest practitioners should take advantage of times when the maximum number of staff is available – for example, in the prelude to mealtimes, when key persons are able to focus on their particular group. A home-based practitioner will have more flexibility over the choice of suitable times. Goldschmied and Jackson suggest creating a quiet area, always the same place, made comfortable with rugs and cushions, which they call an 'island of intimacy'. Here practitioners can give undivided time and attention to an individual child or a group of children, providing opportunities for special conversations and listening to children, thus sustaining relationships and stimulating language and cognitive development.

### Case Study: Roberta – a childminder

Roberta cares for Joshua (aged six months) and his two siblings. She describes below how she considered the 'islands of intimacy' idea in her home-based setting.

> Creating a special time to be with Joshua is not a problem as we have quite a lot of time together during the morning. At midday I pick up his sister Mabel from playgroup, so that's a bit hectic. But then, when Joshua has his afternoon sleep, I have a quiet time with Mabel. It gets really hectic when their older brother Kelvin is home from school. Joshua is tired by then and I'm busy getting the tea ready before they are all collected at 6.30 p.m. I needed to think about how I can create a quiet time for all of us after school. I could do a bit more preparation for tea, both early in the morning and in the afternoon, to create time later.

### Case Study: Pen Green Centre

At Pen Green Centre a different approach was taken to creating quiet spaces. Rather than having baby rooms, toddler rooms and pre-school rooms (as many settings do), staff at the centre opted for a sharing of space and an organisational pattern where six children could have their 'special person' attached to them for their time in the nursery, and siblings could join in the same group.

(Whalley 1994).

As we discussed in Chapter 4, the environments we provide for children are indicative of what we value for them and says a great deal about the conception of childhood that the adults hold.

# Learning through play

In Chapter 6 we looked at the role of play in learning. In this section we focus on particular aspects of play relating to children from birth to three. In both home-based and group settings young children learn from involvement in everyday activities as well as from more specifically planned play experiences. They need a variety of readily available materials to experiment with, for example glue, fabrics, dough, paint and sand and water. Children in this age group need opportunities to be creative, to have contact with living things, for music and opportunities to encounter pattern, shape and number in everyday events. Organising this kind of provision poses challenges for practitioners, including how best to build on children's experiences of learning at home and elsewhere in a positive way.

## Treasure baskets

The idea of treasure baskets comes from observations and recordings that show babies' curiosity and interest in everyday objects such as keys and spoons at mealtimes (Goldschmied and Jackson 1994). In considering treasure baskets, we have in mind a baby who is sitting, perhaps with support, who is not yet mobile and who is able to explore a basket containing a rich array of 'natural' objects (not 'bought toys') in every possible way, with their hands, feet and mouths. Goldschmied and Jackson have recorded babies' intense concentration and systematic exploration when playing in this way. Babies engage with the properties of objects and discover their own power in making things happen. The security of having adults nearby is important, but they don't necessarily need to intervene in the exploration process.

Setting up a treasure basket isn't a once and for all activity. Babies get bored with being offered the same things, so ringing the changes and keeping the objects in good condition is important. Treasure baskets offer the opportunity for exploring:

Touch – texture, shape, weight

Smell – variety of scents

Taste – more limited in scope, but possible

Sound – ringing, tinkling, banging, scrunching

Sight – colour, form, length, shininess

(Goldschmied and Jackson 1994: 97)

*Activity 7.2 Treasure baskets*

Make a list of objects you might include in a treasure basket. Note what you think babies might do with the chosen items and the various senses they might use in investigating them.

The extract below describes how a practitioner has commented on how Andrew (aged seven months) explores objects in a treasure basket.

> He is selective. His personality is quite serious, not unhappy . . . I would say he is quite intelligent and he knows what he wants . . . He does concentrate for a long time . . . He studies things, you can see him thinking . . . The treasure basket is his favourite at the moment, he goes for all the stainless steel things.

Edwards comments:

> [Alex] has observed how much Andrew enjoys the treasure basket and what he chooses most often. If she watches him carefully she may be able to work out what it is about the stainless steel things he likes most. Is it the feel of them, their temperature, their shininess? Andrew is being a scientist, investigating a sequence of problems. What happens when I do this? If I do it again, will it happen again?
>
> (Edwards 2002: 77)

Careful observation during concentrated periods of play helps us to know what interests children – it can show us what they are discovering.

## Heuristic play

'Heuristic play' is a term used by Goldschmied and Jackson (1994) to describe children's absorption in filling and emptying containers. Through this play, children learn what objects can and cannot do and they can explore shape and space. Once children have developed some language, then materials are put to more imaginative use. There is no predetermined design in heuristic play, recommended for children aged 10–20 months. It requires a range of natural materials and the time and space to explore them. Goldschmied and Jackson (1994) have described some important guiding principles:

■ Time: heuristic play should be offered for a limited time in the day, about an hour, and not every day. It can provide the quality time needed by key persons to develop relationships with slightly older babies.

- Materials: there should be provision of varied and plentiful play materials and containers, for example cloth bags and tubs containing things like pom-poms, ribbons, keys, shells, ping-pong balls and pegs.
- Quietness: heuristic play needs a clear, quiet and carpeted space to minimise noise, although it should be large enough to allow up to eight children to play together.
- Adult role: the adult is an organiser and facilitator – collecting and taking care of resources, reordering objects in an unobtrusive way, and encouraging the children to put materials away – and a quiet, attentive observer.

## Activity 7.3 Playing with jelly

In a Baby Unit, a low table has been set out with plates of jelly. (The staff in the unit are careful to emphasise the difference between the play jelly and jelly that is served as food.) Chloe approaches the table hesitantly. She looks round at Nabia, her key person, to make sure she is in sight.

Now read Nabia's comments.

Chloe was initially hesitant in approaching the jelly. She watched as Darius, another child, put his hand into the jelly. She was reluctant to explore the jelly with her hands. I offered Chloe some of the jelly on my hand – she tentatively reached out to touch it, then looked up at me and smiled. Eventually, with some gentle encouragement, she was happy to put her hand inside the jelly on the plate and feel the slippery texture. She eventually became absorbed in exploring the jelly and managed to get quite a lot of it on herself.

What is Chloe learning here? What do you see as Nabia's role?

Nabia's notes show that Chloe is initially apprehensive about playing with the jelly. After some encouragement she becomes more confident, she concentrates hard on the jelly, pushing it and spreading it around. She is eventually absorbed in what she is doing. Quite a lot of jelly seems to be on Chloe, but she doesn't mind and neither does Nabia. The activity has been prepared so that Chloe can really explore the materials in her own way without anyone restricting her.

In considering children's learning through play, we have highlighted the importance of carefully considering the quality of play activities offered to babies and young children. More recently, support has been offered to practitioners in the form of guidance and frameworks for play, development and learning, as we discuss in the next section.

## Policy and provision for children from birth to three years

In this section we look briefly at policy and provision in relation to children up to three years and consider how these can contribute to high-quality experiences for young children.

### Policy initiatives

In recent years a number of government initiatives have been aimed at providing more childcare and early education places, one of the most recent being the government's Ten Year Strategy for early years and childcare (HM Treasury 2004). New guidance and frameworks for children's learning and development have been part of these initiatives to enhance quality provision, to provide support for those working with the very youngest children.

### Frameworks for working with children from birth to three years

In 2002, in England, the first published framework for working with children from birth to three was developed (Sure Start Unit 2002a), with a set of resources to support those who work with babies and toddlers. A national training strategy is supporting this framework. In Scotland, national guidance relating to the care and education of children from birth to three, 'Care and Learning for Children from Birth to Three', will be published in 2005 (LTS Scotland 2004). In Wales, a draft framework for children's learning has identified the need to consider changes relating to a learning curriculum for children aged 0–7 (National Assembly for Wales Learning Wales 2003).

### Birth to Three Matters

The *Birth to Three Matters* framework (Sure Start Unit 2002b) is organised into four aspects: a strong child; a skilful communicator; a competent learner; a healthy child. These aspects reflect the holistic development of children. The framework places relationships and the key person at the heart of healthy development.

The principles that underpin the framework are outlined below.

- Parents and families are central to the well-being of the child.
- Relationships with other people (both children and adults) are of crucial importance in a child's life.

- Learning is a shared process and children learn most effectively when, with the support of a knowledgeable and trusted adult, they are actively involved and interested.

- Caring adults count more than resources and equipment.

- Schedules and routines must flow with the child's needs.

- Children learn when they are given appropriate responsibility, allowed to make errors, decisions and choices, and respected as autonomous and competent learners.

- Children learn by doing rather than by being told.

- Young children are vulnerable. They learn to be independent by having someone they can depend on.

(Sure Start Unit 2002b: 4–5)

## Activity 7.4 Principles into practice

Now highlight those principles that you can readily identify as operating in your practice. Note those you would like to see developed and say why. Are there any principles that you do not agree with or you would like to see modified or changed? If possible, discuss the principles above with a colleague or someone connected with your setting.

Principles are concerned with what we believe in, and should always underpin our work with babies and young children. They provide a foundation for our thinking and practice. Unless we have a clear rationale for our practice, then we cannot defend it or explain it to others, and we cannot be confident about what we do. An understanding of the key principles and the ways in which they are implemented in practice influences the ways in which practitioners work with young children and affects the quality of provision offered.

## The planned and received curriculum

In this chapter we use the term 'curriculum' in a broad sense, to refer to both planned and unplanned activities and experiences designed to achieve particular developmental and educational outcomes. Selleck (2001) distinguishes between the *planned* rather than the *received* curriculum. The former can tend to focus on a group rather than on individual children. Selleck notes that we can never be certain that what we hope to achieve in supporting children's learning is actually realised. Only by careful observation and record keeping can we discover this, as we discuss in Chapter 10. People, relationships, language, objects, time, space, interactions, emotions, needs, interests, meaning-making and intentions are all part of the complex web that is the experienced curriculum. Selleck recommends that we consider three ideas:

- following children's inclinations;
- being energetic and responsive;
- embracing each baby into a community.

(Selleck 2001: 90)

## Review

This chapter has considered how children's experiences in their earliest years are critical in laying the foundations for later learning and development. We now know that children up to age three years have considerable abilities, and that practitioners can build on these by providing rich and stimulating learning experiences. We have seen that practitioners play an essential role as key persons for babies and young children in individual and group settings, and that they can contribute to the ways in which babies think, learn and form relationships. Ensuring quality environments for learning that build on sound principles is a crucial aspect of supporting children's development and learning in the early years.

### Questions for reflection

1 How do relationships with familiar others help young children to learn and to develop a positive sense of self?

2 What relevance does the key person approach have in your setting?

3 In what ways do the adults in your setting provide routines, experiences and interactions that meet the emotional and intellectual needs of the youngest children?

## References

Bowlby, J. (1982) *Attachment and Loss* (Volume 1), 2nd edn, Harmondsworth: Penguin.

Edwards, A.G. (2002) *Relationships and Learning: Caring for children from birth to three*, London: National Children's Bureau.

Elfer, P., Goldschmied, E. and Selleck, D. (2003) *Key Persons in the Nursery*, London: David Fulton Publishers.

Goldschmied, E. and Jackson, S. (1994) *People Under Three: Young children in day care*, London: Routledge.

Gopnik, A., Meltzoff, A. and Kuhl, P. (1999) *How Babies Think: The science of childhood*, London: Weidenfeld and Nicolson.

HM Treasury (2004) in conjunction with Department for Education and Skills (DfES), Department for Work and Pensions (DWP), Department for Trade and Industry (DTI), *Choice for Parents, the Best Start for Children: a ten year strategy for childcare*, London: HMSO, www.surestart.gov.uk/aboutsurestart/strategy/ (accessed April 2005).

Libraries Linking Idaho (LiLI) (2003) *Facts about brain development and how children learn*, Idaho State Library, http://www.lili.org/read/readtome/braindevelopment.htm#brfacts (accessed April 2005).

LTS Scotland (2004) *Care and Learning for Children from Birth to Three* [online], http://www.LTScotland.org.uk (accessed April 2005).

National Assembly for Wales (2003) *The Learning Country: The foundation phase – 3 to 7 years*, Cardiff: National Assembly for Wales.

Rutter, M. (1981) *Maternal Deprivation Reassessed*, 2nd edn, Harmondsworth: Penguin.

Schaffer, H.R. (1977) *Mothering*, London: Fontana/Open Books.

Selleck, D. (2001) 'Being under three years of age: enhancing quality experiences', in Pugh, G. (ed.) *Contemporary Issues in the Early Years: Working collaboratively for children*, 3rd edn, London: Paul Chapman/Coram Family.

Sure Start Unit (2002a) *Birth to Three Matters: A framework to support children in their earliest years*, London: Department for Education and Skills.

Sure Start Unit (2002b) *An Introduction to the Framework*, London: Department for Education and Skills.

Trevarthen, C. (1977) 'Descriptive analysis of infant communicative behaviour', in Schaffer, H.R. (ed.) *Studies in Mother–Infant Interaction: Proceedings of the Loch Lomond Symposium*, London: Academic Press.

Trevarthen, C. (1993) 'The function of emotions in early infant communication and development', in Nadel, J. and Camaiori, L. (eds) *New Perspectives on Early Communicative Development*, London: Routledge.

Whalley, M. (1994) *Learning to be Strong: Setting up a neighbourhood service for under-fives and their families*, London: Hodder and Stoughton.

## Further reading

Abbott, L. and Langston, A. (eds) (2004) *Birth to Three Matters: Supporting The Framework of Effective Practice*, Buckingham: Open University Press/McGraw-Hill Education.

Bruce, T. (2004) *Developing Learning in Early Childhood*, London: Paul Chapman Publishing.

Dahlberg, G., Moss, P. and Pence, A. (1999) *Beyond Quality in Early Childhood Education and Care: Postmodern perspectives*, London: Falmer.

David, T., Goouch, K., Powell, S. and Abbott, L. (2003) *Birth to Three Matters: A Review of the Literature*, London: DfES.

## Website references

http://www.LTScotland.org.uk for information on *Care and Learning for Children from Birth to Three*.

http://www.learning.wales.gov.uk/foundationphase/whats-new-e.htm for information on *The Learning Country: The Foundation Phase 3–7 years*.

www.surestart.gov.uk/aboutsurestart/strategy/ for information on *Choice for Parents, the Best Start for Children: a ten year strategy for childcare*.

# 8 Language and Learning

**By the end of this chapter you will have developed your:**

■ knowledge and understanding of how young children learn;

■ understanding of the importance of language in learning;

■ understanding of your roles and responsibilities in providing contexts and support for children's language and learning.

## Introduction

In this chapter we focus on how children learn and, in particular, on how children learn the language they need to communicate their feelings and intentions, to respond to people and experiences and to develop, refine and reinforce their ideas and understanding. In doing so, we will examine the view of learning that has emerged from and been influenced by socio-cultural theory and the implications for practice in early years settings.

## How young children learn

Perhaps one of the most striking facts to come out of the past three decades of research into learning is just how much young children, even very young babies, know. The Select Committee Report on Education and Employment – Early Years (2000) drew on an overview of studies of brain development in young children to conclude that a rich, stimulating early years environment is important for early development. It also concluded that many skills, such as walking, talking and emotional understanding, develop naturally through play and exploration, whereas others, such as reading, writing and mathematics, require teaching. However, the report says that there is no convincing evidence to suggest that teaching these skills too early (i.e. before the age of six) is advantageous.

So what is learning and how do we know when it is taking place? The 'Start Right' report offers the following definition of early learning:

> ... the development of children's capacity and motivation to acquire knowledge, skills and attitudes, to make sense of their world and to operate effectively within it.
>
> (Ball 1994: 103)

So *what* should children learn? Katz (1993) identified four goals: knowledge, skills, dispositions and feelings. Traditionally, published curriculum documents have emphasised knowledge and skills, particularly for older children, and paid little attention to dispositions or feelings. More recently, the English 'Curriculum guidance for the foundation stage' (QCA/DfEE 2000: 8) noted that 'developing positive attitudes and dispositions towards their learning' is one of the aims for this stage of education. The introduction to the Northern Ireland Curriculum document for primary schools (DENI undated) says that at Key Stage 1, learning experiences should be enjoyable, challenging and motivating so that children will be encouraged to adopt positive attitudes to schools and learning.

## Views of learning

So *how* should children learn? Our views on how children learn are influenced by theories, but while theories can tell us more about how children learn or develop, they do not tell us how best to support children's learning. We can say that theories have implications for practice; however, these need to be interpreted. In this chapter we do not have space to examine all the theories of learning, or their implications for practice, so we have chosen to focus on what is termed a *socio-cultural* view of learning.

Socio-cultural perspectives emphasise the social and cultural context of learning, and in this section we will briefly examine this through the way that knowledge, language, learning, learners and the role of others are viewed. For example, knowledge is viewed as being a social construct built up through the interactions of individuals in particular contexts; knowledge is not viewed as having an existence of its own but is defined by the cultural and social context. Language is viewed as being a form of thought and is considered important because it provides a way of representing the world and an additional and special way of thinking – we will explore this aspect in more detail later in this chapter. In socio-cultural theory, learning is seen as an active process of making sense of the world which is carried out in partnership with others.

Through these partnerships the learner develops understandings, takes these on board or appropriates them, and makes them their own. Social interaction plays a key role in learning, particularly through the support of 'more knowledgeable' others. The main theorist responsible for developing these ideas was Russian psychologist Lev Vygotsky (1978).

One of Vygotsky's key ideas was the 'zone of proximal development'. He suggested that, when learning, children could operate on two developmental levels:

■ their actual level; and

■ their proximal level (i.e. the next level).

He described the interchange between these two levels as the 'zone of proximal development' (ZPD). Within the ZPD, the child operates on the edge of their capabilities. In practice, the difference between the two levels is what the child can do alone and what she or he can do with the help and guidance of a supporting adult. Nutbrown (1994) describes this as the child doing with assistance today what they will do alone tomorrow. The adult can support the child's learning, by helping them to move forward in their thinking, skills and understanding. Play can provide children with opportunities to move between the known and the unknown without fear of failure and to try out new skills and knowledge in a risk-free environment. A skilful adult minimises the risk of failure, encourages high aspirations, encourages independence and so leads children towards the outer limits of their competence.

### Activity 8.1 ZPD

Think about an incident where you helped a child to move towards the edge of their competence. Try to focus upon an incident where you felt the child was at the critical point of almost being able to do something but was in need of adult help in order to progress. Justify why you think you helped to move this child on in their learning. What did you do and say that helped?

Vygotsky's notion of the ZPD has implications for how we support and extend children's learning and development. It can help us to think about the importance of how adults interact with and support young children in different social and cultural contexts. These ideas have been developed further by others such as Bruner (1977). Using a building metaphor, he and his fellow researchers described the process by which adults support learning within the ZPD as 'scaffolding'. When a child builds a new understanding, the structure is at first shaky. Without interfering in that building, the adult must construct a supporting scaffold which allows the child to keep building.

> ### Case Study: Archie, aged 25 months
>
> Archie (25 months) was sitting on his key worker's lap, having just woken from his afternoon nap. He picked up a yellow sticklebrick and held it up, saying 'It's a blue one'. J replied, 'It's a yellow one'. Archie made his sticklebrick into a candle by sticking another short piece into the end to resemble a flame and pushed the whole candle onto a large flat base (the cake). J said, 'Oh look at that cake – put another candle on'. Archie complied and then blew out the candles with a mighty puff.
>
> (Early Childhood Education Forum 1998: 40)

In this example, Archie's key worker responded contingently or sensitively to his idea about the candle. She joined in his play and helped him to extend his idea by encouraging him to put another candle on the cake. In doing so, she entered into his imaginary play and held a conversation with Archie about it. Gradually, she will remove the 'scaffolding' as Archie progresses towards more independent learning.

We can summarise the main implications of socio-cultural perspectives for early years practitioners as:

- knowledge cannot be transferred but must be co-constructed between individuals;
- social interaction is vital to learning;
- learning is a process of enculturation – taking on, or appropriating, shared understandings of the world through interaction with 'more knowledgeable' others (adults or peers);
- language plays a fundamentally important role in promoting children's learning and development;
- learning is an active process that involves learners interacting with others.

However, what can be learnt will depend upon a range of factors, including the knowledge the different participants bring to the learning interaction and their relationship. Practitioners need to be 'tuned in' to the child's level of understanding and skills and to their emotional states. Teaching is important, but it involves determining a child's ZPD and then intervening to co-construct a shared understanding with them, within their ZPD. It is also important to remember that peer–peer interaction, particularly between children with different levels of understanding, can be a powerful vehicle for learning.

The following extract from the English foundation stage curriculum guidance suggests that effective learning involves:

- children initiating activities that promote learning and enable them to learn from each other;
- children learning through movement and all their senses;
- children having time to explore ideas and interests in depth;
- children feeling secure, which helps them to become confident learners;
- children learning in different ways and at different rates;
- children making links in their learning.

(QCA/DfEE 2000: 20–1)

## Strategies to support teaching and learning

A number of researchers and practitioners have sought to interpret socio-cultural theory and develop approaches to supporting children's learning which are based around the ideas we have discussed. The following are some examples.

Rogoff *et al.* (1998) extended the notion of the ZPD in their work with toddlers and caregivers. They use the term 'guided participation' to describe how young children participate in episodes with more experienced 'others'. They emphasise the need to consider different developmental goals relating to the cultural context and early experiences of children prior to joining group settings.

The concept of 'joint involvement episodes' (JIEs) stems from the research of Schaffer (1977) and Bruner (1977), who observed that mothers and babies appear to 'turn take' with each other. This behaviour develops into periods during which the adult and child are both focused on a potential learning episode: for example, they jointly play with a ball, pushing, bouncing and rolling it. The child learns about the properties of the ball within a safe and secure environment with a familiar adult.

The notion of learning partners is another interpretation of the ZPD. In the nurseries of Reggio Emilia in Northern Italy, the adults are seen as more able 'others' who 'co-construct' knowledge alongside children and support their learning (Malaguzzi 1996). The teachers act as the group's 'memory' by documenting visits and children's work through photographs, tape recordings and written notes. The children and adults can then reconstruct, revisit and reflect on what they have learnt. The teachers pose problems and questions to be explored. and offer assistance, resources, and strategies if necessary.

Apprenticeship learning (Edwards and Knight 1994) provides another interpretation of learning partners. In this model the practitioner is 'the expert' and the child an active learner of goals to be achieved. Gradually, the child moves towards more independent mastery of new understandings and skills.

Language and social interaction in the co-construction of knowledge are key elements in socio-cultural perspectives on learning and in the approaches described above. In the following sections of this chapter, we explore the link between language, thinking and learning and your role in supporting children's developing skills and understanding.

## Language and learning

The learning of language is crucial because of the many other kinds of learning that are achieved through the medium of language. Language is central to personal and social development: it supports the development of knowledge and understanding of the world; expressive, aesthetic and creative growth; and mathematical, scientific and technological development. Even some aspects of physical development will be supported by language.

Language features in all the guidance documents for the early years curriculum published in the four countries of the UK and it is also a key element in documents for primary age children. All the authorities opt for the term 'language' rather than 'English' or 'Welsh', and there is good reason for this. A child's mother tongue may well not be the same as the main language used in the early years setting that he or she attends. However, it is this first language that provides the ground on which vital early skills of communication and thinking are developed. A child's first language is an essential part of his or her identity.

## Communication

'Communication' is a broad term, which describes an exchange of information. If we are to communicate successfully with other people, we need to understand what they are communicating to us and to get our messages across to them. This process does not need a spoken 'language'. *Birth to Three Matters* (Sure Start Unit 2003) describes children as 'skilful communicators', which involves being sociable and effective communicators, listening and responding appropriately to the language of others, and making meaning. To become skilful communicators, babies need to be with people who are important to them and with whom they have formed strong and loving relationships. When babies' early attempts at communicating and vocalising are rewarded, they become more confident and learn to communicate their needs and feelings to others. Carers in turn provide a model for language development: being spoken to, sung to, and hearing language patterns from birth make important contributions to children's future language development. In their first year, babies make enormous progress in the sounds they are able to produce. However, some babies may be less equipped to do this, for example if they have an intellectual, sensory or physical impairment, and it is essential that these are noted and acted on, and that sensitive interventions are put in place.

As children grow and develop, they need many varied opportunities to talk and to listen. Taking advantage of everyday conversational opportunities with siblings, other children, and less familiar adults such as neighbours, key workers and other staff is important. They need to experience stories, songs and rhymes, and music as both listening and participatory activities and imaginative play opportunities that reflect the everyday world as well as that of fantasy.

At first, children talk about what they are doing while they are doing it. Gradually, they develop the ability to step back and talk about past or future events. The ability to speak without a supporting context allows them to use words for thinking. This ability, valuable in itself, will also, eventually, enable children to understand written language. However, it is an advanced skill that can only grow out of wide experience of talking in context. Talk fulfils a variety of functions which children have to experience and learn, including:

- communicating meaning, feelings and intentions;
- conveying instructions;
- conveying responses – to people and experiences;
- recalling the past;
- predicting the future;
- reshaping and reinforcing understanding;
- answering and asking questions;
- exploring and developing ideas by externalising thought.

(adapted from Clipson-Boyles 1996: 21)

## Activity 8.2 Children talking

Read the following example from the Scottish curriculum framework (SCCC 1999: 18). Note some of the ways in which this scenario offers opportunities for children to employ each of the 'major functions of talk' in the list above. If there are any for which you feel good opportunities are not provided, try to think how the activity might be developed or extended to accommodate them.

## Case Study: The new baby

Robert came in one morning with news of the birth of his sister. He had brought a photograph of her when she was two hours old.

A group of children gathered round with one of the staff to hear the news and look at the photograph. The child was asked to describe how he had visited his mum and the baby in hospital and had held the baby. He talked well about the visit and told everyone how excited he had been. The children listened carefully and some asked questions. Many of them began talking about their own smaller brothers and sisters. Everyone in the group took part in the conversation. More photographs appeared the following day, some showing the children as babies. A display was made and children looked at the photographs. They were encouraged to talk about how they had grown and changed since the photographs were taken. They also talked about some of the things that they could now do on their own. Many of the children painted expressive paintings of babies in their families.

You will have had little difficulty in identifying opportunities for talk. The excitement of the event entailed the sharing of feelings as well as facts. Over time, the talk moved from the straightforward recounting of events to more speculative and exploratory talk: for example, about how babies learn and grow, what they need in order to thrive, and how the children themselves expect to grow up. Further activities designed to promote collaboration, either between children or between children and adults (such as using LEGO to build a bedroom for the baby), would encourage the language of instruction and response, as well as the development of ideas in the process of planning. The practitioners also have the opportunity to model precise scientific language related to growth and development.

Talking and learning are not always the same thing, and careful planning is needed to ensure that children can develop their skills in talking for different purposes. As we saw in Chapter 6, play offers many opportunities. Children acting out events in a doctor's surgery, for example, will have the chance to communicate meaning and feelings, to respond to each other's speech and actions, and to ask and answer questions. They will be able to learn and practise necessary vocabulary, such as the naming of body parts. More formal group activities, such as storytime, will allow them to talk about the future and the past, and to explore and reshape ideas. Where children work together on more focused activities with clear goals (perhaps rehearsing for a puppet show, designing and building a model or carrying out a scientific investigation), talk may be used to give and respond to instructions, and to test and develop ideas. No doubt you can think of many other examples from your own setting or school.

## Language for thinking

As you know from observing children in your setting, they do not have to be working with others to engage in talk. Many solitary activities will be accompanied by a kind of running commentary, like this one:

> [Child playing in the water tray] 'Ooooooh! Cold! That's cold, that is. Fill it up. Right to the top. Careful. Careful.'
>
> (Clipson-Boyles 1996: 11)

Vygotsky called this 'speech for oneself' (Britton 1994: 260). Vygotsky's research led him to the conclusion that although we hear less of it as children grow older, this speech does not disappear but continues silently, first as inner speech and then as verbal thinking. Personal monologues, then, are of vital importance to children's development as thinkers and they continue to be important throughout our lives.

In Chapter 6 we discussed symbolic play – an activity in which children choose an object to represent some other thing with which they want to play. Words may be used as symbols in just the same way.

> James:  (waving a full bottle at his carer) Bottle!
> James:  (without his bottle, wanting a drink) Bottle!

In the first example, the word 'bottle' accompanies the object: James has probably never said the word without being able to see his bottle. In the second example, the word and the object are separated, and James is using the word to 'stand for' the object – that is, the word becomes a symbol of the object. Later, words can stand for a whole class of objects, not just a particular one. Although children may begin by using the word 'bottle' to refer just to their own bottle, over time they learn to apply the word to everything they consider to be a bottle.

Both play and language introduce children to symbolic thought, through which they are able to think about things that are not immediately present. Verbal thought allows children to consider possibilities and past events without any physical support: they can do it all in their own head. Words (and phrases and sentences) allow us to organise our thoughts: we can make comparisons, or show relationships of cause and effect.

Listening to what children say will give us valuable insights into their thought processes. Duffy (1998: 137) compiled the following questions for practitioners to ask themselves when observing young children's talk.

- Are children hypothesising, predicting, speculating, questioning?
- Are they relating new ideas to previous experiences and understanding?
- Do they express/justify feelings and opinions?
- Can they organise, interpret and represent ideas and information?
- How is the children's knowledge and understanding of the world around them reflected in their talk?
- How does the adult support all this?

## Supporting language development

It is important to be a good listener, handling what children say positively and with respect. Skilful prompts and questions will allow them to explain further and to reflect on what they are saying. Replies provide an opportunity to model different forms of language, confirm ideas and stimulate further thought. Much of any child's talk will be with other children, so it is important that the experiences and activities children are offered present them with the kinds of challenges and problems that can be approached collaboratively. Such opportunities will stimulate talk for planning, speculation, agreement and disagreement, expressing opinions, comparison and many other purposes. The more children are free to choose their own way of tackling a task, the resources they are going to use and the people with whom they are going to work, the more decisions they will have to make. All this involves plentiful and varied use of language.

As children's powers of communication and knowledge of the world grow, the need to keep things simple, and to stress, exaggerate, repeat and rephrase decreases. However, the strategy of rephrasing what children say in more complete or conventional sentences continues to be useful. The following exchange, between a bilingual child and her teacher, is a good example:

Child (4 years): Judy, this where? (Holds a piece of puzzle up and points to the puzzle).
Teacher: Where do you want to put that piece?
Child: A cat.
Teacher: You're making a puzzle about a cat.
Child: A eye.
Teacher: Yes, that's right. It might fit here (she points to the place where it will fit).
Child: One more eye.
Teacher: That's right. It's got two eyes. Somewhere near the other one? Oh, good shot (the teacher nods her head as the child tries to fit the piece in).

(Clarke 1996 cited in Siraj-Blatchford and Clarke 2000: 24)

Maclure (1992: 107) calls this process, of giving back children's words in a more adult form, shaping: 'A cat' becomes 'You're making a puzzle about a cat'; or 'One more eye' becomes 'It's got two eyes'. Shaping is one of Maclure's 'four S's' – four key strategies for supporting children's language. The other three are:

- sharing information and emotions – in the example above, the teacher shares her feelings about the child's success ('Oh good shot') as well as sharing in the task itself;

- supporting – the child is given enough help to succeed, but not so much that the adult takes control;

- and finally, stretching – using questions and prompts to extend both language and understanding.

In Maclure's terms, stretching is achieved through shaping, supporting and sharing. Stretching involves working with children in the areas of skill and understanding in which they are not completely secure – the 'zones of proximal development'; (Vygotsky 1978) and scaffolding children's learning until the child's understanding is secure (Bruner 1985).

## Asking the right questions

Questions may be used for a range of purposes: to stimulate thought or discussion, or gain information about what a child has learnt. Questions that have only one possible answer (e.g. 'Where did the bears find Goldilocks?') are known as closed questions. Where there is more than one possible answer (e.g. 'What do you think happened next?') they are called open questions.

Wood and Wood (1983, 1984) examined children's responses to five adult 'conversational moves':

- Enforced repetition: 'Say, "It's a bottle".'
- Two-choice questions: 'Is it a big one?'
- 'Wh-' type questions: 'What did you do?'
- Personal contribution: 'I thought that story was better.'
- Phatic comment: 'That's great.'

They suggested that the first three types of conversational move could be considered as 'controlling moves': the child has relatively little choice over what to say next. Extensive use of controlling moves leads to short and unelaborated responses: children are less likely to volunteer their own ideas or ask questions, and more likely to show signs of confusion or misunderstanding.

The final two types of move produce longer and more elaborate responses, even though they are not really questions at all. The researchers discovered that when adults speculate and hypothesise, children speculate and hypothesise in turn. When adults offer suggestions, children reply with speculation.

## Activity 8.3 Talking with children

Record a sample of your conversation with children. If you are a childminder or a nanny, you may wish to keep a tape recorder with you, switching it to 'record' when you are about to engage in some experience or activity that involves talking. If you work with a larger group of children, you may want to organise an activity and then record your discussions with a succession of children as they work on it. Aim to 'collect' about fifteen minutes of conversation.

Listen to the recording several times and, as you do, make notes about the strategies you use to support children's speech. In particular, consider the following points.

■ What is the proportion of adult talk to child talk? Are you enabling the children to express their ideas, or are you 'hogging the microphone'?

■ Listen to how you deal with pauses and hesitations.

■ Can you find examples of all four S's (shaping, sharing, supporting and stretching)?

■ What examples are there of open and closed questions? Do you use other strategies to stimulate talk?

■ Finally, think about how you could improve the way in which you talk with children. Jot down one or two things you will try to do in future.

Children quickly get used to the style of interaction preferred by the adults they are with. If they think that you will sooner or later give them the answer to whatever you are asking, they will learn to wait for it – and let you do all the talking. If they know that you are asking a genuine question to which you want to know their answer, then they will talk at greater length and be prepared to risk giving you an answer you weren't expecting.

## Review

In this chapter we have briefly looked at socio-cultural perspectives on learning and considered how some of these ideas have been interpreted by researchers and practitioners and what this might mean for your practice. We have focused in particular on children's language development and the role of talk because of the central role this plays in children's overall learning, and we have suggested some areas you might like to reflect on and consider in planning your support for children's learning.

## Questions for reflection

1  How do you draw on children's previous experiences in providing experiences and activities to support their learning in your setting?

2  How much time to do you spend listening and responding to children and how much telling them what to do?

3  To what extent do you build planning for talk into your overall planning?

## References

Ball, C. (1994) *Start Right: The Importance of Early Learning*, London: RSA.

Britton, J. (1994) 'Vygotsky's contribution to pedagogical theory', in Brindley, S. (ed.) *Teaching English*, London: Routledge.

Bruner, J. (1977) 'Early social interaction and language acquisition', in Schaffer, H.R. (ed.) *Studies in Mother Infant Interaction*, London: Academic Press.

Bruner, J. (1985) 'Vygotsky: A historical and conceptual perspective', in Wertsch, J.V. (ed.) *Culture, Communication and Cognition: Vygotskyan perspectives*, Cambridge: Cambridge University Press.

Clipson-Boyles, S. (1996) *Supporting Language and Literacy: A handbook for those who assist in early years settings*, London: David Fulton Publishers.

Department of Education Northern Ireland (DENI) (undated) *The Northern Ireland Curriculum Key Stages 1 and 2 Programmes of Study and Attainment Targets*, Belfast; the Stationery Office.

Duffy, B. (1998) 'Listening to young children', in Smidt, S. (ed.) *The Early Years: A reader*, London: Routledge.

Early Childhood Education Forum (1998) *Quality in Diversity in Early Learning: A framework for early childhood practitioners*, London: National Children's Bureau.

Edwards, A. and Knight, P. (1994) *Effective Early Years Education: Teaching young children*, Buckingham: Open University Press.

Katz, L.G. (1993) *Dispositions as Educational Goals*, University of Illinois: ERIC Digest, September.

Maclure, M. (1992) 'The first five years: the development of talk in the pre-school period', in Norman, K. (ed.) *Thinking Voices: The work of the National Oracy Project*, London: Hodder and Stoughton.

Malaguzzi, L. (1996) *The Hundred Languages of Children, Reggio Emilia*, Italy: Reggio Children.

Nutbrown, C. (1994) *Threads of Thinking: Young children learning and the role of early education*, London: Paul Chapman.

Qualifications and Curriculum Authority (QCA)/Department for Education and Employment (DfEE) (2000) *Curriculum Guidance for the Foundation Stage*, London: QCA/DfEE.

Rogoff, B., Mosier, C., Mistry, J. and Göncü, A. (1998) 'Toddlers' guided participation with their caregivers in cultural activity', in Woodhead, M., Faulkner, D. and Littleton, K. (eds) *Cultural Worlds of Early Childhood*, London: Routledge.

Schaffer, H.R. (ed.) (1977) *Studies in Mother–Infant Interaction*, London: Academic Press.

Scottish Consultative Council on the Curriculum (SCCC) (1999) *A Curriculum Framework for Children 3 to 5*, Dundee: SCCC.

Select Committee on Education and Employment (2000) *First Report: Early Years*, http://www.publications.parliament.uk/pa/cm200001/cmselect/cmeduemp/33/3303.htm (accessed April 2005).

Siraj-Blatchford, I. and Clarke, P. (2000) *Supporting Identity, Diversity and Language in the Early Years*, Buckingham: Open University Press.

Sure Start Unit (2003) *Birth to Three Matters: A framework to support children in their earliest years*, London: Department for Education and Skills.

Vygotsky, L.S. (1978) *Mind in Society: The development of higher psychological processes*, Cambridge, MA: Harvard University Press.

Wood, D. and Wood, H. (1983) 'Questioning the pre-school child', *Educational Review*, 35, 149–62.

Wood, D. and Wood, H. (1984) 'An experimental evaluation of the effect of five styles of teacher conversation on the language of hearing impaired children', *Journal of Child Psychology and Psychiatry*, 25 (1), 131–47.

## Further reading

Anning, A. and Edwards, A. (1999) *Promoting Children's Learning from Birth to Five*. Buckingham: Open University Press.

Jordan, B. (2004) 'Scaffolding learning and co-constructing understanding', in Anning, A., Cullen, J. and Fleer, M. (eds) *Early Childhood Education: Society and culture*, London: Sage Publications.

Whitehead, M. (2002) *Developing Language and Literacy with Young Children*, London: Paul Chapman.

 **Inclusive Settings**

## By the end of this chapter you will have:

- gained insights into what inclusive education and equal opportunities mean in practice;

- recognised the various ways in which discrimination can impact on children's development and learning;

- increased your knowledge of practices that can support inclusive education and anti-discriminatory practice.

## Introduction

In this chapter we look at inclusion and equal opportunities and explore what these concepts mean for the children you support in your setting. We also consider the impact of discrimination on children's learning and we look at how early years practitioners can apply the values and principles underpinning inclusion, equal opportunities and anti-discrimination to their work with children and parents. In one chapter it is impossible to cover all aspects of inclusion, so we focus here on children with learning difficulties and disabilities, children growing up bilingually, and gender and anti-discriminatory practice.

## Creating inclusive cultures

The development of inclusive cultures in early years settings is about 'creating a secure, accepting, collaborating, stimulating community in which everyone is valued' (Booth and Ainscow 2000).

Inclusion is about providing equal opportunities for all children and about promoting the practice that will make it a reality (DfEE 1999). The Curriculum

Guidance for the Foundation Stage suggests practitioners should follow the principle that 'no child should be excluded or disadvantaged because of ethnicity, culture or religion, home language, family background, special educational needs, disability, gender or ability' (QCA/DfEE 2000: 11). One way of doing this is by providing 'a safe and supportive learning environment, free from harassment, in which the contribution of all children is valued and where racial, religious, disability and gender stereotypes are challenged' (QCA/DfEE 2000: 17).

The Primary National Strategy in England (DfES 2004) emphasises that learning should be focused on the needs and abilities of individual children and talks about 'a tailored approach' which 'enables knowledge about individual children to inform the way they are taught and learn' (DfES 2004: 3). Scottish guidance also focuses on how the curriculum, teaching and learning should support individual needs.

> The curriculum should be inclusive and promote equality of opportunity. It should help develop in children the knowledge, skills, capabilities and dispositions that they will require in order to gain the best from school and from life. It needs therefore to build progressively on what they learn, offering challenge, rewarding success and celebrating achievement.
>
> (Scottish Executive/Learning and Teaching Scotland, 2000: 3)

Curriculum documents also highlight the need for practitioners to work with children to overcome prejudicial attitudes. In Scotland, the document 'A Curriculum Framework for Children 3 to 5' states that young children should be helped to recognise the different ways of seeing and understanding the world, and that these 'depend on a range of cultural, social and religious viewpoints' (SCCC 1999: 54).

## Prejudice and stereotypes

Prejudice is a judgement or opinion that is formed with little or no prior information about a person. We can all be prejudiced and suffer from prejudice, but this does not make it right and the reality is that some people are more prejudiced than others and some people experience more prejudice than others. Our views of different people are learnt and often based on stereotypical images perpetuated by the media, books and visual images, as well as by the misinformation passed on to us by others. Stereotypes are assumptions made about groups of people which do not take account of individual differences. For example: Asian girls are not all passive; African-Caribbean boys are not all good at sports; not all blind people like dogs; working class parents are not all indifferent to education; not all Irish men drink a lot or have 'the gift of the gab'; not all Jewish people are rich; and girls are not all incapable of playing football (Lane 1999: 8). Whether such stereotypes are positive or negative, they exert a powerful influence on our attitudes and behaviour towards individuals belonging to different groups, and on our expectations of them.

Prejudice can lead to the stereotyping of children, their families, and the values and practices of communities. The following case study illustrates how even the most well-intentioned actions may be influenced by stereotypical attitudes and how underlying stereotypes can lead to low expectations and self-perpetuating behaviour.

## Case Study: Joe

Joe, a four-year-old African-Caribbean boy, joins a local pre-school playgroup. There is only one other black child, a girl, and he doesn't know any of the other children. He feels a bit shy and so plays alone on a bicycle for a few minutes. No one interrupts him and he moves on to play on the slide. He then returns to the bicycle. He gets braver and starts going quite fast, riding it all over the place.

One of the playgroup workers, Rita, has a particular responsibility for Joe and is pleased to see him occupying himself. Although she would not actually say it, she has some idea that black boys have difficulty in concentrating and that they like physical activity.

Several days later, Joe is still mainly occupied on the wheeled toys. No one suggests that he plays elsewhere, with jigsaws or painting or looking at books. No other child is unsupervised in this way. Because Rita's assumption, based on a stereotype, is that Joe is doing what he is best at doing and what he likes doing, she is happy for him and happy that he appears to be content. But Joe has had no opportunity to develop learning skills or to cooperate with other children. Rita's assumptions have helped to create the behaviour that Joe is displaying – and he is being denied access to vital parts of his all-round development.

Rita's discrimination is unintentional, but it is based on hidden stereotyped attitudes that can remain hidden and may have serious and long-term consequences.

(Lane 1999: 7)

## Developing children's understanding

It is important to empower children to express their feelings and opinions from a young age and help them to feel secure and confident so that they can learn and develop. The adult's involvement in children's play is stressed in the Welsh QCA document 'Desirable Outcomes for Children's Learning before Compulsory School Age': 'Good early years educators are there to help children, to guide their play, to offer choices, to challenge children with care and sensitivity, to encourage them to move their learning along' (ACCAC, 2000: 3). Role-play, circle time, stories and community projects are all ways of helping children to explore their values and beliefs. Using persona dolls is another method of doing this.

Persona dolls can be used to help children construct positive identities and a sense of belonging to, understanding of, or empathy with, a particular group. These 20–30-inch fabric dolls are given personalities and characteristics by practitioners and parents, including agreed details such as gender, ethnicity, class, family structure, type of home, religion, cultural background, languages spoken, physical features, skin colour, special abilities and disabilities, likes and dislikes. Children are encouraged to share and identify with the feelings and situations that the dolls experience during storytelling. The dolls can also be used to discuss or introduce children to issues such as racism, bullying, discrimination and social diversity, and to provide children with ways of dealing with their fears and anxieties (Brown 2001). In the following example, the doll is used to support problem-solving and the development of empathy. In this example, the doll is called John and he is a traveller.

## Case Study: John

John says he wishes children would stop teasing him because he lives in a trailer. He thinks living in a trailer is fun and he's glad he doesn't live in a house. But really he doesn't like it when children are horrible to him. He thinks it isn't fair. What should he do?

(Brown 2001: 94)

Through the doll, the children are able to become involved in suggesting what John might do and what they can do to help him. Practitioners can help them to understand how John is feeling, and learn more about travellers' lifestyles and preferences.

## Activity 9.1 Listening to children

Consider the following questions, and make a note of your answers.

Are there any particular issues or events in your early years setting that could be discussed with the children by using persona dolls?

How could a persona doll be used to develop children's understanding and empathy with a child who experiences difficulties in learning?

You may be able to remember how an adult listened to you and understood how you felt during a difficult event that occurred at home or at school. Perhaps you can recall how their empathy reassured you and reduced your sense of isolation. Maybe you kept an aspect of your identity a secret, for fear of being seen as different and not accepted by others – for instance, your religion or your language. Persona dolls can be useful tools in helping young children to express their feelings and understand the impact of prejudice and discrimination on other people's lives.

## Children with learning difficulties or disabilities

The term 'special educational needs' (or 'SEN') was first introduced into education law in England and Wales with the 1981 Education Act and in Scotland in the 1980 Education Act. According to the SEN Code of Practice (DfES 2001), children have special educational needs if they have a learning difficulty which calls for special educational provision to be made for them.

Children have a learning difficulty if they:

a) have a significantly greater difficulty in learning than the majority of children of the same age; or

b) have a disability which prevents or hinders them from making use of educational facilities of a kind generally provided for children of the same age in schools within the area of the local education authority;

c) are under compulsory school age and fall within the definition at a) or b) above or would do so if special educational provision was not made for them.

(DfES 2001: 6)

It is worth noting that the Centre for Studies on Inclusive Education (CSIE) has challenged the use of the term 'special educational needs', as it is considered to be an all-encompassing label and a barrier to the development of inclusive practice. Labelling children can lead to lowered expectations, such that children with a label are seen as a 'problem'. Children can then be thought of as the responsibility of specialists rather than the responsibility of mainstream class teachers or early years practitioners (Booth and Ainscow 2000). Booth and Ainscow have argued:

'Inclusion' or 'inclusive education' is not another name for 'special needs education'. It involves a different approach to identifying and attempting to resolve the difficulties that arise in schools.

(Booth and Ainscow 2000: 13)

## Identification and early intervention

The Special Educational Needs Code of Practice, introduced in England in 1994, and revised in 2001, outlines procedures for identifying and supporting children's difficulties. All settings in England are expected to follow these procedures. Scotland, Northern Ireland and Wales have their own, but similar, versions of the SEN Code of Practice. The SEN Code of Practice in England covers children of three and above in all early years settings that receive government funding (including childminders working as part of an approved network). The revised document sets out how children should be supported in terms of a 'graduated approach' to the identification, assessment and recording of any difficulties they may experience. This is seen as a way of allowing schools and early years settings to maintain responsibility for the process of identifying children's difficulties, and differs from the 'staged approach' of assessment outlined in the previous Code of Practice.

In 2004 the government published *Removing Barriers to Achievement: The Government's Strategy for SEN* (DfES:2004) for England, which was designed to build on the proposals for integrating children's services outlined in the Green Paper *Every Child Matters* (DfES 2003). The strategy covers four areas: early intervention; removing barriers to learning; raising expectations and achievement, and delivering improvements in partnership. The document highlights some of the barriers children can face and aims to support an increase in partnerships between parents and service providers in education, health and social services, leading to early and effective intervention and support provision.

### Activity 9.2 An observation activity

Observe a child you are concerned about for 30 minutes, and write down your observations. Sometimes, thinking of a question directly related to the child you are observing can help to focus your observation. For example, how does the child communicate with his or her friends? In particular, consider any difficulties the child may have, and think about how he or she overcomes them or how you could help them to do so. Also think about any barriers to learning the child may be experiencing and how you could help to overcome these.

Observations of children as part of ongoing practice help to ensure that any learning difficulties children have are identified early and planning and provision are adapted to meet children's needs.

# Growing up bilingually

Research evidence clearly shows that growing up bilingually, far from being a disadvantage, is in fact advantageous in terms of a child's personal and educational development. However, children growing up in an environment that does not recognise and value their home language are likely to be confused and to feel that a part of them and their home culture is not valued, as we saw in Chapter 4. Parents may need to be reassured that it is the quality of the language interaction between them and their children that is important in supporting overall language development, rather than the particular language used in the home. In the following example, Turner (1997) describes a conversation with a mother whose daughter, Rameen, is the only Urdu-speaking child in her infant school.

## Case Study: Rameen

Rameen's mother was already sharing books with her in both Urdu and English. Rameen had some dual language books in the nursery and they both enjoyed using them. Rameen's mother was pleased to be reassured that Rameen was not going to be confused by speaking Urdu; she had felt that it was sad, but inevitable, that Urdu would be eroded by the 'dominant' school language. She was interested to hear that it would be useful to talk about number work and class topics in Urdu, to help Rameen to sort out her ideas in her stronger language.

(Turner 1997: 138)

Many children join early years settings unable to speak English but well able to speak in their mother tongue. Drury (2000) compared the experiences of a monolingual child and a bilingual child at an early stage of learning English, when they had just started nursery school. She looked at the children's experiences in terms of how they adapted to the expectations and procedures of their nursery, how they were enabled to build on their home backgrounds, and the opportunities for language learning. She suggests that the organisation and procedures in an early years setting – what she calls 'the culture' – are complex. Children's knowledge and understanding of what to do, and how to respond and behave, are mediated through the sharing of a common culture and language. Children's ability to engage in tasks, and with other children and adults, will depend on their familiarity with the kind of things they are required to do and how these build on their experiences.

Some children may initially choose not to talk when they are in a new setting, especially if there is no one there who speaks their home language. However, it is important that staff continue to talk to them and ensure that they are engaged in activities which support their social interaction and language development. During this time, children will be actively listening, watching and exploring their environment, and developing meanings from their experiences. They will be trying to relate their new experiences to their previous knowledge and understanding. Children will not just 'absorb' language by being immersed in an English-speaking environment, and practitioners need to plan activities to support children's language development alongside curriculum tasks.

Finding out about the language experiences of children and providing opportunities for children to maintain and extend their skills in their home languages while they are learning English is crucial. Bilingual staff are in the best position to do this, but monolingual practitioners can support children's language development too: they can listen to children even if they do not understand what is being said, and they can learn a few words of the language. There are many dual-language storytapes available which can be used with individual children, and parents can be encouraged to record songs and rhymes for use with all the children. The print environment can also reflect children's different languages, with labels and displays sending the message to bilingual children and their parents that their home languages are valued and enabling all children to appreciate the diversity of written languages.

Kenner (2003) highlights the need for practitioners to regard bilingualism as a resource rather than as a problem and to engage directly with children's bilingual learning, so that they can identify ways of integrating home and school language and literacy development in the curriculum. She also suggests they need to ensure that children's home and community learning is recognised and valued by the school as a whole. Children's home languages should not be used as decorative additions to the classroom, but as learning resources for bilingual and monolingual pupils.

## Gender and anti-discriminatory practice

The move to combat discrimination, and promote equal opportunities and inclusion, is premised on the belief that their experiences make a substantial contribution to how children see themselves and what they can achieve. Developing anti-discriminatory practice depends on our being willing to reflect on our current knowledge and understanding, and to challenge some of the views we may hold, as young children can be heavily influenced by the stereotypes we may be perpetuating.

You may have observed the way in which certain activities tend to be dominated by boys and others by girls: for example, construction activities. A common approach in settings keen to provide equal access to the full range of activities for boys and girls is to set aside time for girls to engage in such activities. This was the approach adopted by Epstein (1995) when she was working as a Year 1 teacher, following a complaint from three of the girls in her class that the boys would not allow them to play with the bricks.

However, as Epstein acknowledged, setting time aside for girls to do these activities will not, on its own, change children's perceptions of what are boys' and what are girls' activities. Practitioners need to take an active role in enabling children to reflect on their views and attitudes, and in challenging their stereotypical perceptions of roles and behaviour.

At first, this may appear to run contrary to notions of 'child-centred' pedagogy, which are closely related to ideas of natural development stemming from the work of people like Piaget and Froebel, and endorsed in the Plowden Report (CACE 1967). These notions tend to focus on providing stimulating resources and a rich learning environment in which the practitioner's role is to facilitate learning and encourage children to grow and develop through making their own choices. Adult direction is often limited because it is seen as conflicting with children's need to learn through self-discovery and experimentation.

Working to implement anti-discriminatory policy, however, requires practitioners to evaluate whether such an approach is, in itself, sufficient to bring about equal opportunities and establish inclusive settings for all children. This is not to suggest that resources, the environment and the practitioner's role in facilitating learning are not of fundamental importance. However, adults also need to adopt active strategies to counter negative stereotypes, validate children's experiences and give them opportunities to question their own assumptions.

An example is behaviour management, for which much of the current training encourages practitioners to ignore 'bad behaviour' (unless it is likely to cause injury) and to praise 'good behaviour'. The notion here is that children will 'see' and 'learn' what adults approve of and adapt their behaviour accordingly. However, this will not automatically help the children to develop any understanding of why the 'bad behaviour' was unacceptable.

## Activity 9.3 The role of adults

Compare the two scenarios outlined below, which could occur in any early years setting. How does the behaviour of the adult confirm or challenge the children's stereotypical views and their behaviour?

Then think of similar situations in your own setting. How do you react when children ask you to intervene in situations where boys or girls are dominating activities? Make a note of these.

## Computers

Joshua and Martin are working on the one computer in the primary classroom, doing research for the class project on the weather. Each pair of children has been allocated a 15-minute slot but the boys have been at the computer for 20 minutes. Emma and Tracy have told them twice that it is their turn, but have been told to 'go away'. The girls complain to the teaching assistant, who asks the boys to let the girls go on the computer. The boys say 'yes, just finishing' but continue for another five minutes, until the teaching assistant comes over and asks them again to stop. The teaching assistant doesn't say anything to the boys, but tells the girls that they can have a go now. The girls settle down to do their research but ten minutes later all the children are asked to get ready for break. The teaching assistant doesn't make any reference to the boys' behaviour.

## Hospital play

The role-play area has been set up as a hospital, and a group of boys and girls are involved in the play. Voices are raised, and an adult joins the group. The boys are insisting that the girls should be the nurses and the boys should be doctors, but one of the girls is adamant that she wants to be a doctor. The adult asks the children about doctors they know who are women and nurses who are men. She encourages them to tell her about whether their own doctor is a man or a woman. She explains that both men and women can be doctors and nurses, and suggests that the children take turns in the different roles.

Although an adult was involved in both situations, the children concerned will have received very different messages. In the first scenario, the boys may have ended up feeling disgruntled at being asked to stop or satisfied that they were able to keep using the computer for longer than their turn. They will have learnt nothing about why the girls are as entitled as they are to access this activity. In the second scenario, both the boys and girls have been helped to reflect on their perceptions of the different roles of women and men, and to participate in a situation where they can each experiment with different roles through their play.

Adopting an anti-discriminatory approach is not about making boys more like girls or girls more like boys. It is about enabling all children to participate in activities and to learn through their experiences, without those experiences being constructed around gender or limited by assumptions that they are gender-specific. Boys and girls *are* different biologically, and all children grow up with different characteristics and attributes, some of which are more evident in boys and others in girls. The challenge is to enable children to experience a full range of opportunities without feeling that they are denying their masculinity or femininity, or their culture, language or identity.

## Review

In this chapter we have examined the effects that discrimination can have on children's development and learning, and we have provided you with opportunities to reflect on your own views and attitudes. We have also looked at how you can support children by challenging prejudicial attitudes and helping them to respect and value difference. Racism and sexism affect everyone, including the children and families with whom we work. We all have a responsibility to counter prejudice and discrimination – in our day-to-day interactions with children, parents and colleagues, and at an institutional and structural level. To ensure the inclusion of children in your setting, you need to work closely with parents to create an environment and ethos that support children's learning. The implementation of inclusion for children with disabilities or learning difficulties is not unproblematic. However, barriers to learning can be overcome through careful, thorough and sensitive reflection and action by practitioners.

### Questions for reflection

1 What would you do if you were concerned about a child's learning or behaviour?

2 What do you know about the language backgrounds and literacy practices of the children in your setting?

3 Do boys and girls in your setting receive the same amount of your time and attention?

## References

Awdurdod, Cymwysterau, Cwricwlwm ac Asesu Cymru (ACCAC, or the Qualifications, Curriculum and Assessment Authority for Wales) (2000) *Desirable Outcomes for Children's Learning before Compulsory School Age*, Cardiff: ACCAC.

Booth, T. and Ainscow, M. (2000) *Index for Inclusion*, Bristol: Centre for Studies on Inclusive Education.

Brown, B. (2001) *Combating Discrimination: Persona dolls in action*, Stoke on Trent: Trentham Books.

Central Advisory Council for Education (England) (CACE) (1967) *Children and their Primary Schools*, The Plowden Report, London: HMSO.

Department for Education and Employment (DfEE) (1999) *Social Inclusion: Pupil support* Circular 10/99, London: DfEE.

Department for Education and Skills (DfES) (2001) *Special Educational Needs Code of Practice 2001*, Nottingham: DfES.

Department for Education and Skills (DfES) (2003) *Every Child Matters*, Norwich: The Stationery Office.

Department for Education and Skills (DfES) (2004) *Removing Barriers to Achievement: The Government's Strategy for SEN*, London: DfES.

Department for Education and Skills (DfES) (2004) *The National Primary Strategy*, London: DfES.

Drury, R. (2000) 'Bilingual children in the pre-school years: different experiences of early learning', in Drury, R., Miller, L. and Campbell, R. (eds) *Looking at Early Years Education and Care*, London: David Fulton Publishers.

Epstein, D. (1995) ' "Girls don't do bricks": gender and sexuality in the primary classroom', in Siraj-Blatchford, J. and Siraj-Blatchford, I. (eds), *Educating the Whole Child: Cross-curricular skills, themes and dimensions*, Buckingham: Open University Press.

Kenner, C. (2003) 'An interactive pedagogy for bilingual children', in Bearne, E., Domby, H. and Grainger, T. (eds) *Classroom Interactions in Literacy*, Buckingham: Oxford University Press.

Lane, J. (1999) *Action for Racial Equality in the Early Years*, London: National Early Years Network.

Qualifications and Curriculum Authority (QCA) and Department for Education and Employment (DfEE) (2000) *Curriculum Guidance for the Foundation Stage*, London: QCA.

Scottish Consultative Council on the Curriculum (SCCC) (1999) *A Curriculum Framework for Children 3 to 5*, Dundee: SCCC.

Scottish Executive/Learning and Teaching Scotland (2000) *The Structure and Balance of the Curriculum 4–14 National Guidance*, Dundee: Learning and Teaching Scotland

Turner, M. (1997) 'Working in partnership: parents, teacher and support teacher together', in Gregory, E. (ed.) *One Child, Many Worlds: Early learning in multicultural communities*, London: David Fulton Publishers.

## Further reading

Connolly, P. (1998) *Racism, Gender Identities and Young Children: social relations in a multi-ethnic, inner city primary school*, London: Routledge.

Hyder, T. and Kenway, P. (1995) *An Equal Future: A guide to anti-sexist practice in the early years*, London: National Early Years Network.

Siraj-Blatchford, I. (1994) *The Early Years: Laying the foundations for racial equality*, Stoke on Trent: Trentham Books.

Siraj-Blatchford, I. and Clarke, P. (2000) *Supporting Identity, Diversity and Language in the Early Years*, Supporting Early Learning series, Buckingham: Open University Press.

# 10 Assessment for Learning

## Introduction

> . . . where educators observe children and use their observations to generate understandings of their learning and their needs, they are contributing to the development of a quality environment in which those children might thrive.
>
> (Nutbrown 2001: 69)

In the previous chapters you have explored the ways in which children learn and the importance of understanding the teaching and learning process. This enables practitioners to gather reliable evidence of learning, and make judgements about what the learner has achieved. We begin this chapter by asking you to consider what is meant by 'assessment' and why practitioners assess the learning of young children. We explore ways of assessing, particularly through observation and by building up 'learning stories' that portray children as learners. Finally, we focus on the inclusion of the voices of the child and parent.

## Assessment and learning

Assessment is a process that must enrich [children's] lives, their learning and development. Assessment must work for children.

(Drummond, 1993: 13)

Assessment is about gathering evidence of what children can do, know or understand. In early years settings, practitioners use this evidence to determine the learning that has taken place. Being able to assess learning is an important skill, for the information that you gather will inform future experiences and extend learning for children. Assessment requires a wealth of knowledge and skills, especially:

- how children grow and develop;
- learning and how children learn;
- assessment purposes;
- techniques and ways of gathering evidence;
- how to use the information gathered effectively to support the learner.

Making informed judgements about what a child can do and possible lines of development are dependent on professional and objective analysis. As Edgington (1998: 120) says, 'the highest priority should be given to the learning needs and development of the individual child', echoing Drummond's earlier thoughts.

## Assessment and the teaching and learning cycle

Starting from *where the child is* means finding out or assessing what each child knows and can do in order to provide appropriate experiences and curricula. Assessment occurs on a day-to-day basis and involves practitioners modifying and adjusting their interactions, provision and support, and providing feedback to children. Assessment is an intrinsic part of the teaching and learning process and can be formal or informal, depending on the depth, value and purpose of the assessment.

How do you, as a practitioner, set about finding out what children can do? To assess effectively means to be able to judge the worth or importance of information gathered. Drummond (1993) suggests that the assessment process has three elements: evidence, judgement and outcomes. Evidence is that the information gathered, and the kind of information gathered, in a multitude of ways, will influence the kinds of judgements and outcomes that follow.

Providing formal tasks for young children to do, and 'marking' their responses against a set of criteria, gives a very different picture to watching or listening to what they can do in situations that they have chosen for themselves or that you have provided for them. The amount of commitment and involvement that children show reflects their interest in the experience and the extent to which they think it is relevant to them. Early years practitioners generally set up environments that are interesting, stimulating, challenging and fun, and that encourage children to join in, play and learn; see Chapter 6. As Hurst and Lally have noted:

> Young children's learning is context dependent, and it is important that we [practitioners] recognise the impact that an unfamiliar setting has on achievement. We gain a much clearer view of what children know and can do when we observe them setting their own challenges and taking responsibility for their learning.
>
> (Hurst and Lally 1992: 56)

The first activity below illustrates the importance of giving children the choice to participate in activities, and provides a starting point for you, as a practitioner, to consider why you assess and what you assess when working with young children.

## Activity 10.1  What does Laura know?

Read the following case study and then consider the questions that follow.

### Case Study: Laura's 'homework'

Laura (aged two years and eleven months) is sitting making marks or 'writing' at the table with her childminder's two older children (aged twelve and fourteen years), who are doing their homework. The two older girls are moaning about how to do their work and writing notes in their workbooks. Laura asks for paper and a pen to do her own 'homework'. She kneels and puts her elbow on the table, and rests her head on her left hand as she writes with her right hand on the paper. The two older girls are writing in a similar way. Laura stays with them for about 20 minutes, mirroring and modelling their body language and their moans and groans. When the childminder asks Laura to get ready to go home, Laura sighs and says that she is just finishing her sentence! The childminder is surprised, and asks Laura what she thinks a sentence is. Laura replies, 'It's lots of words,' and then finishes the bottom line of her 'homework'. When Laura's mum arrives, the childminder shows her Laura's work (see Figure 10.1). Laura's mum takes it with pleasure to share with Laura's dad.

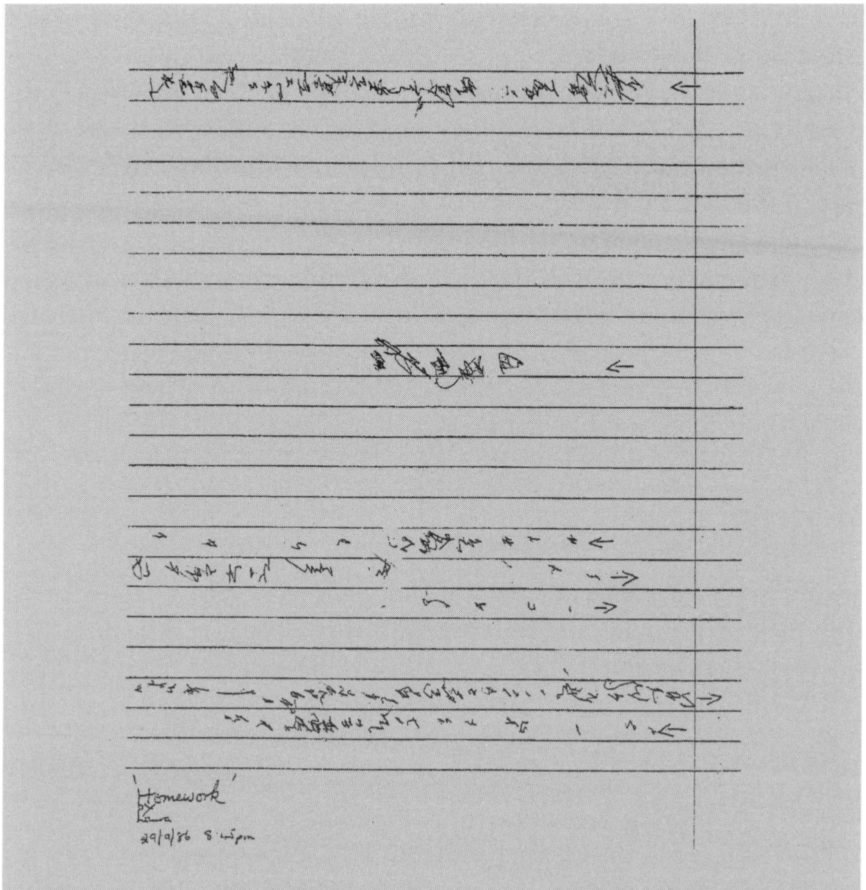

**Figure 10.1**    Laura's 'homework'

Look at Laura's mark-making carefully and note the arrows that were added later to show the direction in which she had written.

■ What do you think Laura knows and understands?

■ What judgements can you make about Laura from this observation? What evidence do you have to support your claims?

■ What outcomes, in Drummond's (1993) terms, are possible from this observation, if any?

■ What might you do to extend Laura's understandings and develop her interest?

■ Why is it important to gather information like this?

This observation of Laura shows that she is interested in mark-making in a way that is unusual for children of her age. However, in analysing what Laura can do and understand, it is important to be cautious about your possible conclusions: this observation is only one instance. It is important not to make judgements about what a child can do or has achieved *without sufficient information*. Nevertheless, it does offer some indication of Laura's possible interests and the skills she is trying to develop. Providing opportunities for Laura to make marks and represent what she is doing in a variety of contexts may provide further evidence of just how interested and skilled she is. Such activities as painting and drawing, sharing books, using building blocks and small-world play toys will extend her understanding of ways of representing her world and provide breadth to her interest in mark-making.

## Why assess?

There are many questions that, as a practitioner, you need to consider when talking about assessment and learning, not least what it is. The next activity explores why you assess.

### Activity 10.2 Why do you assess children?

Consider the following questions.

What aspects and areas do you assess for the children in your care? Why do you do this? What aspects and areas do you focus on in particular when you are working with a child who is new to your setting? Why do you do this? How do you involve children in the process? Why is this important? Whom do you share your findings with and what records do you keep and why?

You may have wondered where some of the information on children in your care has come from. Was it from formal assessment or does it form part of a picture that you have built up over time? Perhaps you feel that you have always known this information – in which case, you would have obtained it in some way. Maybe you talked with other adults, or asked the children to share what they had done; or perhaps you looked at and talked about their work with someone else, or observed and listened to them playing.

Being able to assess children will provide you with information on:

■ what children can do, know and understand;

■ their approach to learning;

■ any difficulties, strengths and interests they may have.

This information will enable you to:

- monitor children's progress;
- inform curriculum planning;
- evaluate what you do;
- help children to understand themselves as learners and to think about their learning;
- have a focus for communication with others;
- make your job enjoyable and rewarding;
- show how competent, confident, imaginative and creative children can be.

# Types of assessment

Information or evidence gathered through the process of assessment can be used either formatively, summatively or for diagnostic purposes.

Information or evidence that is used directly to inform and possibly change how practitioners work with particular children on a moment-by-moment or day-to-day basis is referred to as *formative assessment*.

Information or evidence that is presented as a summary of what a child can do or has achieved over a period of time, or at the end of an activity or project, is called *summative assessment*.

## Formative assessment

In early years settings, formative assessment is most useful and necessary when practitioners work alongside children and involves watching and talking with children about what they are doing, and providing support through interaction. Feedback must be seen as useful to children (as learners), otherwise its value is lost (Black *et al.* 2002). This means asking children about the support they would like, the activities they are finding difficult, and ways in which you might help. Your presence may be all that is needed to give a child the confidence to try something new or take a risk to learn something new. The case study below illustrates the sensitivity this requires.

## *Case Study: Alex*

Alex (aged three years and two months) is learning how to walk across the climbing apparatus that the children have constructed for themselves outside. Alice, the practitioner, spends several hours over a period of days supporting Alex as he gains the skills and confidence needed to walk across the apparatus unaided. For several days after he first succeeds, Alex calls Alice over to stand by while he walks across for the first time each day. A week after his initial success, Alice meets him on his way to the climbing apparatus and suggests that he has a go without her being alongside. She stands some distance from the apparatus and watches as Alex slowly starts to walk across. He looks to Alice for reassurance. She smiles and he smiles back, and he goes across. After this attempt, Alex never calls on Alice to help again.

This is the kind of situation where, as a practitioner, you are continually using your judgements (or assessments) about what is happening to inform whether you intervene or interact and how you do this.

## Diagnostic assessment

Gathering evidence of some of the problems a child may have with learning, with the aim of identifying appropriate support, possibly using special diagnostic tests, is termed *diagnostic assessment*. Such assessments may have particular programmes, support packages or resources linked to them, which help children to better access the learning experiences offered, as the following case study illustrates.

### Case Study: Suad

When Suad (aged four years and three months) starts at nursery school, she has already been identified as having learning difficulties because of significant hearing loss. After several weeks at the nursery, and despite being fitted with special hearing aids linking her to a key worker and enabling her to communicate, Suad is not making the progress that the practitioners have been expecting. Suad seems to have difficulty making sense of some communications, and her key worker has highlighted concerns. Following discussion with Suad's parents, other agencies are called in to carry out some diagnostic tests to analyse the problems she is having. These show that Suad has difficulty processing certain combinations of sounds, although it is not known at first if this difficulty is related to her hearing loss. An expert helps to develop an action plan to support the practitioners working with Suad.

When observations of and interactions with a child cause concerns, it is important to share these with colleagues and, if possible, to gather more evidence. Sharing ideas and information, and involving others in observing, may confirm whether or not other agencies with more expertise in identifying difficulties and supporting a child's particular needs should be consulted.

## Summative assessment

Summative assessment involves making judgements and providing an overview of what children have achieved over a period of time, during a topic or theme, and their stage of development at that point. Often these judgements are related to developmental criteria based on research showing the different stages of understanding that children normally go through – for example, as they learn to count. Pound (1999) has described clearly some of the significant principles that children need to understand in order to count effectively (see Chapter 14). These principles could be used as criteria to determine or assess how well a child is able to count in different situations and against accepted norms. Summative assessment information could be used to evaluate the effectiveness of a setting and deployment of resources and personnel.

# Learning and assessment

Nurturing positive attitudes to learning, and developing the confidence to cope with problems, are key to progression in learning. Formative assessment – that is, assessment for learning – must have the child at the centre, controlling their own learning. Teaching children does not mean that they will learn, unless you take careful notice of their styles of learning, their interests, and their ways of thinking about learning. To become lifelong learners, children need to enjoy learning and the challenges that it presents and so it is important that you reflect on children's dispositions to learn.

The downward pressure exerted on early years settings by the impositions of national curricula has resulted in inappropriate practice in some settings. For example, children are often required to work in groups but on individual tasks, or they are placed in 'ability groups' in which they are not able to share and work with others from whom they might learn. Carr (2001) suggests that practitioners need to be careful that their work is not compromised by the more formal, summative assessment that has been emerging in England, particularly with the introduction of Standard Attainment Tests (SATs) for seven-year-olds. Wales has abandoned these tests, whilst Scotland and Northern Ireland did not embrace formal testing at seven but adopted approaches based on how children learn. Children can be assessed easily through careful observation of their everyday activities. Practitioners and parents can encourage children to develop interests in all areas of learning by acknowledging, celebrating, supporting and extending the range of resources and contexts they make available, and they can model ways of learning that help children to gain the confidence to take risks in a safe and supportive environment.

Moving backwards and forwards within the teaching and learning process, assessing and observing children, supports learning (see Figure 10.1). As Drummond (1993: 13) suggests, assessment is 'the ways in which, in our everyday practice, we observe children's learning, strive to understand it, and then put our understanding to good use'.

## Ways of assessing

For young children, learning is deeply embedded in the context in which they work and play. If they are intensely involved in what they are doing, then the level at which they can operate is much higher and the potential for learning much greater. To assess children's learning, there is a range of tools and ways of gathering evidence, some more useful and appropriate than others.

### Gathering evidence

By observing and listening to what children are doing, it is possible to make judgements about what children can do and need. For example, Marvin (aged four years and five months) is 'reading' a favourite story book to a group of soft toys, which are set up as if it were storytime. He reads the whole story in the correct order but with his eyes closed.

Marvin says he can read and he is displaying knowledge about reading and stories but, as with the earlier example of Laura, we do not have sufficient information from this one observation to make a judgement. To build a more holistic picture, more detailed observations of Marvin engaging with books and environmental print in different contexts are needed to assess his competence and plan the next steps in his learning.

Alongside such evidence, a clear understanding of what would be an appropriate curriculum for the child being observed is needed (Hurst and Joseph 1998). Knowing the different stages and common order in which most children achieve certain skills or understandings provides an indication of what you might expect. However, as a tool, stages need to be used with caution and as a guide rather than a straitjacket that limits expectations and provision.

### Developmental checklists

Developmental checklists exist for many different aspects of development and growth such as height, weight and language, and each of these provides a normative guide on what most children at that age or stage are expected to be able to do or understand. They do not provide detailed information on how a child learns or on individual differences in learning styles, and so have limited use in supporting day-to-day provision and interaction. Checklists are often context-free and do not always enable practitioners to make detailed sense of what they have observed with a child. Nevertheless, if practitioners have concerns about a child's progress, completing such lists is a useful trigger to seek more help from parents, carers and other professionals.

## Sharing observations and insights

Sharing information between home and early years settings on the ways children acquired particular skills and knowledge is another way of gathering evidence of children's learning. Parents and carers have inside knowledge of their children, which practitioners need to tap into in order to gain a full picture of each child, for example the child who is very agile at climbing or using books when they enter an early years setting.

Listening to children involves engaging children in conversation about what they are doing and noting what is said. Clarke (2003) suggests drawing on the following types of evidence:

- descriptions of what you saw that do not provide interpretations or judgements as you write – for example, the entry 'Jamil was carelessly scribbling on the paper' could also be written as 'Jamil was making marks quickly all over the paper';
- video and photographs that capture significant stages or points in play or in constructing models or artefacts;
- artefacts to show what children have made;
- other samples of children's work;
- observations of what children said or did – these could be transcripts and recordings;
- children's comments on their thinking, what they were trying to do, and how they were trying to do it;
- children's comments on their achievements and learning.

A variety of evidence ensures that reliable and valid judgements are made and can be used to inform planning. Agreeing norms of who or what to observe should be informed by evidence and judgements (Drummond 1993).

## Learning stories

Carr (2001) has developed the recording of children's experiences as narrative. Learning stories are a way of building a picture of the child as a learner in a holistic way. Part of the process of developing learning stories is sharing the evidence gathered with children, talking with them about what they think they have achieved and how they set about the learning. Learning stories, made up of individual stories, are recordings of what children do, think and say over periods of time. Together these build a rounded picture of what children can do and their attitudes to learning. Carr (2001) and Clarke (2004) highlight the importance of listening to and valuing *the voice of the child* in thinking about how and what each child learns. The following lists provide guidance on the assessment process and highlight the benefits of a narrative approach.

*Learning stories:*
- acknowledge the unpredictability of development in assessing learners;
- seek the perspective of the learner;
- reflect the learning better than performance indicators;
- indicate that collaborative interpretation of collected data is helpful;
- show that many tasks provide their own assessment.

(Carr 2001)

*Assessment:*
- contributes to children's learning dispositions;
- protects and enhances the early childhood setting as a learning community;
- is possible for busy practitioners;
- is useful to practitioners.

It is important for learners to recognise what they know and can do, but also important that they know and understand how they function as learners.

## Learning dispositions

The process of children considering their own thinking is called *metacognition* and enables them to develop an interest in and disposition towards learning. Katz (1993) sees a disposition as 'a tendency to exhibit frequently, consciously, and voluntarily a pattern of behaviour that is directed towards a broad goal' – for example, of curiosity as a desirable disposition to encourage.

Carr (2001) has identified five 'domains' (areas) of learning dispositions to encourage:

- taking an interest;
- being involved;
- persisting with difficulties or uncertainty;
- communicating with others;
- taking responsibility.

To each of these domains, Carr ascribes three 'dimensions', which she calls 'being ready', 'being willing' and 'being able'. O'Connor (2003) has described each of Carr's dimensions as follows:

- being ready – children see themselves as being able to participate in learning;
- being willing – children see that the place they are in has opportunities and is safe for learning;
- being able – children have the developing knowledge and abilities that support their inclinations and contribute to their being ready and willing.

For children to make best use of the five domains of learning dispositions, they need to manifest all three dimensions. Table 10.1 illustrates how these manifest themselves.

The next activity asks you to explore one of these learning dispositions in more depth with a child you know.

### Activity 10.3 Learning dispositions

Focusing on a child you are responsible for in your setting, think about which learning disposition he or she exhibits best. Think about the evidence you have, and may still have to gather, to support this tentative judgement. Table 10.1 will help you to think about the elements of your chosen learning disposition. What other evidence might you need to gather before you can be sure that the child has developed all three dimensions of that learning disposition?

In exploring any one of these dispositions, such as encouraging curiosity in children, Carr (2001) suggests that *being ready* to be curious requires the child to have interests. Do you know the interests of the child you have chosen for this exercise? If not, how might you gather this information? How might you develop the child's interest in things? *Being willing* suggests that children are prepared to make contact and engage with the provision you make for them. If they do not, do you need to reconsider what you provide rather than making

**Table 10.1** Learning dispositions: the three dimensions

| Domain of learning dispositions | Being ready | Being willing | Being able |
|---|---|---|---|
| Taking an interest<br>*Children are developing:* | expectations that people, places and things can be interesting; a view of self as interested and interesting. | preparedness to recognise, select or construct interests in a place or occasion; abilities to make connections between artefacts, activities and social identities across places. | abilities and funds of relevant knowledge, which support their interests. |
| Being involved<br>*Children are developing:* | readiness to be involved and pay attention for a sustained length of time; a view of self as someone who gets involved. | informed judgements on the safety and trustworthiness of the local environment. | strategies for getting involved and remaining focused. |
| Persisting with difficulty or uncertainty<br>*Children are developing:* | enthusiasm for persisting with difficulty or uncertainty; assumptions about risk and the role of making a mistake in learning; a view of self as someone who persists with difficulty and uncertainty. | sensitivity to places and occasions in which it is worthwhile to tackle difficulty or uncertainty and to resist the routine. | problem-solving and problem-finding knowledge and skills; experience of making mistakes as part of solving a problem. |
| Communicating with others<br>*Children are developing:* | an inclination to communicate with others in one or more of 'the hundred languages' (Edwards et al., 1993) to express ideas and feelings; a view of self as a communicator. | responses to a climate in which children have their say and are listened to. | facility with one or more languages, widely defined; familiarity with a range of context-specific 'genres'; script knowledge for familiar events. |

| Taking responsibility *Children are developing:* | a habit of taking responsibility in a range of ways, to take another point of view, to recognise justice and to resist injustice; a view of self and others as citizens with rights and responsibilities. | recognition or construction of opportunities to take responsibility. | experience of responsibility, making decisions, and being consulted; an understanding of fairness and justice; strategies for taking responsibility. |

*Source:* Adapted from Carr (2001, pp. 24–25)

them do things they are not captivated by? *Being able* means children can and do raise questions and show curiosity about what objects are, and they are observant, seeking out things to do, look at and explore for themselves. Do you respond to their queries and comments constructively? To be curious requires children to have the knowledge and personal resources to support their interests and may include developing other learning dispositions, such as taking responsibility and persisting with difficulties in order to succeed.

Depending on the age, experiences, dispositions and stage of development, you may obtain only a partial picture of how the child sees himself or herself as a learner. The more children are asked to talk about their learning, the more they begin to know themselves as learners. If you know that some children find it difficult to do things for themselves and to handle failure, talking about their learning and progress will help them to succeed more. It will develop self-esteem and confidence in their own abilities, as well as dispositions for learning that will serve them throughout life.

According to O'Connor (2003: 13), developing children's dispositions towards a desire to learn involves practitioners considering the following:

- providing time, access to a wide range of resources, and space for children to initiate enterprises;
- planning for open-ended activities or projects;
- providing a workshop environment where children can return to and work on longer-term projects;
- providing quiet areas where children can work uninterrupted;
- providing long periods of outdoor play or open access to the outside;
- talking with children about their learning and encouraging them to take risks;

## Activity 10.4 Children talking about learning

This activity is in two parts.

1. First, we would like to you to observe a child engaged in a task for about 10–15 minutes. (The child needs to be old enough to talk about what they have been doing.) The task can be something that the child has chosen or a challenge that you have set. The purpose of the task is to provide a starting point for you to talk to the child about what they are trying to do and learn.

As you watch, consider the following questions:

What is the child trying to do or learn?

How do you know?

What evidence do you have to support this judgement?

2. After 15 minutes, as the child continues to play/work, talk to them about what they are doing. Use your questions help the child to explore their learning. Listening to children means that they should do most of the talking! Your questions and probing should arise naturally from your interest in understanding more about the child's perceptions of their learning. This should not be a question and answer session. Possible questions for this activity could be:

What are you doing? Why?

Is it easy or hard?

How are you sorting it out? Have you sorted it out in your head?

Have you talked to anyone else about what you're doing?

Has anyone been helping you?

What do you like to do/learn about?

How do you think you learn best?

What/who helps you most?

- supporting them through difficult patches, making mistakes and showing by example;
- developing with them the language to talk about their learning;
- encouraging children to question and puzzle over things;
- observing what they do, noting their comments and how they solve problems, for example recording their learning stories as they develop and sharing these with the children, other practitioners and parents;
- reflecting on the progress and problems, using displays and discussion to help.

# Review

Assessment of, and for, learning therefore involves, as Hutchin (1999: 26) has summarised, a number of principles that, when followed, enable effective assessment. Assessment should be based on what is seen or heard, recording what children can do rather than what they cannot do, and with parental contributions forming a significant part of the process. The voice of the child should also be given priority, allowing them to express their own views on their achievements and the ways they learn. Observing children in action regularly as they go about their experiences and activities is the best way to assess very young children, rather than setting up formal assessments. Keeping notes and samples on all aspects of significant development and experience, as they happen, will provide the evidence needed to justify the kind of provision made for each child. Sharing our judgements with parents and other professionals should be an ongoing process that informs planning and feeds children's end-of-stage records and reports, which follow them to their next setting.

## Questions for reflection

1 What ways do you currently use to gather evidence of children's learning?

2 What new ways would you like to try, and why?

3 What kinds of records do you keep and how could you improve these?

# References

Black, P., Harrison, C., Lee, C., Marshall, B. and Wiliam, D. (2002) *Working Inside the Black Box: Assessment for learning in the classroom*, London: King's College London, School of Education.

Carr, M. (2001) *Assessment in Early Childhood Settings: Learning stories*, London: Paul Chapman.

Clarke, A. (2003) 'Listening to children', in Miller, L. and Devereux, J. (eds) *Supporting Children's Learning in the Early Years*, London: David Fulton Publishers.

Drummond, M.J. (1993) *Assessing Children's Learning*, London: David Fulton Publishers.

Edgington, M. (1998) *The Nursery Teacher in Action*, London: Paul Chapman.

Edwards, C., Gandini, L., Forman, G. (eds) (1993) *The Hundred Languages of Children: The Reggio Emilia approach to Early Childhood Education*, Norword, New Jersey: Ablex Publishing Corporation.

Hurst, V. and Lally, M. (1992) 'Assessment and the nursery curriculum', in Blenkin, G.M. and Kelly, A.V. (eds) *Assessment in Early Childhood Education*, London: Paul Chapman Publishing.

Hurst, J. and Joseph, J. (1998) *Supporting Early Learning: The way forward*, Buckingham: Open University Press.

Hutchin, V. (1999) *Right from the Start: Effective planning and assessment in the early years*, London: Hodder and Stoughton.

Katz, L.G. (1993) *Dispositions as Educational Goals*, University of Illinois: ERIC Digest, September issue.

Nutbrown, C. (2001) 'Watching and learning: the tools of assessment', in Pugh, G. (ed.) *Contemporary Issues in the Early years: Working collaboratively for children*, London: Paul Chapman Publishing/Coram Family.

O'Connor, A. (2003) 'Stick at it', *Nursery World*, London: TSL Education Ltd, 8 May, p. 12.

Paley, V.G. (1985) *Wally's Stories*, London: Heinemann.

Pound, L. (1999) *Supporting Mathematical Development in the Early Years*, Buckingham: Open University Press.

## Further reading

Carr, M. (2004) 'A folk model of assessment – and an alternative', in Miller, L. and Devereux, J. (eds) *Supporting Children's Learning in the Early Years*, London: David Fulton Publishers.

Devereux, J. (2004) 'Observing children' in Miller, L. and Devereux, J. (eds) *Supporting Children's Learning in the Early Years*, London: David Fulton Publishers.

Webber, B. (1999) 'Assessment and learning', in David, T. (ed.) *Teaching Young Children*, London: Paul Chapman Publishing.

# Acknowledgement

Grateful acknowledgement is made to the following sources for permission to reproduce material within this product:

Table 10.1, from Carr, M. (2001) *Assessment in Early Childhood Settings: Learning stories*, reprinted by permission of Sage Publications Ltd. Copyright © Margaret Carr, 2001.

# Part 3

# Curriculum in Practice

# Introduction to Part 3: Curriculum in Practice

Part 3 of this book is concerned with the curriculum children and their parents experience in early years settings. Curriculum guidance for children from three to eight exists in all four UK countries in the form of statutory and non-statutory guidance or recommendations. Guidance has tended to differentiate between 3–5-year-olds and those of primary school age, although there are indications that they this may change in the future. Guidance for practitioners working with children from birth to three years old has recently been published in England and Scotland. In addition, some practitioners work within settings guided by particular philosophies or approaches to learning. The challenge for practitioners is in interpreting guidance on areas or aspects of learning or subjects to meet the individual and collective needs of the children and parents with whom they work. The six chapters in this section aim to explore some of these areas of learning, the challenges for practitioners, and ways of supporting children's learning and development.

Chapter 11 focuses on a key area for children's learning and one that will impact on all their other learning: the development of self-esteem. We look at the importance of children's personal, social and emotional development and consider how practical activities and experiences which promote young children's growth and development in these areas can be included in the early years curriculum in ways that will encourage children to be aware of their individuality, to value secure relationships, to trust and rely on their own abilities, and acquire social confidence, competence and self-esteem.

Chapter 12 explores two areas that reach across the curriculum, creativity and information and communications technology (ICT). The development of children's understanding, skills and abilities in both these areas is of fundamental importance in the 21st century. In this chapter we examine creativity, not only in terms of developing children's interests in the creative or performing arts, but also in terms of helping children to become creative thinkers and learners by stimulating their curiosity, and their ability to problem-solve and engage in 'possibility thinking'. We examine what children need to learn about ICT but, perhaps more importantly, how they can learn with ICT and the potential of these powerful tools to support learning.

Chapter 13 focuses on literacy and what it means to be literate in the 21st century. Children need to become effective communicators, readers and writers and, therefore, an important task for early years practitioners is to provide the kind of support that will help to prepare them for the demands of a rapidly changing society. In this chapter we explore how young children learn about literacy through everyday interactions in families, communities and early years settings and examine the connections between family literacy practices and those in early years settings. We consider some major theoretical perspectives that have contributed to our current understanding of literacy learning and consider how early years practitioners can support children in this area of learning.

Chapter 14 examines how children learn mathematics and what is involved in this process. Learning to use mathematics is a complex process, although we all use mathematics in quite sophisticated ways in our daily lives, whether we are aware of it or not. In this chapter we consider what children have to achieve in learning to count. We examine the ways in which very young children begin to develop the abstract thought necessary for mathematical competence and confidence, and we consider the importance of language in the development of mathematical thinking. We discuss the importance of incorporating not only adult-led activities that support mathematical learning, but also child-initiated opportunities that enable children to reflect on and make sense of their own learning.

Chapter 15 explores the development of children's knowledge and understanding of the world. As children grow and develop, they explore their world and the people and places in it. They develop new ways of seeing, understanding and manipulating time, space, matter and the objects and processes that they encounter. They make sense of their experiences through experimentation, investigation and problem-solving. In this chapter we look at the holistic development of knowledge and understanding of the world as well as the subjects that contribute to this area of learning, and we examine the different ways that the environment and community can contribute and be drawn on to support children's learning.

Chapter 16, the final chapter in this part, and indeed in this book, invites you to reflect both on your own practice and that of others. Sometimes the changes and challenges posed by new curriculum policy initiatives can make it easy to lose sight of the assumptions that underpin day-to-day practice, and to 'get on with the job' without building in time to think or reflect. Taking time to look at the ways in which others work with young children will help you to reflect on and gain insights into your own practice, and to see what you do in a new light. In this chapter we explore five approaches to early childhood curricula: Steiner, Montessori, Schema, Reggio Emilia and Te Whāriki. These examples illustrate how and why different ideas about teaching and learning have developed, and how practitioners successfully weave and synthesise a range of ideas into their practice alongside published guidance.

# 11 Self-esteem and Identity

## By the end of this chapter you will have:

- developed your understanding of the importance of self-esteem and a strong personal identity for children's learning and development;
- extended your knowledge and understanding of personal, social and emotional development, and the implications for your practice;
- considered experiences that will promote children's personal, social and emotional development.

## Introduction

This chapter considers children's personal, social and emotional development and how this relates to children developing self-esteem and a strong personal identity. We consider how practical activities and experiences contribute to children's personal, social and emotional development, the ways in which these can be included in the early years curriculum and the ways in which you can promote young children's growth and development in these areas. You can develop skills, and plan and evaluate experiences, that will encourage children to be aware of their individuality, to value secure relationships, to trust and rely on their own abilities, and to acquire social confidence, competence and self-esteem. Children who can do all these things are strong, healthy children.

## Developing a sense of self

As young children grow and develop, they learn to see themselves both as individuals and in relation to the people around them. They receive powerful messages about who they are and how they should behave from the views and opinions of the adults with whom they are in contact. Parents, carers, families, communities and practitioners all have an influence on the values children form. Through these interactions, children discover how they feel about themselves and develop their sense of self-worth, or self-esteem. If children receive positive messages about themselves from the people around them and from their environment, they will grow and develop secure in their knowledge of their self-worth. Conversely, if they receive negative messages, they may become unsure of themselves, their feelings and abilities, and may develop low self-esteem.

## Emotional relationships

Children's emotional development starts from birth with the attachments formed within the family and with the development of trust in the people who care for them, as we discussed in Chapter 7. Attachments and trust are vital in setting the foundations for healthy emotional development. Making a child feel loved, wanted, valued and cared for provides a safe and supportive environment, from which they can explore their world. This opportunity to explore independently in a secure environment is the beginning of children seeing themselves as separate from their parents. They begin to develop feelings of self-confidence and self-esteem, and skills such as self-control.

### Activity 11.1 Observing child/adult interactions

Observe a child aged 6–12 months with their carer – perhaps a parent or someone with whom the child has a close attachment. In particular, look carefully at how the child explores the environment and refers back to the carer. If you can, spend about half an hour watching. The following questions may help you to focus your observation.

- How does the child involve the adult in their exploration?
- How often does the child appear to check the location of the adult?
- What happens if the adult goes away for a while?
- What happens if another child makes contact with the same adult?

Perhaps you noticed how the child checked the location of the carer at points during your observation. Or maybe you saw how the child reacted with tears and anxiety when the carer was out of sight. Separation can raise lots of issues for children: some children have lengthy rituals they must go through in order to move from their special adults into an early years setting; some children may feel threatened if other children get the attention of their special carer. Your own experience of working with children in an early years setting may mean that you have seen a range of children's reactions to these kinds of scenarios.

All young children are intensely curious as they try to understand the world around them. This innate curiosity leads them to puzzle over new experiences in ways that help them to understand the nature of the physical environment as well as more abstract qualities like feelings. This fosters in young children a positive disposition to learn, which can be nurtured by encouraging them to follow their concerns and interests, and to make discoveries about their environment and the people who live and work within it.

## Transitions and new experiences

Experiencing transition can be a critical time for the emotional well-being of babies and young children, as we discussed in Chapter 3. Transition happens not just when, say, a baby moves from his or her parent to the childminder, or when a young child moves into a reception class; it can also occur during a single day, when activities are changed or children move from one building to another. How practitioners help young children to cope with separation and transition will promote social and emotional independence. Some children will cope with the change of moving from home into an early years setting easily and happily, while others will feel anxious and distressed at the separation from their parents. It may be misguided simply to try to 'jolly along' children in such situations. Much patience and sensitivity is needed to help them make this transition independently. For example, many children find that the size and sounds of buildings create anxiety, especially when they are required to move from classroom to hall to dining area. The thoughtful design of a setting can do much to alleviate potential stress.

Yet even the best designed environment cannot replace the sensitive practitioner who takes the time to understand the needs and requirements of each child in his or her care. Dowling (2000) points out that there is a need for practitioners to be constantly proactive and to observe children closely, as they may appear to be coping with a situation when in fact they are not:

> I visited a reception class three days after children had started school. I wanted to find out how much of an understanding children had about school life in this short space of time. I approached Gavin and asked him 'What do you do in this school?' He

paused for a moment and then told me 'Well, we paint and draw and go outside to play. Sometimes we have a story and we must try to sit and cross our legs.' After another pause, Gavin continued, 'That's not all. We have lunch and then we go to the hall. I like that. We have to take off our clothes and put them together, 'cos they will get lost. Then our mummies come to take us home.' Over the other side of the class I approached Joe with the same question. Joe avoided looking at me. He simply hung his head and muttered, 'I dunno, I dunno.'

(Dowling 2000: 36)

Practitioners can do much to structure the environment and induct children into new situations so that they can make transitions smoothly. In the following account, Mrs Singh, a teacher in a reception class, explains her approach to helping children cope with transitions.

At the beginning of the year I always talk to the children about where things belong, how to put them away and why it is important to care for them. We often talk about what would happen if they leave the lids off the pens, or fold the pages of books. The children come up with rules for themselves. I don't have rules saying things like 'only four children in the sand' because it seems to me that the children can be self-regulating and will appreciate that when activities are overcrowded play is damaged. I depend on the children to sort things out for themselves and mostly they do. I find that when I don't have to be busy making sure that they are keeping to imposed rules I have more time to really interact with them or observe them.

(Smidt 2002: 52–3)

Mrs Singh realised that it was more effective to talk sensitively about caring for classroom items than to create a lot of rules for the children to remember and follow. In this way, she was able to ease their transition into school and help them to gain independence through being in control of what they did. Young children are more likely to develop emotional well-being successfully if they are familiar with the situations in which they find themselves and are able to predict what will happen in their environment. It is essential that early years practitioners understand the impact of young children's emotional development on their early learning, if they are to equip them for life now and in the future.

In the day-to-day activities of your setting there will be many tasks, routines and activities that are familiar to you but which may, initially, be unfamiliar to the children with whom you are working. Coming into a new environment that has several children in it may be a daunting experience for a child who has been used to the close, one-to-one relationships of home. The time it takes for individual children to feel part of a setting, and able to join in the experiences offered, may vary enormously.

## Activity 11.2 Making transitions easier

How do you support children in engaging with new experiences and how much time and space do you give to this in any one day? Note down your responses to the following questions.

- How do you get to know children as individuals?
- What do you do to support children in developing familiarity with the routines and practices in your setting?
- How do you support children in developing independence?
- Have you observed and kept notes on the behaviour of individual children?
- How have you used this information?

## Case Study: Jo and Alison

Jo cares for Alison, who is two and a half years old. Jo has mixed together some sand, soap and water for Alison to play with. Alison spends a long time exploring the soapy sand. It feels so lovely, she makes different patterns in it with her fingers. Jo admires the designs and patterns that Alison is making, and encourages her to make some more.

## Case Study: Shereen, Sarah and Brian

Shereen works in a nursery. She is watching Brian, who has Down's syndrome, and Sarah as they play outside together. Sarah decides to go on the slide. She climbs the ladder and slides down successfully. She does this several times while Brian watches. Brian decides to have a go, and climbs up the ladder. But when he tries to turn round, his legs get tangled up. Brian persists and, with Sarah shouting instructions to him, he finally manages to turn round so that he can come down the slide. Shereen and Sarah clap and cheer at Brian's success. Brian climbs the slide again and again, becoming more skilful each time.

In the above examples, both practitioners are providing the children with new experiences to explore. By extending the activity or applauding the children's achievement, Jo and Shereen encourage them to take a positive approach to new activities. The two practitioners observe the children's response to the activities, and this provides them with information they can use to plan further experiences using different materials. In this way, they can ensure that the children develop increasing independence and confidence in what they are doing.

## Children's personal, social and emotional development

Personal, social and emotional development can be defined as an accumulation of experiences that stimulate and challenge, and promote strong relationships, personal identity and self-esteem. Through valuing the home and cultural context, and planning appropriate experiences into their provision, early years practitioners can help young children to develop:

- self-confidence and self-esteem;
- good relationships with peers and other adults;
- understanding of how to behave in a wide range of situations;
- self-control and a sense of community.

Personal, social and emotional development encompasses a wide range of experiences, indoor, outdoor, linked to a child's nurture or to their emotional and physical health. When all aspects of children's development are enabled, they will become whole and strong. 'The strong child' is a term taken from the English framework *Birth to Three Matters* (Sure Start Unit 2002). Paying attention to all the primary needs of young children has implications for the early diagnosis of children with learning difficulties, and for identifying and alleviating child abuse and poverty.

The Green Paper, *Every Child Matters* (DfES 2003: 14), identifies five key outcomes relating to the well-being of young children:

- being healthy;
- staying safe;
- enjoying and achieving;
- making a positive contribution;
- economic well-being.

To achieve these outcomes, there needs to be improved prevention and early intervention. The Green Paper proposes a wide range of strategies to meet those aims, and it is evident that all those working with young children have a central role to play in achieving them. Developing the whole, strong child depends on far more than simply stimulating intellectual development: it is about fostering personal and social qualities that are grounded in emotional well-being.

The English Curriculum guidance for the foundation stage (QCA/DfEE 2000) also highlights the importance of supporting and promoting children's personal, social and emotional development across the curriculum:

> [the] curriculum for the foundation stage should underpin all future learning by supporting, fostering, promoting and developing children's:
> - **personal social and emotional well-being** . . . by supporting the transition to and between settings, promoting an inclusive ethos and providing opportunities for each child to become a valued member of that group and community so that a strong self-image and self-esteem are promoted;
> - **positive attitudes and dispositions towards their learning** . . . in particular an enthusiasm for knowledge and learning and a confidence in their ability to be successful learners;
> - **social skills** . . . by providing opportunities that enable them to learn how to cooperate and work harmoniously alongside and with each other and to listen to each other.
>
> (QCA/DfEE, 2000: 8)

Edgington (2002) welcomes the move to a more social curriculum. She argues that early education programmes which encourage the development of cognitive, emotional and social skills, through play and exploration, result in lasting social and educational benefits. Where the curriculum is characterised by narrowly defined academic goals in reading, writing and number, and children are taught through instructional approaches, they are more likely to suffer from social and behavioural problems in later years.

## Working within the culture of the setting

The cultural context, values and ethos of a setting will all have an impact upon the personal, social and emotional well-being of the children who are in it. In Chapter 4 we discussed the importance of a learning environment in which young children are listened to, treated with respect and surrounded by things they are familiar with as well as things that are new. If the values of the home clash with the values of the setting, children are likely to be confused, which will impact on their sense of self and their feelings of self-worth. Discontinuity between the home and the setting can occur in many contexts and situations, and not just in those where another culture prevails or a different language is spoken in the home. In all their planning, practitioners have to respond to the challenge that the children they work with come from very diverse backgrounds. Settings must aim to meet the needs of boys and girls, children from different social and economic backgrounds, children with learning difficulties or disabilities, more able children, as well as children from minority backgrounds such as travellers, asylum seekers and refugees. Parents need to be included in the work of sharing and understanding different home experiences and cultural backgrounds, and practitioners and parents need to consider ways of providing a range of social and cultural experiences in the setting. For example, learning that letters, words and numbers can be written in different scripts, or about different child-rearing practices or conventions.

> Children who have experienced different cultural conventions are already able to understand how to manipulate different symbols to mean different things, sometimes with sophisticated layers of meaning. Because they know intimately about differing cultural conventions and symbols, they are not destined to be narrow 'culture-bound specialists'.
>
> (Bruce 2001: 13)

In the curriculum guidance for all four UK countries, personal, social and emotional development is clearly identified as a key element or dimension of the curriculum. It is also linked to those activities in settings and schools which involve wider participation – for example, with parents and the local community.

## Case Study: Jasmine (aged 4)

The children have been brought together to watch a mother bathing her baby. All the children talk about their younger brothers and sisters, and about babies in general and how they are cared for at home. Jasmine says, 'My mum puts oil on my baby brother's skin when he has had a bath.'

In this example, the children were able to discuss differences within their individual communities, and to use that as a starting point for learning about what happens in other communities. Jasmine's practitioner provided an experience that helped create an atmosphere of openness, so that the children were able to learn from one another and from each other's family experiences.

## Building good relationships

An important aspect of personal and social development is the ability to form good relationships with other children and adults. By the time children reach the age of three, they have usually established, with the help of their parents, a number of different relationships with adults and other young children. If they have managed to form only a small number of social contacts, they may find the early years setting, with its greater numbers of children and adults, a challenging experience. Learning to make friends is crucial if a child is to develop strong self-esteem and self-worth; failure to do so can lead to great unhappiness.

As children grow and develop, they become aware of others' views and feelings, and learn to interact with others. The ways in which children do this will depend on the kinds of experiences they have, and the support and modelling they are given when mixing with other children and adults.

## Case Study: Nasma (aged 4)

Nasma has a new toy, a windmill, which she brings to the nursery to show everyone. Three-year-old Josh is attracted to the windmill because it is shiny and catches the light. He grabs the toy and won't let go. Other children in the group push Josh away, and Nasma takes back her new toy. Later, Nasma is seen sharing the toy windmill with Josh. Together, they are blowing on it and making it move.

Nasma is learning social skills. In this example, she demonstrates her ability to recognise, empathise and respond in a positive manner to a younger child's wants. As a practitioner, you need to be aware of the stages that children pass through in terms of their ability to think beyond their own needs and how you support children when they find themselves in situations that are new, challenging, excitable, aggressive and frightening. Children need to be helped to make sense of what they see and hear. Helpful, supportive feedback helps children to develop their social skills. For example, some of the children in the example above might benefit from input about how they could help someone more effectively next time, rather than pushing.

Understanding the viewpoint of another person is an important aspect of friendship. When young children are in a place that is familiar to them, they often show considerable understanding of the emotions and feelings of others (Donaldson 1978). Even babies can be sensitive to those close to them, and toddlers will show some understanding of how older brothers and sisters will react when annoyed or teased (Dunn and Kendrick 1982). Dowling (2000) suggests that while young children may be unable to appreciate another's perspective in an intellectual task, they work from a sharp social intelligence. By around four years old, the complex social skills involved in making friends have grown to include the ability to:

- gain entry to group activities;
- be approving and supportive;
- manage conflicts appropriately;
- exercise sensitivity and tact.

The early years curriculum in each of the UK countries is divided into distinct areas or aspects of learning. However, it is intended that practitioners use these areas/aspects to provide an integrated education for children in their early years. The more links that are made across the curriculum, the deeper children's understanding of what they are learning. Although the division of the curriculum into 'subject' areas may appear to be greater in curriculum guidance for primary-aged children, an emphasis on providing for children's personal, social and emotional development remains. The Primary National Strategy (DfES 2004) sees personal, social and emotional development as a condition for successful learning and identifies five affective aspects, or domains, as being critical – managing feelings, social skills, motivation, empathy and self-awareness.

Some aspects of personal, social and emotional development are integral to the daily activity of the setting, such as taking turns, sharing, showing concern and caring for the environment. Practitioners will want to pay particular attention to other aspects, such as going on outings, settling in new arrivals and dealing with challenging behaviour. There are also certain activities that practitioners will want to use to support children in making friends, learning to wait or sitting quietly at specific times.

Many young children struggle to find out who they are and to develop confidence and self-esteem in their own identity. Giving them a positive view of themselves is one of the practitioner's most important tasks. Children learn a great deal through imitation, so you and the other adults in your setting need to reflect these positive qualities in your own behaviour and treatment of children, and seek to be positive role models for them. However, it is important that you are consistent; it can be very confusing for children when different adults expect different things.

Being a good role model involves not only how you interact on a daily basis with parents, other adults and children but being aware of how you react and respond to specific incidents.

## Case Study: The missing cake

Carl found that the cake in his lunchbox had disappeared. He discovered that James had taken it; James was hungry because his au pair had forgotten to pack his lunchbox properly. The teacher took both upset children aside. She gently asked

James to think if there might have been any other solution to the problem. Together they agreed that a better line of action would have been for James to have told an adult that he was hungry. James himself suggested that in recompense he would bring Carl a cake from home tomorrow. At the end of the day (with the permission of James and Carl) the teacher shared this episode with the other children. Everyone agreed that taking things without permission was not good and should not happen in the nursery.

(Dowling 2000: 95)

Handling situations such as this one can be challenging. The practitioner skilfully used the incident to teach all the children how to control the impulse to take items that did not belong to them. It is hoped that a social and moral lesson was learnt, and the children were encouraged to reflect on what had happened. The practitioner considered the behaviour of the two boys and helped them towards a solution. She then used the incident to further the personal, social and emotional development of all the children. Responding to and utilising situations that arise means that planning needs to be flexible enough to respond to these incidental opportunities for learning.

## Activity 11.3 Developing social skills

Consider what you do to support the social development of children in your setting. The following questions may help to guide your thinking.

- How does the way in which the setting is organised help children's social development?

- How do you encourage adults to interact with the children?

- In what ways do you support and develop children's social skills?

- How do you react if there is conflict between children?

- How do you help children to make sense of an incident and learn from the experience?

- What activities do you regularly provide to allow children to play together?

- How do you encourage and develop children's ability to take turns and to share?

- How do adults serve as role models for positive interactions between each other within the setting?

Early years settings provide ideal surroundings for children to meet new people, share their experiences and feelings, and enjoy new experiences. Children chat as they engage in activities and play together or alongside each other. Encouraging them to take turns, listen to others, and acknowledge and accept differences are important ways to support their social development and a strong sense of self-identity.

## Promoting children's self-esteem

When children have a high sense of self-esteem, they are more likely to take risks. This enables them to gain confidence in acquiring new skills and to make bigger leaps in their understanding. Table 11.1 lists five key aspects of self-esteem and summarises some of the ways in which you can help to promote the self-esteem of children in your setting.

**Table 11.1**  Promoting children's self-esteem

| Aspect of self-esteem | Suggested activities/actions |
| --- | --- |
| Age | With age, children learn increased control, gain memory, develop cognitively, learn language, and gain a sense of how to plan for the future. This development can be supported in the following ways:<br>    (pre-school) building on the child's interests, and involving them in real tasks to give them a sense of accomplishment;<br>    (school age) respecting their strengths and helping them to set goals. |
| Supported waiting | Children have difficulty waiting, but can be supported while they wait. Talk to them. For example, 'Dinner will be ready in five minutes . . . I know you can wait that long . . . Let's do a puzzle while we wait'. |
| Follow through | Follow through after a child waits. Do not imply a reward will come if you don't intend to give one. This is part of the build-up of trust. Adults need to be consistent in their approach. |
| Modelling | Adults who control their own anger, aggression, language and needs provide positive models for the children in their care. Showing that you are cross about a child's behaviour but you are not rejecting the child can be part of this process. |
| Feeling in control | Provide children with age-appropriate choices. Offer two choices you can live with, and give the child an opportunity to learn to make decisions. Too many choices too early can lead to confusion or children hoarding activities. |

*Source:* Katz, L. (1996)

## Review

In this chapter we have looked at the personal, social and emotional development of young children. This is a complex and under-researched area of children's development which has, in the past, been assumed to happen rather than being considered and planned for. We hope that you have enhanced your knowledge of this area of learning and of strategies and ideas for enhancing your practice. Young children's personal, social and emotional well-being will affect not only how they behave in the early years setting and the ease with which they learn generally; it also provides the foundation for a strong sense of self-identity, something that they will carry with them into adulthood.

### Questions for reflection

1 How often you invite children to explore their understanding of an incident or problem they encounter, as opposed to providing them with an explanation or answer?

2 How consistent are you in the way you deal with incidents involving different children in your setting? What kinds of messages may you be sending to children?

3 How do you support children in becoming more independent and in taking risks?

## References

Bruce, T. (2001) *Learning through Play: Babies, toddlers and the foundation years*, London: Hodder and Stoughton.

Department for Education and Skills (DfES) (2003) *Every Child Matters*, Norwich: The Stationery Office.

Department for Education and Skills (2004) (DfES) *Primary National Strategy Excellence and Enjoyment: Learning and teaching in the primary years*, London: DfES.

Donaldson, M. (1978) *Children's Minds*, London: Fontana.

Dowling, M. (2000) *Young Children's Personal, Social and Emotional Development*, London: Paul Chapman Publishing.

Dunn, J. and Kendrick, C. (1982) *Siblings: Love, envy and understanding*, Cambridge, MA: Harvard University Press.

Edgington, M. (2002) 'High levels of achievements for young children' in Fisher, J. (ed.) *The Foundations of Learning*, Buckingham: Open University Press.

Katz, L. (1996) 'How can we strengthen children's self-esteem?', ERIC Clearinghouse on Elementary and Early Childhood Education website, http://www.kidsource.com/kidsource/content2/strengthen_children_self.html (accessed April 2005).

Qualifications and Curriculum Authority (QCA)/Department for Education and Employment (DfEE) (2000) *Curriculum Guidance for the Foundation Stage*, London: QCA.

Smidt, S. (2002) *A Guide to Early Years Practice*, 2nd edn, London: RoutledgeFalmer.

Sure Start Unit (2002) *Birth to Three Matters: A framework to support children in their earliest years*, London: Department for Education and Skills.

## Further reading

Leach, B.J. (2003) *Personal, Social and Emotional Development*, 'Goals for the Foundation Stage' series, Leamington Spa: Scholastic.

Moseley, J. (1996) *Quality Circle Time*, Cambridge: LDA.

Siraj-Blatchford, J. and Siraj-Blatchford, I. (1995) *Educating the Whole Child: Cross-curricular skills, themes and dimensions*, Buckingham: Open University Press.

# 12 Creativity and ICT

## By the end of the chapter you will have:

- learnt about creativity as 'possibility thinking' and the connections between creativity and learning;

- explored some practical approaches to fostering a creative climate in your setting;

- considered the nature and role of information and communications technology (ICT) and its place in the curriculum and as a medium for play and learning;

- explored ways in which the appropriate use of ICT can enhance young children's learning.

## Introduction

This chapter focuses on creativity and ICT. Both have relevance across the curriculum for children's learning and lives. In the first part we explore what is meant by children's creativity, broadening the definition of creativity beyond art and craft, dance, drama, music and imaginative play to include the notion of 'possibility thinking'. We explore reasons why it is important to foster this in young children's lives and look at creative learning and strategies to encourage creativity. In exploring how to support young children in their learning *with* and *about* information communication technology, we consider your role as an early years practitioner in deciding how best to use such powerful tools in your practice. We explore the place of ICT in the early years curriculum.

## The importance of creativity

What do you imagine when you think of encouraging young children's creativity? Perhaps in your mind's eye you see children experimenting with colour and texture, for example painting, or playing with wet sand. Creativity is often taken to encompass the creative and performing arts and self-expression, and these are important dimensions of children's learning and development. Other definitions of creativity, though, are broader than the arts alone, and a commonly used one is 'imaginative activity fashioned so as to produce outcomes that are both original and of value' (National Advisory Committe on Creative and Cultural Education 1999: 29). Consider the following three scenarios.

### Case Study: Jacob (aged 1 year and 5 months)

Jacob, sitting in the back seat of a car, was holding a stick found in the park earlier. He held it up. 'Umbrella!' he said. Then, 'Flowers!' and then, 'Wand!'

### Case Study: Georgia (aged three)

Georgia, together with two older children, is making an apple cake with their childminder when they discover that they have no apple juice, one of the critical ingredients. 'Oh, dear,' says the childminder, 'I wonder what we could do about that?' Whilst the older children ponder, Georgia pipes up, 'Why don't we use orange juice instead?' and with that she scrambles off her chair to collect some.

### Case Study: Natasha (aged 9 months)

Natasha is sitting on the kitchen floor whilst her childminder prepares a meal. She has been given some empty upturned metal cooking pots and a wooden spoon. She bangs the different pots with her spoon, loudly, and then discovers, after knocking one pot over, that when it is the right way up, she can make a different sound by bashing the edge of it.

Each child is confident in exploring possibilities, acting as though it were unproblematic and obvious, actively considering alternatives, using imagination, asking 'what if? This is what is sometimes called 'possibility thinking', and it is at the heart of being creative, whether in everyday life – for example cooking, in early mathematics or imaginative play (Craft 2000, 2002). It involves a child moving in their thinking, from 'What does this do?' to 'What can I do with this?' and, in the case of difficulties, 'How can I get around this problem?' Possibility thinking involves and encourages a move from the concrete into the more abstract. In other words, a child moves from the very practical, for example: 'How can I make a roof for my play-house?', or 'What happens if I bash the pot the other way up with my wooden spoon?' to the more abstract or ideas-based 'What sort of play-house is this – a mouse hole, perhaps?', or 'What sort of mood does this rhythm conjure?' The roots of possibility thinking can be seen in the concrete (practical) experiences of very small children and is a way individual learners develop the capacity to find their way through the life experiences they meet, even those which appear problematic, with a creative attitude and approach. It is distinct from problem-solving, as it encompasses 'problem-finding' – i.e. noticing the potential for a new idea or a new question, as well as solving problems.

## Activity 12.1 Reflecting on creativity

Recall a scenario of your own where you think you may have witnessed a child or children engaged in possibility thinking. Write down:

- what the child did;

- why you think this involved the child in possibility thinking;

- what, if anything, in their learning environment encouraged their possibility thinking.

You may have noticed children being creative, in the sense of possibility thinking, in other areas of the curriculum, such as early mathematics, physical education, and information and communications technology. Here is an example of a child being creative with a computer. Rowan, the child involved, identifies and then solves a problem.

## Case Study: Rowan and the computer game

Four-year-old Rowan is playing on the computer, whilst his teacher works on the play mat nearby with other boys. Rowan completes the game, which was on the screen, which is a teddy bear with 'clothes' that need to be placed over the correct part of his body. He looks around at his teacher, and seeing him occupied, deftly finds the menu screen to select a new game. He concentrates hard and after a few seconds succeeds in bringing up a new game involving sorting. His teacher notices what he is doing and comes over. 'Did you manage it all by your-self, Rowan?' he asks, appreciatively. Rowan nods and smiles. As this is a game he is unfamiliar with, he seems puzzled about what to do. His teacher asks, 'What do you think you might need to do for this game?' Rowan is unsure but another child notices and calls out a suggestion. His teacher warmly acknowledges the sugges-tion, whilst at the same time encouraging Rowan to consider what the game might require. Rowan eventually decides on his own rules for the game, which involve putting all the pieces into the 'rubbish bin', although this is not 'officially' the way the game works. Rowan also sorts each of the fruits verbally by fruit type, as he puts them into the bin. Rather than criticising this, his teacher praises his idea and his grouping and encourages him to continue to think about how this game works.

Children (and adults) are capable of developing creative ideas in any aspect of life. Fostering and valuing creativity are important because it is the key to encouraging independence of thought, an increasingly important skill in today's world. As early years practitioners, we need to be sensitive to the potential for children to express and develop their creativity in any part of the curriculum. This means considering what possibilities might be offered by the outdoor play area, early literacy and numeracy, the computer, in social and emotional experiences – in fact, in all aspects of a child's experience in the setting.

## Why is possibility thinking important?

The development of possibility thinking is increasingly important for survival in a world of decreasing certainties. The pace of change is becoming ever faster and family and local community structures, as well as the world of work, seem to be fragmenting and shifting. What was accepted as a 'given' in the past is no longer the case, for example having a career or job for life. Early years settings therefore need to stimulate the creativity of children in a way that will enable them to make the most of opportunities they are faced with. The importance of creativity is increasingly recognised. As Learning and Teaching Scotland suggest, 'in today's world, creativity is fundamentally important for our personal social, economic and cultural well-being' (LTS 2001: 4).

# Creative learning

Creativity enhances learning because it involves encouraging children's imaginations. Beetlestone (1998) suggests that learning any subject is integrally combined with the development of creativity, because the process of learning involves making new sense of knowledge and skills and this in itself is a creative act. For Beetlestone, aspects of creative learning include curiosity, problem-solving, investigation, conversation and other interactions, and experiential learning. She suggests that creativity involves practitioners in:

■ helping children propose unusual combinations, for example thinking of different ways of combining ingredients in making a salad;

■ connecting sense-impressions ('images') and developing ideas from sensations, for example making up a poem about a windy day;

■ helping children express feelings, for example encouraging them to express their feelings in small or big groups;

■ offering children access to diverse possibilities;

■ providing an outlet for the subconscious, releasing un-expressed feelings, like fear and worries, for example through dramatic play or music;

■ being the 'engine' of much of children's play, which helps children develop their understanding of the world, and their place in it, providing a safe place to take risks and explore worries and fears.

Woods (1990) identified four elements to being creative in the classroom:

■ innovation – the activity the child was engaged in should involve something novel for them;

■ relevance – the activity should feel relevant to the child;

■ control – the child should feel some control over the activity;

■ autonomy – the child should be able to express their independence through the activity.

The work of Beetlestone (1998) and Woods (1990) has implications for practice. The features of creativity which they each write about are often present in, and can be developed through, children's play. But other activities can foster creativity too.

> ## Activity 12.2 Fostering creative learning
>
> Look at the different aspects of creative learning, identified by Beetlestone and Woods. Then write responses to these questions.
>
> Which of these form a part of your practice in your own setting?
>
> In what other ways does your setting encourage creative learning and imagination?
>
> What benefits do you see in stimulating creative learning, and what challenges are there in doing so?

## Fostering a creative climate

Establishing a creative climate is fundamental to early years education and care. In an ever-changing world, future generations will need to think beyond what is given to them, to generate ideas, to use their imaginations, to be innovative, simply because many of the 'templates' for activity, behaviour and interaction are evolving so fast. A creative approach to life means the capacity to self-direct; it is built on positive self-esteem and it both rests on and inspires confidence.

Early years environments need to offer children opportunities to develop their creativity in their own preferred styles of learning. This means providing ways of building children's self-esteem and confidence, with awareness of culture, gender and social context. It means offering children the opportunity to develop and express their gross and fine motor skills, their artistic, musical and kinaesthetic abilities and encouraging different modes of expression in verbal and non-verbal ways. Most importantly of all, it means offering opportunities for children to make informed choices.

Duffy (2003) suggests that observing children can reveal a great deal about what interests, motivates and stimulates a child's creativity. It can also help us to notice how children are supported in their creativity, by their environment and in their interactions with other children as well as by early years practitioners. Researchers have noticed that a number of things can contribute to the successful stimulation of children's creativity.

These include:

- offering children sufficient space, which includes physical play areas, but also finding ample opportunities to listen to children – and to hear what they say – as well as offering opportunities for them to be quiet and reflective;
- 'good teaching', which includes a feel for what is appropriate for individual learners, backed up by flexibility and imagination;

- providing stimulating materials and resources and modelling creativity by being inspired oneself;

- setting aside areas for potentially messy activities and enabling children to return to unfinished work over a period of time;

- encouraging children to take risks and supporting their self-confidence;

- asking questions, describing what you see them doing, offering analysis, and sometimes being controversial with them;

- negotiating with children where appropriate, showing them that ideas, procedures and possibilities are always open to refinement and change;

- using events when things do *not* happen as creative learning opportunities.

Which of these strategies seem most helpful to you? In the case study of Rowan we saw how ICT can be used to foster creativity, and the next part of this chapter explores ICT further.

## What is ICT?

Technologies of many kinds are a feature of everyday life and are becoming ever more commonplace as the pace of change increases. Flexible technologies that allow people to communicate with each other through a variety of media are becoming increasingly accessible. For example, mobile phones can take and instantly transmit photographs as well as let us talk or send text or e-mail messages across the room or around the world. We are not surprised that we can make connections between different devices like phones, computers and the Internet to do all manner of things, even though not everyone is actually using them all yet. Devices which have electronic components, which allow us to store, manipulate and represent information can be classified as information communication technology.

Tales about the technological prowess of small children are part mythology, but whilst some of these stories are exaggerations they do contain an element of truth. We are frequently taken by surprise by the speed at which children seem to discover what various devices, such as tape activity centres, do and how comfortable they are with the interactivity they offer.

### Activity 12.3 Everyday technology

Make a list of the technological devices you think the young children you know or work with might have encountered. Sort the devices into groups of your own choosing. For example, you might make groups of:

- everyday domestic things;

- things that children see around them;

- things that children actually use.

Alternatively, you could group them using the following criteria:

- things you think have improved our everyday lives;

- things you feel children should be encouraged to use;

- things you feel children should not be allowed to use.

There isn't a right or wrong way of doing this, but think carefully about your groupings. When you are satisfied with the way you have grouped all the devices on your list, make a note that describes each group in a few words. Now think about any items that were difficult to place or that could have gone into more than one of your groups. Did these have anything in common?

It is easy to see just how much of our lives has been influenced by technology and how quickly new products and 'improvements' come along and make us rethink the way we do things. In doing this activity, you will have started making judgements about the advantages and disadvantages these devices bring. By making judgements about which devices you feel children should be allowed or encouraged to use, you will have started to evaluate what part these devices have to play in children developing their understanding of their world and their part in it.

## ICT and appropriate use

The term ICT is most often thought about in connection with computers, and it is these that have probably had the most impact on our thinking about learning in early years settings. However, developers are looking at materials for technological play and learning that do not have screens, keyboards, input devices such as a touch pad or a mouse, cables or even hard surfaces – these devices will be more responsive than anything we have at the moment.

There has been considerable debate about the suitability of young children using what can be very powerful tools, and we need to think very carefully about when, how and for what purposes we use them. Papert (1996) argues that computers have a great deal to offer young children's learning and reminds us that computers, like any other tools, can be used in different ways and can be used well or badly. He argues strongly that computers should not be 'babysitters' or 'baby stimulators' or just motivators, as he suggests that computers offer 'new ways of learning' that are particularly well matched to the exploratory nature of children's learning.

Judgements about the appropriate use of ICT should be based on the same criteria as judgements about the appropriateness of any resources or activities for particular children in a particular setting at a particular time. We need to think about developmentally appropriate practice, where children are seen as active learners who build their understanding of the world on cultural knowledge, as well as all the physical and social experiences of their everyday lives (Bredekamp and Copple 1997).

When thinking about ICT and learning we need to be clear about the difference between learning about ICT and learning with ICT. Teaching ourselves to surf the Internet or programme a video machine includes developing the knowledge, skills and understanding needed, and is therefore learning about ICT. When we use our new skills to locate information on the Internet about the early learning goals or care standards, for example, we are learning with ICT. The information and communication facilities have helped us to get to what we are interested in learning more about.

## Play and ICT

We have discussed the importance of play in learning in earlier chapters and what we say applies equally when we are thinking about learning *about* and *with* ICT.

In general, children under three are not often considered as users of information communication technology. However, there are many child-friendly audio recorders, play phones, programmable toys and other devices that provide worthwhile learning opportunities. If the significant people in young children's lives are users of ICT, then it is only natural that the children will be interested in, and want to be part of, these interactions. This happens in just the same way as any other sharing of everyday involvement, such as story telling or mark-making or cooking. Encouraging and supporting children's interest in similar ways is appropriate, but what is really important is that the adult and children play together. The technology is just a part of this involvement.

### Case study: Nina and Sam

Nina, who is four, and Sam, who is four and four months, are busy in the imaginative play area. For the past few days it has been an estate agents just like the one near their nursery that they visited. They know about moving house and they are helping Susie, the nursery teacher, to look through the pictures in the area to find a house with a garden for her baby to play in, a garage for her car and enough bedrooms for everyone. Renata, who is a little younger, has come along to see what's going on and to decide if she wants to play too. They have a good selection of resources in their play area and lots of mark-making equipment, including an electronic notepad. Sam is busily scrolling back through the display screen to find the '5' he knows he keyed in when they were talking about the bedrooms. The others are all watching him very carefully. He is the estate agent and he is creating his record of the customer's requirements. Later he can print this out and his teacher will see that it gets included in the play props.

Sam is clearly interested in the mark-making aspect of what he is doing; he knows about numbers and he knows that his number should still be there. He is learning about number symbols [*with* ICT] and he is learning about how the notepad keyboard works by exploring his actions and ideas [*about* ICT]. The resources area and activity have been carefully structured and contextualised. Susie planned visits to the estate agents as one of the activities linked to this role-play development. She clearly thinks that seeing how ICT is used in a specific context is a significant element of the play provision. The children are learning *about* ICT and *with* ICT too and they have been given the opportunity to play with symbolic representations of numbers and letters in a serious way.

## Adult roles

Play that involves ICT presents many opportunities for meaning-making and symbolic activity, and both of these things are very important to the development of thinking and making decisions about actions. The children in the case study above were comfortable and secure in their play environment, and their understanding was helped by their efforts to make sense of the symbol systems and by the opportunity to 'try on the various roles for size'.

With some adult help, play is allowing them to extend their ability to:

- handle equipment confidently;
- use language to construct a dialogue between and within themselves;
- engage in discussions to compare understandings and interpretations;

■ jointly solve problems and resolve any differences between them;

■ organise their learning efforts and seek support from an adult when they need it;

■ take increasing responsibility for the equipment;

■ develop their understanding of the purpose of ICT in the world;

■ gain repeated practice of important manipulative skills.

(adapted from Cook and Finlayson 1999: 33)

Your key role as a practitioner is to ensure that play remains the primary means of learning and that ICT activities are presented to young children in meaningful ways and children are given support whenever and wherever they need it. However, it isn't always possible for adults to become directly involved in children's play. The availability of support when and where children need it is crucial to the quality of learning with ICT, as is planning for the integration of ICT activities into the overall programme of provision.

## Learning about ICT

We need to be aware how individual children behave when using ICT and to ensure that children's ICT skills improve so that they become increasingly capable and self-reliant. We also need to consider how we manage the considerable differences there may be between different children's interest, engagement and persistence and encourage them to discuss and reflect on what they are doing and to develop appropriate behaviours.

## Supporting children's learning *with* ICT

As early years practitioners, we need to ensure that everyone has access to appropriate learning. There are many ways in which access to learning can be supported by ICT. Speech recognition systems, special input devices, access buttons and switches, overlay keyboards and tape recorders are just some of the ways that ICT has been used to help children with learning difficulties or disabilities. It is equally important that we do not promote inequality by being unaware of how children are accessing ICT in our settings. Anecdotal comments from practitioners suggest that some children love to engage with computer activities, for example, while others do not. There is some concern that the children who don't choose this type of activity are the ones who may need to have their confidence and competence actively supported by adults. Some people are concerned that boys and girls behave differently, especially girls as they get older. Some children may only engage in computer activity when adult support is available. Some like to spend a long time just watching others before they are prepared to have a go themselves. Others may have no access to computers in their homes and so may be very unconfident about their usage. All these factors have implications for your planning and the support you provide, as does the cost of equipment. Although prices are falling, equipment is still relatively expensive and the view is sometimes taken that 'older' equipment is good enough for young children. There are equity issues here for both practitioners and children. Whatever you have available, it is as important to be familiar with the ICT equipment you have as it is with any other equipment you use, and to find out about its potential use.

## Computer software

Practitioners use a variety of computer software or programs, many of which are generic, content-free programs, such as art or word-processing packages, and some of which are curriculum specific. The important thing is to use the resources to support children's learning in interesting and imaginative ways. Curriculum-specific programs can be imaginative and creative in design but some are very limiting and repetitive. Some experts (Papert 1996; Davis and Shade 1999) are strongly against the use of any 'drill and practice' programs in early learning contexts. The key is knowing how the software will enable us to support children's learning. This means we need the chance to use the program ourselves to find out what we can make it do. Insights gained in this way help us to anticipate ways in which children might be able to make good use of that resource in a particular area of learning.

Stephen and Plowman (2002) feel that evaluating software for early childhood is quite complex. They suggest that, as well as ensuring that software promotes all the positive values essential for any equipment, we need to check:

- how supportive a product is of collaborative working;
- what level of adult support is required;
- the reading demands it makes of learners;
- its operational simplicity;
- the degree of 'distractibility', e.g. be easy to load and run;
- how easy it is for children find their way around, or navigate.

(Underwood and Underwood 1997)

## Working with parents

Parental interest in new technologies and the contribution they can make to learning is a significant factor underpinning the growing use of computers at home. A recent study looking at popular culture media texts and literacy showed that the research family diaries of the three- and four-year-olds included activity with computer games, with only four out of the eighteen families having neither a games console nor a PC (Marsh and Thompson 2001). Many practitioners comment on the noticeable change from year to year in the skills levels and experiences with computers that young children have, but this means there are equity issues to think about if some children are not to be disadvantaged.

Parents rightly seek information about the computer activities that children engage in outside their family homes. As practitioners, we also need to know about the formative experiences children have had, so that we can build upon existing foundations.

For ICT to be a powerful tool in their learning, children must be able to use the technology in meaningful situations, and its use must be integrated into the wider activities of the setting and linked to the learning objectives for the children. Enabling children to make links between the use of technology inside and outside the home, and inside and outside the setting, is crucial to developing children's understanding of the rapidly changing use of ICT in society today.

## Review

In this chapter, we have explored creativity as possibility thinking and thought about 'creative learning'. We have considered how we can use ICT in supporting young children's learning. We have seen how imaginatively and creatively everyday equipment can be exploited when used thoughtfully and playfully by practitioners. Both ICT and creativity can support children's learning in each of the areas of learning when activities are carefully planned to exploit their potential.

### Questions for reflection

1 What action will you take to enhance the creative learning opportunities for the children in your setting?

2 How do you plan for creativity and ICT in your setting?

3 How do you link both creativity and ICT to the wider experiences children have?

# References

Beetlestone, F. (1998) *Creative Children, Imaginative Teaching*, Buckingham: Open University Press.

Bredekamp, S. and Copple, C. (1997) (eds.) *Developmentally Appropriate Practice in Early Childhood Programs*, Washington, DC: National Association for Education of Young Children (NAEYC).

Cook, D. and Finlayson, H.M. (1999) *Interactive Children, Communicative Teaching*, Buckingham: Open University Press.

Craft, A. (2000) *Creativity Across the Primary Curriculum*, London: Routledge.

Craft, A. (2002) *Creativity in the Early Years*, London: Continuum.

Davis, B.C. and Shade, D.D. (1999) *Integrating technology into the early childhood classroom: the case for literacy learning, Information Technology in Childhood Education Annual 1999 (1)*, pp. 221–54.

Duffy, B. (2003) 'Creative and imaginative experiences', in Devereux, J. and Miller, L. (eds) *Working with Children in the Early Years*, Buckingham: Open University Press.

Learning and Teaching Scotland (LTS)/The IDES Network (2001) *Creativity in Education*, Dundee: LTS.

Marsh, J. and Thompson, P. (2001) 'Parental involvement in literacy development: using media texts', in *Journal of Research in Reading*, 23 (2), 149–57.

National Advisory Committee on Creative and Cultural Education (NACCCE) (1999) *All Our Futures: Creativity, culture and education*, London: DfEE.

National Association for the Education of Young Children (NAEYC) (1996) *Technology and Young Children – ages 3 through 8*, http://www.naeyc.org/resources/position_statements/positions_intro.htm (accessed April 2005).

Papert, S. (1996) *The Connected Family: Bridging the digital generation gap*, Atlanta, GA: Longstreet Press.

Stephen, C. and Plowman, L. (2002) *ICT in Pre-school: A 'Benign Addition'?* Dundee: Learning and Teaching Scotland.

Underwood, G. and Underwood, J. (1997) *Children's interactions and learning outcomes with interactive books*, paper presented at the CAL (Computer Assisted Learning) conference, Exeter, April.

## Further reading

Duffy, B. (1998) *Supporting Imagination and Creativity in the Early Years*, Buckingham: Open University Press.

Siraj-Blatchford, J. and Whitebread, D. (2003) *Supporting ICT in the Early Years*, Buckingham: Open University Press.

Wegerif, R. and Dawes, L. (2004) *Thinking and Learning with ICT: Raising achievement in primary classrooms*, London: RoutledgeFalmer.

## Useful websites

http://www.ioe.ac.uk/cdl/datec – website for Developmentally Appropriate Technology for Early Childhood (DATEC).

http://www.naeyc.org/ – the North American Early Years Curriculum (NAEYC) website.

http://www.ltscotland.org.uk/earlyyears/ictinpreschool.asp – the Scottish Early Years Online site.

http://www.ltscotland.org.uk/earlyyears/ICTstrategy.asp – the Scottish ICT strategy for early years.

# 13 Supporting Literacy Development

## By the end of this chapter you will have:

■ increased your understandings of children's literacy learning and considered the implications for practice;

■ explored the ways in which adults support children's literacy learning at home and in early years settings.

■ considered some theoretical perspectives on literacy learning.

## Introduction

To be literate is essential in the 21st century; therefore, an important task for early years practitioners is to support children in becoming effective communicators, readers and writers. In this chapter we explore how young children learn about literacy through everyday interactions in families, communities and early years settings. We look at the connections between family literacy practices and literacy in early years settings. We consider how early years practitioners can support children in this area of learning and help to prepare them for the demands of a rapidly changing society. We begin by looking at what we mean by literacy learning. We move on to consider briefly some major theoretical perspectives that have contributed to our current understanding of literacy learning in the early years.

## Perspectives on literacy learning

'Literacy' is broadly defined as 'the ability to read and write' (*Concise Oxford Dictionary*). Before we consider how children learn about literacy, both at home and in early years settings, we would like you to think about your own experiences.

In the extract below, a learning support assistant in a key stage 1 class recalls her experiences as a young child.

---

### Case Study: Josie

I don't remember being taught to read or write. My mother was always reading. A family friend worked as a cleaner in the local library and I would go with her in the early morning when the library was empty and read whatever I liked. I loved to listen to stories on a radio programme called *Listen with Mother*. In the 'babies' class' in primary school, I remember an alphabet frieze and I recall puzzling over why there was a 'k' and a 'kite' on the picture. I didn't make the connection. I used to race through school reading books.

---

### Activity 13.1 Learning about literacy

We all experience different sorts of literacy learning at different rates. Make a timeline (from birth to about age ten years) to show significant events in your life that helped you to become a reader and writer and consider the following questions.

- At what age did you learn to read and write?
- Where did you learn?
- Who helped you and how did they help?
- What did you like or dislike about learning to read and write?
- What made this learning difficult or easy?

---

What can you learn from this activity that will help you support the children you work with? For example, would you want to know more about their home literacy experiences? Would you want to review any resources you use? Like Josie, you may remember people who helped you in this learning. What seems to be important about Josie's experience is that she had opportunities to read books and listen to stories with familiar adults who were able to spend time with her.

In the next section of the chapter we consider some ideas on how children become literate. However, we only have space to consider briefly some major theoretical perspectives that have contributed to our understanding of how young children learn about literacy.

## Maturational and developmental perspectives

In the early 1970s the notion of 'reading readiness' prevailed (Smith 1978; Barratt-Pugh 2000). This was linked to ideas on 'mental age' and led to a view that the teaching of reading should not begin until the ages of five to seven. Parents and carers were thought to have little influence on the learning process and were discouraged from helping their children to read and write. Children were assumed to have no knowledge of reading and writing before they began school. Later research showed that the learning process *could* be influenced by teaching and by children's experiences. Consequently, 'readiness programmes' were developed for use in schools as a means of preparing children for reading. These were highly structured and sequential, favouring a 'drills and skills' approach to learning through workbooks and worksheets (Barratt-Pugh 2000).

## The emergent literacy perspective

Ideas relating to emergent literacy challenged the developmental view of literacy learning. Research showed that, for almost all children living in a literate society, learning about literacy begins very early in life and there is no specific point at which children are 'ready' to read and write (Clay 1977; Smith 1978). Yetta Goodman (1984 cited in Miller 1996: 7) coined the phrase 'roots of literacy' to describe the beginnings of reading and writing. This metaphor suggests that the home and the surrounding community provide fertile environments in which the roots of reading and writing can flourish. So literacy 'roots' are nourished in the pre-school years by literacy experiences, which take place in real-life contexts. Reading, writing and language development are interrelated and take place over time through children's participation in everyday literacy events (Miller 1996), and depend on factors such as culture, economic situation and time available for children and familiar adults to spend together. This view of literacy learning led to a change in the teaching of literacy. Practitioners and teachers were encouraged to use a 'whole language' or 'holistic' approach, which emphasised the interaction of reading, writing, listening and speaking through opportunities involving reading and writing for real purposes; for example, children writing shopping lists in literacy play, rather than teaching reading and writing as separate skills in isolation and through systematic direct instruction (Campbell 1995).

## Socio-cultural perspectives

During the 1990s, socio-cultural perspectives (see Chapter 8) emphasised that an individual's literacy knowledge and competence differ according to the social and cultural context in which they are learnt. This view acknowledges that there are different forms of literacy and different types of literacy practices. Barratt-Pugh (2000: 5) has summarised the socio-cultural perspective on literacy as:

- Children learn how to 'do' literacy through participating in a range of activities in their families and communities.
- Literacy practices are carried out in culturally specific ways and contribute to children's sense of identity.
- Children have different understandings of what counts as literacy and how literacy is carried out in everyday situations.
- Literacy practices are carried out in specific ways and for particular purposes.
- The pattern of literacy learning varies between children as they become relative experts within different literacy events.
- Literacy practices are valued differently in different social and educational contexts.

## Becoming a literacy learner

One way of understanding early literacy development is to think of skills such as knowing the names and sounds of the letters as the 'tip of the iceberg'; the visible signs of literacy development as shown in Figure 13.1 (Miller 1996). Below the iceberg are the incidents and activities in daily life that have contributed to the development at the tip. So, the fact that some children informally acquire skills that prepare them well for literacy in school is *a consequence of* their experiences in the pre-school years; for example, the adult naming familiar letters and their associated sounds when sharing a book with a child. However, teaching such skills formally to very young children does not seem to help their later reading achievement. Literacy is a complex and diverse activity, which children learn about through everyday literacy practices and with the support of adults. However, literacy learning also involves specific skills such as 'decoding' words and understanding the role of sounds and letters, but as part of an holistic approach as we note above and as we discuss below.

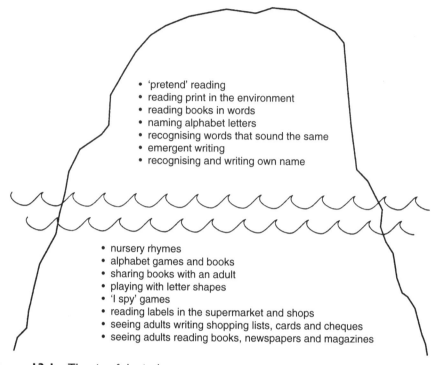

**Figure 13.1** The tip of the iceberg

# Becoming a reader

Most definitions of literacy emphasise the ability to read and write. When young children begin to investigate print and to explore writing, they learn an enormous amount about reading. Children develop the knowledge and skills required to become proficient readers – for example, being able to recognise and manipulate the sounds of language (known as phonological awareness) and learning about how print 'works' through everyday activities such as hearing nursery rhymes, sharing books and encountering print in the environment.

## Phonological awareness: learning about words, sounds and letters

'Phonological awareness' refers to the general awareness of sounds that children might acquire for reading. Phonemic awareness is one aspect of this and is associated with children's progress in reading (Campbell 1995). The phoneme is the smallest unit of sound and typically each letter (grapheme) has an associated phoneme. For example, in the word 'cat' are three phonemes c-a-t. Phonemic awareness refers to the ability to recognise the sound units of language and to manipulate them – for example, knowing that there are two syllables in the word 'don-key', and recognising that sounds like 'pin' and 'win' rhyme and that 'sock' and 'sun' begin with the same sound (alliteration). Another important aspect of sound awareness is the ability to tap out the number of sounds in a spoken word, and to detect how sounds are broken up into smaller units, for example 'spr/ing' (Goswami 1994).

Phonological awareness is a main strand of the National Literacy Strategy (DfEE 1998) and children do need to understand that there are systematic correspondences between the sounds of language and the letters of the alphabet if they are to become successful readers and writers. Research has shown important links between phonological awareness and later reading development. In a study of children who learnt to read at an early age, Stainthorp and Hughes (1999) found knowledge of the alphabet to be an important indicator of later success. Goswami (1994: 32) notes, 'It is now well established that there is a strong connection between children's ability to detect and manipulate the sounds making up spoken words and their reading development'. However, in the teaching of literacy the word 'phonics' has become an emotive term. The debate has centred on *how* this knowledge is taught to young children – that is, formally or informally, or through a combination of these approaches. For young children phonological awareness can be developed informally through nursery rhymes and books that emphasise rhyme and alliteration.

In previous chapters we have discussed the importance of the adult's involvement in all aspects of children's learning. In the next section we consider the adult's role in drawing children's attention to the print that surrounds children and in helping them to associate it with their own words, ideas and experiences.

## Print in the environment

Environmental print is basically any form of writing in children's natural environment. As Campbell (1995) notes, most children in the developed world are surrounded by print in their own homes and the immediate environment and, importantly, this print is 'contextualised' for the child. Common examples include supermarket names such as Tesco, where the whole experience of shopping assists the child in determining the word. Kenner (1997) aimed to discover the kinds of understandings of print that 3–4-year-old bilingual children were bringing from their home literacy experiences to school. She created a home corner containing a range of literacy materials – including items in the children's home languages, which they used in their role-play. One child, Meera, brought in a calendar from home, and identified some of the writing as Gujarati. She would try out writing in both English and Gujarati. Kenner concluded that these experiences supported the children's interaction with print and helped the teacher to recognise the importance of texts that were familiar to the children. We know from Chapter 9 that if children are supported in building up a strong cultural identity, their academic development is encouraged. Therefore, practitioners need to ensure that culturally relevant encounters with environmental print are part of children's everyday experiences.

## Sharing books

Children and adults sharing books together is a familiar practice in many families. Stainthorp and Hughes's (1999) study, referred to earlier, of children who could read by the time they started school, showed that early encounters with texts seem to put children at an advantage. Other studies support the view that listening to stories read aloud is significantly related to children's knowledge of literacy on entry to school and to their later reading achievement (Brice-Heath 1982; Wells 1985). Re-reading familiar books plays an important role in reading development and can help children to understand what written language does and how it 'works'; however, it is important to remember that books are not central in all homes. Early years and primary settings can offer support, for example by loaning book bags and story sacks to children to take home. Many national projects have attempted to build bridges between home, schools and early years settings.

## 'Concepts about print'

Experiences with books and print enable children to develop 'concepts about print' (Clay 1977). These are expressed in their learning about the features of letters, naming letters, identifying letters, words and sounds, and reading familiar words. Some researchers have suggested that children acquire this knowledge in a particular sequence. Table 13.1 summarises the stages that children pass through in their development of word reading and spelling.

Such 'stages' will be influenced by linguistic and cultural context. In addition, each child's development is individual, so children will proceed through stages at different rates and may even skip stages. Development will also be affected by learning styles, cognitive ability, literacy experiences and teaching. As Rohl (2000) notes, 'stages' can offer a window or lens through which we can look at the process of learning in children and then plan for appropriate learning experiences, but they should not be used rigidly.

**Table 13.1** Stages in the development of word reading and spelling

| | Logographic/ pre-phone-mic stage | Novice alphabetic/ semi-phone-mic stage | Alphabetic/ phonemic stage | Orthographic stages |
|---|---|---|---|---|
| How words are read | Cues, such as the colour or shape of the word, are used to recognise words as visual wholes. | Phonetic cues based on individual known letters (usually letter names) are used in word recognition. | Knowledge of sound–symbol relationships is used to blend letters into words. | Sophisticated knowledge of single- and multi-letter units is used to recognise words automatically. |
| How words are spelt | Word spellings bear little or no resemblance to target words. | Spellings include some letters, usually capitals to represent some sounds. | Knowledge of sound–symbol relationships is used to spell words. Spellings usually include all sounds. | Sophisticated knowledge of single- and multi-letter units is used to spell words conventionally. |
| Some signs of development | Looks at books; forms scribble and letter-like shapes. | Recognises and writes some words using initial and final consonants. | Reads and spells short, regularly spelt words; includes vowels in syllables when spelling. | Over time, becomes able to read most words automatically and spell conventionally. |

*Source:* From Barratt-Pugh and Rohl, 2000: 63

# Early writing development

In this section we briefly trace the development of children's writing. Examples can include letters, notices, stories, party invitations and home-made books. Collecting and documenting examples of children's writing can provide valuable evidence of ongoing literacy development.

## Emergent or developmental writing

In order to write conventionally in an alphabetic system, children need to have knowledge of the letters of the alphabet and to be able to map letters to sounds. As we outline below, early writing takes many forms before it becomes conventional writing. Understanding these different forms can help practitioners to locate where children are in their development and so support their learning effectively. However, these forms of early writing should be regarded as an indication of general trends rather than as representative of any kind of 'norms'.

## Scribble

Scribble is one of the earliest forms of children's mark-making and meaning-making, which begins as soon as children have some form of motor control – when they can grasp an implement such as a crayon and make to-and-from lines. This undifferentiated scribble then develops into scribble for writing and scribble for drawing, although children move freely between the two until age 2–3 years, as we see in the example below.

**Figure 13.2** 'An elephant' by Katie (aged three years and nine months)

## Writing with letters

Learning letter names and forms begins with children writing letter-like shapes, as we see in Figure 13.2. Often these reflect children's culture and early experiences of print and writing. A child's name is often the first stable string of letters produced. Figure 13.2 shows Katie's attempt to write the letters of her name.

## Non-phonetic letter strings

Children begin to compose stories or messages using strings of letters that have no phonetic relationship with what they are meant to say. These are known as 'non-phonetic letter strings'. Children often use elements of their name combined in numerous ways, as shown in Figure 13.2.

## Invented spellings

Invented spellings emerge from children's letter strings. Bissex (1980) describes how her son Paul, having failed to gain her attention, had stamped a note to her 'RUDF' (Are you deaf) with rubber letter stamps. Such creative attempts in children's writing are important in that they show how they are actively constructing knowledge of writing and spelling systems; similar abbreviations are now frequently used in texting on mobile phones.

> ### Activity 13.2 What Katie knows
>
> Look again at Figure 13.2. Using Table 13.1 and using your own ideas, consider what Katie knows about the writing system.

Practitioners need to create opportunities for young children to write and mark-make so that they can demonstrate what they know. Below are our ideas on what Katie's mark-making and drawing tell us about her knowledge of the writing system:

- pictures can represent objects;
- drawing is different to writing;
- writing (in Katie's culture) goes from left to right;
- letters represent sounds;
- a combination of letters makes up a name.

In this section we have briefly outlined the development of reading and writing and emphasised the importance of providing for literacy learning in contexts that make sense for children. In the next section we look more closely at linking literacy learning at home to settings outside the home.

## Literacy practices in the home and community

Most children learn about ways of communicating, reading and writing through experiences in their homes and communities. These literacy experiences will differ according to their educational, cultural and linguistic backgrounds, and their social circumstances (Brice-Heath 1982; Gregory and Rashid 1993).

---

### Activity 13.3 Home literacy practices

List the home literacy practices that you use with children in your setting, such as reading books, writing recipes or reading the Koran or the Bible. How do you link children's home literacy practices to the literacy experiences available in your setting? Note two ways in which you could build closer links between home literacy practices and the experiences that you provide for children.

---

Kenner (1997: 4) says it is important to find out about children's 'literacy worlds' at home and in their local communities. She describes how Meera, to whom we referred earlier in this chapter, demonstrated home literacy practices in her nursery class by bringing in home-language videos so that other children in the setting could watch excerpts. She also brought in a poster that her mother had made, showing the film title in Gujarati and English. Meera identified some of the writing and knew the purpose of the numbers.

Practitioners involve parents in their children's literacy development in many different ways. For example, on a school trip for a primary school class, parents and children took part in a 'print search', which involved looking for road signs, directions and advertisements.

## Techno-literacy

'Techno-literacy' refers to literacy practices that are mediated through technologies such as television, films, computer games and mobile phones. Marsh (2002) suggests that young children engage with a range of media texts and artefacts in the home that are not reflected in national curriculum guidance and practice in early years settings. Young children's home literacy practices show that they engage with a range of visual texts relating to popular culture. There is evidence that children are not passive viewers of television, but ask questions and talk about and act out what they are viewing. Some homes have toys, books and dressing-up clothes associated with television characters, which children can use as part of their development and learning – for example, three-year-old Kieran re-enacted the character of Cruella Deville from *101 Dalmatians* in his mum's high-heeled shoes.

The place of techno-literacies needs to be embedded in a curriculum that prepares children for life in the 21st century. Here are some ideas on how you can use items of popular culture to support children's learning:

- draw attention to environmental print such as stickers and labels on videos, computer game boxes and computer magazines;

- encourage attention to print used in television programmes and computer games;

- read books based on television characters;

- provide dressing-up clothes and toys so that children can act out aspects of television programmes;

- use text messaging on mobile phones.

## Assessing literacy learning

The National Literacy Strategy (NLS) in England (DfEE 1998) has been part of the government's drive to raise literacy standards and remains a key part of the Primary National Strategy (DfES 2003). Many practitioners will already be observing and recording children's literacy learning through a range of approaches (see Chapter 10). Since the introduction of the National Curriculum in England, formal assessment processes have become more evident in both nursery and primary settings. For example, the Foundation Stage Profile (QCA/DfES 2003) has a section on communication, language and literacy linked to early learning goals. The framework is based on formative assessment, leading to a profile for each child. However, attempts to assess young children's knowledge through formal approaches can be misleading. Children's responses depend on how questions are asked and how well they have understood the assessment task. In Wales standard assessment tasks for seven-year-olds have been discontinued, and in Scotland there is no national assessment for children under compulsory school age. It is important that there should not be any 'downward pressure' to assess young children because of national curricula. Rather, assessment should be used for getting to know children, seeing what they can do, and planning their future learning.

## Review

In this chapter we have reviewed how young children learn about literacy through everyday interactions with adults and other children, in their families, communities, and in early years settings. We have considered the connections between family literacy practices and early years settings, and the ways in which you can build on these experiences. We have said that practitioners should offer literacy experiences to young children that replicate and extend their encounters with literacy learning in the home and community. We hope that, as an outcome of reading this chapter, you will be helped to prepare children for the demands of a rapidly changing society in which being literate is an essential attribute.

### Questions for reflection

1 How can you involve parents from your setting in their children's literacy development?

2 How can you use items of popular culture to promote children's reading development in your setting?

3 How can you promote and plan for literacy through play in your setting?

## References

Barratt-Pugh, C. (2000) 'The socio-cultural context of literacy learning', in Barratt-Pugh, C. and Rohl, M. (eds) *Literacy Learning in the Early Years*, Buckingham: Open University Press.

Bissex, G.L. (1980) *Gnys at Wrk: A child learns to write and read*, Cambridge, MA: Harvard University Press.

Brice-Heath, S. (1982) 'What no bedtime story means: narrative skills at home and at school', in *Language in Society*, 11, 49–75.

Campbell, R. (1995) *Reading in the Early Years Handbook*, Buckingham: Open University Press.

Clay, M. (1977) *Reading: The Patterning of Complex Behaviour*, London: Heinemann Educational.

Department for Education and Employment (DfEE) (1998) *The National Literacy Strategy: A framework for teaching*, London: DfEE.

Department for Education and Skills (DfES) (2003) *Excellence and Enjoyment: a strategy for primary schools*, Nottingham: DfES Publications.

Goswami, U. (1994) 'Phonological skills, analogies and reading development', in *Reading*, 28 (2), 32–7.

Gregory, E. and Rashid, N. (1993) 'The Tower Hamlets work: monolingual schooling, multilingual homes', in Gregory, E., Lathwell, J., Mace, J. and Rashid, N. (eds) *Literacy at Home and at School*, London: Goldsmiths College, Faculty of Education.

Kenner, C. (1997) *Home Pages: Literacy links for bilingual children*, Stoke-on-Trent: Trentham Books.

Marsh, J. (2002) *The Sound of Silence: Emergent techno-literacies and the early learning goals*, paper presented at the British Educational Research Association (BERA), University of Exeter, September.

Miller, L. (1996) *Towards Reading: Literacy development in the pre-school years*, Buckingham: Open University Press.

Qualifications and Curriculum Authority (QCA)/Department for Education and Skills (DfES) (2003) *Foundation Stage Profile*, London: QCA/DfES.

Rohl, M. (2000) 'Learning about words, sounds and letters', in Barratt-Pugh, C. and Rohl, M. (eds) *Literacy Learning in the Early Years*, Buckingham: Open University Press.

Smith, F. (1978) *Reading*, Cambridge: Cambridge University Press.

Stainthorp, R. and Hughes, D. (1999) *Learning from Children who Read at an Early Age*, London: Routledge.

Wells, G. (1985) *Language Learning and Education*, Windsor: NFERNelson.

## Further reading

Hall, N. and Robinson, A. (2000) 'Play and literacy learning', in Barratt-Pugh, C. and Rohl, M. (eds) *Literacy Learning in the Early Years*, Buckingham: Open University Press.

Marsh, J. and Hallett, E. (eds) (1999) *Desirable Literacies: Approaches to Language and Literacy in the Early Years*, London: Paul Chapman Publishing.

Whitehead, M. (2002) *Developing Language and Literacy with Young Children*, London: Paul Chapman Publishing.

## Website reference

www.standards.dfes.gov.uk/primary – for information on the Primary National Strategy.

# 14 Supporting Mathematical Development

## By the end of this chapter you will have:

■ developed your understanding of the ways in which young children develop mathematical skills;

■ gained insights into the challenges facing children as they learn about mathematics;

■ reflected on the learning experiences that you provide in your setting to support mathematical learning.

## Introduction

In this chapter we consider how children learn mathematics and what is involved in the process of learning. We begin by considering the complexity of the mathematics that we use and what children have to achieve in learning to count. We examine the learning that occurs in infancy and the ways in which very young children begin to develop the abstract thought necessary for mathematical competence and confidence. We consider the importance of language in the development of mathematical thinking and discuss the importance of incorporating not only adult-led activities that form the basis of classroom planning for mathematics, but also child-initiated opportunities that enable children to reflect on and make sense of their own learning.

## Attitudes to mathematics

At three I fell in love with numbers . . . Numbers were toys with which I could play.

(Devi 1990: 9)

Before I was two years old I had developed an intense involvement with automobiles ... It was, of course, many years later before I understood how gears work; but once I did, playing with gears became a favourite pastime ... *I fell in love with the gears.*

(Papert 1980: vi–viii)

Few people would describe their early contact with mathematical ideas in the joyful terms expressed above by writers Shakuntala Devi and Seymour Papert. Early memories of mathematics for many people are coloured by the intense anxiety they felt at having to respond to teachers' questions quickly and without error. Anxiety, boredom and confusion, which characterise so many adults' memories of mathematics in school, have led to a situation where a high proportion of the population does not have the skills needed to use mathematics confidently and competently in everyday life.

---

### Activity 14.1 Early experiences of mathematics

Think back to your own experiences of mathematics when you were at school. Write a brief account of events that trigger either positive or negative feelings in you.

Does it matter if children develop negative attitudes to mathematics? Consider some possible consequences and jot these down.

---

Negative attitudes to mathematics may come about for a number of reasons: even an off-hand comment from an adult, that a child's efforts are silly or wrong, can have a personal and far-reaching impact. Positive attitudes to mathematics enable children to take on new learning – a vital skill in a world where knowledge is constantly changing. Mathematics also helps children to develop particular skills such as identifying patterns, sequencing and logic. More generally, mathematics impacts on large areas of everyday life. If children feel that this aspect of understanding is beyond their reach, they may develop a sense of helplessness or inadequacy that they carry with them into adulthood.

## Using number in everyday life

While number is by no means the only important aspect of mathematics, numbers are integral to much of everyday life. There are five main contexts in which we encounter numbers:

Non-numerical contexts – The numbers in telephone numbers, PIN numbers, security codes and bus numbers are used as labels: they do not actually quantify anything. A number 46 bus, for example, is not bigger than a number 45 bus.

Everyday contexts – Many of the ways in which we use numbers every day are not wholly accurate. We ask children to wait two minutes. We think it is about thirty miles to a friend's house. More confusingly, when answering questions relating to one category of measurement, we often respond in terms of another: 'How far is it to the superstore?' 'Only half an hour!'

Cardinal contexts – When we buy eggs or shoes, we want to be certain that we are getting the right number. It matters that we apply the appropriate rules of counting and come up with the correct quantity of objects. However, confusions may arise for children. In counting a group of children, we may point at individuals and say, 'You're number one, two, three, four, five, six . . .' At some point one of them will say, 'But I'm not six – I'm four.' The child has thought of his or her age in a non-numerical context.

Measurement contexts – Time is a particularly difficult concept for children to understand: '1.35 pm' can be the same as '13.35' or '25 minutes to two'. As for the passing of time – for children, one minute can feel like an hour or a year like a lifetime. Our use of number in other measurement contexts can be equally confusing. The label of a short fat bottle says that it holds 1,000 millilitres of orange juice; the label of the tall container says that it contains one litre of orange juice, yet it appears to be so much bigger.

Ordinal contexts – Further confusion awaits children as they discover that the words used to signify a position in a sequence, row or line ('first', 'second', 'third') are different from those used to simply count objects.

In all of the five contexts outlined above, children have to learn about *written numbers*. Numbers may be written in words (one, two, three) or in figures (1, 2, 3; or I, II, III). In books and newspapers, figures and letters are frequently combined, and children have to learn to differentiate between two distinct systems.

## Learning to count

To use counting, children have to understand the potentially confusing contexts described above. However, the process of counting is itself complex, having five distinct elements, or principles (Pound 1999).

### Cardinal principle

The *cardinal principle* and the *cardinal context* are similar in that the term 'cardinal' relates to an accurate number. Children have to learn that the last number name they recite when counting identifies the size of the group of items being counted.

## Case Study: Georgie

Georgie successfully counted a group of five small cars: he used the number names in the correct order, and attached just one number name to each car. However, after he had counted each object, he continued to recite the number names until he reached the number ten in the sequence. He then proudly repeated the word 'ten', and announced that there were ten cars. Georgie understood some important aspects of counting, but had not yet fully understood that he should stop reciting when he ran out of things to count.

## One-to-one principle

Young children begin to develop the one-to-one principle of counting when they take part in games like 'This little pig went to market', which emphasise the individual nature of each toe or finger being pointed to in the game. Children can better understand this principle when the uniqueness of each object is highlighted through emphasis when counting: for example, by slowing the pace of counting each tread of a stairway to match a child's speed. As children grow older, adults can encourage their understanding of one-to-one correspondence by asking, for example, that they make sure there is a mug for every child at drink time.

## Stable-order principle

To count accurately, the number names must be used *in the same order every time*. If a child gets the one-to-one principle right (matching fingers to words when counting) but the order of the words wrong (saying, for example, 'One, three, eleven, nine, six'), he or she will not arrive at an accurate answer.

If you have ever tried to learn to count in a language other than your first language, you will be aware of how difficult it is to remember an exact sequence of words. Adults who are implicitly aware of these difficulties can make use of songs and rhymes to help children remember the correct order of counting words. Songs like 'One, two, three, four, five – once I caught a fish alive' are effective because:

■ music and rhythmic chanting support memory, helping children to memorise number names;

- the physical movement involved in the actions stimulates the brain, supporting memory and thought;

- there is a close association between the areas of the brain associated with the fingers and with counting;

- the use of fingers and actions provides children with a mental and visual image of numbers – they quickly learn that all the digits on one hand equal five, two hands equal ten, and so on.

## Abstraction principle

It is important that children know that counting can be applied to *anything*, even things that cannot be seen, that are similar or that are dissimilar. This understanding is what children are learning as they meet numbers in the range of counting contexts discussed earlier. Numbers can be applied to birthdays, grams and fruit.

## Order-irrelevance principle

No matter the order in which you count a group of objects, there is still the same number of objects. This principle becomes increasingly important as children develop, as it informs so much arithmetic. Adults do not always realise the difficulty children can have with this principle and the need to probe children's understanding, as the practitioner does in the following example.

### Case Study: Jo

Jo seemed confident about counting objects. When shown a small group of toy farm animals, she was able to identify correctly that there were four. The practitioner working with her asked her to count them again, but this time to make sure that the cow was number one. Jo was hesitant, despite her earlier confidence. Then, when that task was successfully achieved, the practitioner asked her to count the animals *again*, this time ensuring that she counted the horse last. After several false starts, Jo refused to try, simply saying, 'Well, I can't do that!'

Jo knew that the order in which she recited the words was important (stable-order principle), that she had to say only one number name for each object (one-to-one correspondence), and that the last word she recited denoted the size of the group she was counting (cardinal principle). She even knew something about the abstraction principle, since she was counting dissimilar objects (various farm animals). She was, however, less certain of the idea that the order in which she counted them didn't matter – the number of animals would still equal four. Suggesting to Jo that she might move the animals once she had counted them helped her to achieve more confident counting and better understanding of this principle.

---

### Activity 14.2 Observing children counting

Spend ten minutes observing a child in your setting who seems to be having difficulties in counting or who is in the early stages of learning to count. When you have done this, reflect on what you have observed and try to identify which of the five principles seem to be confidently applied and which have not yet been fully established.

---

It is important that you take time to reflect on just how difficult it is to learn to juggle the contexts and principles of counting. Children must decide what kind of counting it is they are doing, why they are doing it, and whether a guess will do or an accurate figure is required. They must also remember to apply all five principles simultaneously – for example, remember not only the number names in order but also to stop when there are no more objects to be counted. This process has been called *orchestration*: it demands that children decide which instrument (context or principle) is relevant in any particular situation.

Careful analysis of the difficulties children face in counting accurately and consistently will help you in thinking about how best you can support their learning. If a child is having problems getting the number names in order, you could plan more opportunities for reciting and singing poems, songs and chants that include number names; or perhaps counting a wide range of different items will help children establish the abstraction principle. However, it is important that the contexts are meaningful for children and that the activities are integrated into your overall planning.

## Language and mathematics

In Chapter 8 we discussed the importance of language in learning. Language supports the development of abstract thought that is essential to mathematical development.

*Mathematical communication* supports mathematical thinking, since communication and thinking are linked. Long before babies and toddlers are able to converse easily, they seek to communicate a wide range of ideas, including mathematical ideas, using all the means at their disposal. They may use gesture (spreading their arms wide to indicate the enormous size of the Great Dane dog they have just seen for the first time). They may use single words ('up' to denote direction that may be either up or down). They may use their fingers (extending the index fingers of both hands to represent 'two', one for each hand).

*Cause and effect* is one of the process skills integral to mathematical thinking. Often when a one-year-old is carrying out an activity, the watching adult will give a sort of running commentary. As the child piles toys into a basket or places a row of objects on a table, the adult may say things like 'One more or another one', perhaps adding, 'Oh dear, it's all fallen down!' In this way, the child comes to associate language and action: words and phrases are uttered which link with what he or she is doing. The adult highlights 'cause and effect' – piling bricks up high may lead to them tumbling down.

*Categorisation*, or sorting, is an aspect of mathematical understanding which is supported by adults when they respond to a question frequently asked by young children, 'What's that?' At this stage of development, children suddenly extend their vocabulary at a much faster rate than they have been able to do before. By a process known as *fast-mapping*, they begin to 'cluster' (sort) words into groups (categories) – for example, 'cat', 'dog' and 'sheep' – making the words themselves easier to learn. This period of intense linguistic activity coincides with physical action as children become 'little "sorters" [who] spend hours of playtime separating objects into different categories' (Karmiloff-Smith 1994 : 194).

Practitioners can help children engage with these processes in a variety of ways – for example:

- using visual materials and resources that are of interest to children;
- providing that 'running commentary' as children carry out activities in the setting;
- being willing to respond when children are developing vocabulary that will promote mathematical thinking.

As children grow older, thinking in action is gradually supplemented by language. Children's vocabulary is extended so that they learn to distinguish between 'up' and 'down' instead of making 'up' stand for both directions. They need time and experience to understand the appropriate use of words and phrases like 'in front of' and 'behind'. 'More' is often learnt in the context of wanting more ice cream, more stories, more television. But 'less' is harder to grasp: if a child does not like cabbage, he or she is unlikely to negotiate for less of it; more likely, the child will be holding out for none at all!

Using language to represent mathematical ideas enables children to think more clearly and to clarify the concepts involved. Language is further extended when adults encourage children to describe the properties of objects, define the sequence of a pattern or compare two different ways of finding out, for example, how much money is left in the shop till. In England, the National Numeracy Strategy (DfES 1999) placed a strong emphasis on encouraging children to talk about what they are doing when they solve problems, giving both adults and children insights into children's thinking. The Primary National Strategy for England (DfES 2004) also places great emphasis on the importance of developing children's speaking and listening skills across the curriculum. Children's talking promotes their thinking: trying to explain how they know that three plus one more makes four gives them greater awareness of their *metacognition* (their 'thinking about thinking').

As we saw in Chapter 8, the type of questions that adults use with children is important in scaffolding learning. Open questions allow children to make use of their understandings without exposing their fledgling ideas. Open questions are much more supportive of children's mathematical thinking and development than closed questions, which have only one answer, right or wrong. For example, if you show a child a triangular shape and ask, 'What is this?' (a closed question), the child may not know that the shape is called a triangle, and may feel anxious about being unable to give the correct answer. However, it may be that the child knows the name of the shape but finds it difficult to say so without a cue of some sort. If you ask, 'What does this remind you of?' (an open question), you give the child the option of either producing the name or not. In the process, however, they can talk about sails, tents, flags, ice-cream cones and trees, setting up all sorts of connections in the brain which support their understanding of triangularity.

## Activity 14.3 Using mathematical questions

Jot down questions you have observed your colleagues asking children in mathematical contexts. You could also include questions that you know you ask regularly. To inform your response, you may want to observe a colleague or tape yourself carrying out an activity. As you make your notes, consider the following points.

■ Are they open or closed questions?

■ Do they encourage children to use their imaginations and take risks; or do they make them afraid of getting the wrong answer or encourage them simply to guess what you want them to say?

■ Which questions are most effective in getting children to engage with mathematical ideas?

Open questions offer the benefit of allowing adults to have greater insight into children's thinking. They remove from children the stress of worrying about giving the wrong answer, and help them to understand that mathematics is not just about right or wrong answers but about processes of thought.

Mathematical questions, or questions that promote mathematical thinking, are not only found in specifically mathematical contexts. Mathematics permeates everyday life, occurring whenever children are playing in the home corner, helping with household tasks, riding bikes or tidying up before bedtime.

## Moving towards abstract mathematical thinking

We have suggested that mathematics is an abstract subject demanding high levels of reasoning and thought. If children are to attain abstract thought, they need time and opportunity to play with and explore a wide variety of materials with a wide variety of characteristics. Thinking in action (exploration and talk) is an important part of the process; however, there are other experiences that will lead children towards this ability. For example, games encourage children to think about what they cannot see:

- Children describe what they can feel inside a 'feely-bag' while other children guess what the item is; this promotes the process of 'creating images in the head'.

- Two or three objects are put inside a bag or box, then one or more of the objects is added or subtracted. Children are asked to identify the number of objects in the bag, even though they cannot see them.

- Children are invited to imagine things they have never seen, such as a jug big enough to hold all the water in a swimming pool, or a toy for an ant.

- Children imagine things they have seen but which are not currently visible: for example, 'What shape are the two halves of my big round pizza?'

- Children are invited to guess what objects might become: for example, what does a piece of folded paper or cloth remind them of? What shape might it become as it is unfolded?

---

### Activity 14.4 Developing abstract thinking

Choose one of the suggested activities above and try it out with a group of children. Try to write down immediately afterwards what you observed and learnt. How could you plan for similar activities on a regular basis?

Recording in writing is another means of promoting abstract thought. Research by Martin Hughes (1986) showed how disadvantaged were children who, by the end of primary school, had not fully grasped the ways in which mathematical ideas are represented by sums. For children to understand the power of written mathematical forms, they need first to understand the power of symbolic representation. This process can be supported by:

- representing mathematical ideas in a variety of ways – drawings, tallies, plans, counters – and encouraging children to use a similar variety;

- illustrating mathematical ideas through photographs, drawings, models, plans and stories;

- promoting the use of invented or have-a-go symbols, by simply asking children to write or draw something that will help them remember a number, perhaps as part of a game or so that they will not have to count items all over again.

Hughes (1986) conducted an experiment in which children were given three small, lidded boxes, and asked to place respectively one, two, and three objects inside them. A fourth identical box had no objects inside. The children had then to create labels for the four boxes to remind them how many objects were inside each. They were able to develop and record invented symbols, which made it possible for them to identify how many objects each box contained. Subsequent studies have shown that children use a range of strategies, including invented symbols or hieroglyphs, pretend- or play-writing such as the kind of zigzags often used by children, tally marks and pictograms (e.g. five circles to represent five balls). Researchers found that many children used numerals *iconically* (Munn 1994), that is, they mirror the one-to-one correspondence they have learnt in order to count objects. For example, rather than writing '3' on the lid of the box containing three objects, the child might write '123' – one number for each object. Research of this sort helps us to understand and thus plan to clarify children's misconceptions or misunderstandings.

## Adult-focused and child-initiated mathematical learning

Traditionally, mathematics has been thought of as a subject that children can only learn when adults take an active lead. Adult-led or adult-focused activities support mathematical development by:

- modelling strategies for working out mathematical problems or investigations;

- modelling the use of mathematical language and methods of recording;

- introducing unfamiliar materials and resources;

- planning experiences, introducing new vocabulary and asking thought-provoking questions that challenge children's thinking;

- grouping children in ways that will enable them to learn from each other, since peer support has been found to have a beneficial effect on mathematical thinking.

Children benefit from the vital input that adults make; however, play and exploration are also of fundamental importance in supporting mathematical development. When children are given sufficient time and space, they will use play and exploration to think in action, rehearsing and re-presenting their ideas. In this way, they are both 'thinking to learn' and 'learning to think'. Informal talk with peers and sensitive intervention from adults help children to modify ideas, face up to misunderstandings and refine their thinking. Well-planned and well-resourced early years settings (including home settings) offer children opportunities to rehearse and re-present mathematical learning in a wide range of contexts, as the following examples illustrate.

## Case Study: Lee (aged 2)

Lee found some lengths of chain and ribbon in the treasure basket, which he was able to slide into a tall cylindrical tin. However, the hairbrush would not fit. This was a source of frustration for Lee, until he noticed a box into which the brush could be comfortably fitted, along with all the objects he had placed in the first tin.

## Case Study: Tom (aged 4)

On his birthday Tom arrived at his playgroup wearing a badge that proclaimed he was '4 years old'. During the course of the morning, he went to the sand tray and made a birthday cake with four straw 'candles', singing 'Happy Birthday' to himself as he worked. With a spade, he cut the cake into four pieces and touched each piece in turn – 'One for Mummy, one for Daddy, one for Grandma and one for me! Trina's too little.' He went to the writing-and-drawing area and drew the pictures that had been on his birthday cards that morning. The number 4 figured large in his drawing, as he bordered the paper with several 4s. In the block area he found four cylindrical blocks and stood them on end on the carpet, blowing on them and knocking them over as he sang 'Happy Birthday' again. In the outdoor sandpit, he turned out a large sandcastle and placed four pine cones on top to represent candles.

---

### Case Study: Jasmine (aged 6)

Jasmine is very interested in the idea of doubling. She rehearses verbally 'One and one are two; two and two are four; three and three are six . . .', and so on up to 'twelve and twelve'. She makes a long list of numbers, checks with an adult that 'thirteen and thirteen make twenty-six', then seems satisfied.

She moves to the workshop area and finds some sticky-paper shapes. She finds two triangles that together make a square. She finds some other triangles that will not make a square, but will make a rhombus or diamond.

She finds two circles and puts them together, telling her friend that they are glasses and then a number 8. She jokes, 'Two fours are glasses!' Moving to the role-play area, Jasmine puts two plates together, re-creating the shape she has just made with the sticky paper.

She finds two square plates, and says that they are a rectangle. Jasmine is very purposefully exploring a mathematical idea that interests her.

---

## Home learning

The benefits of working in partnership with parents to support children who are learning to read are well documented. Less well known are the results of studies showing that the children who succeed in mathematics on entry to statutory schooling are usually those whose home life has given number a high profile (Young-Loveridge 1989). Where mothers in particular regularly refer to calendars, use calculators, tot up how much they have spent on the day's or week's shopping, children become confident young experts in mathematics. Children who have been exposed at home to mathematical ideas applied within meaningful contexts arrive at settings or school with a built-in advantage.

## Review

In this chapter we have considered the development of mathematics in young children and we have considered the centrality of number to mathematical thinking and development. Despite apparently innate abilities to understand aspects of number, counting remains a highly complex activity, and we have examined some of the factors that make it so complex. We have considered the link between language and mathematical development and the place of adult-led and child-initiated activities, and we have made some suggestions as to how you can enhance the mathematical thinking and learning of children you support.

## Questions for reflection

1 How do you find out about children's home experiences of mathematics and build on these experiences in planning for children's learning?

2 Look around your setting. How is the world of mathematics represented?

3 Do you know how to count in any other languages? Could you learn from or with the children and parents you work with?

# References

Department for Education and Employment (1999) *The National Numeracy Strategy*, London: DfEE.

Department for Education and Skills (2004) *Primary National Strategy Excellence and Enjoyment: learning and teaching in the primary years*, London: DfES.

Devi, S. (1990) *Figuring*, London: Penguin Books.

Hughes, M. (1986) *Children and Number: Difficulties in learning mathematics*, Oxford: Blackwell.

Karmiloff-Smith, A. (1994) *Baby It's You*, London: Ebury Press.

Munn, P. (1994) 'Counter intelligence at work', *Times Educational Supplement*, 5 April.

Papert, S. (1980) *Mindstorms: Children, computers and powerful ideas*, Brighton: Harvester Press.

Pound, L. (1999) *Supporting Mathematical Development in the Early Years*, Buckingham: Open University Press.

Young-Loveridge, J.M. (1989) 'The relationship between children's home experiences and their mathematical skills on entry to school', *Early Child Development and Care*, 43, 43–59.

# Further reading

Pound, L. (2004) 'Born mathematical', in Miller, L. and Devereux, J. (eds) *Supporting Children's Learning in the Early Years*, London: David Fulton Publishers.

Pound, L. (2004) 'A curriculum for supporting mathematical thinking', in Miller, L. and Devereux, J. (eds) *Supporting Children's Learning in the Early Years*, London: David Fulton Publishers.

Warren, V. and Westmoreland, S. (2000) 'Number in play and everyday life', in Drury, R., Miller, L. and Campbell, R. (eds) *Looking at Early Years Education*, London: David Fulton Publishers.

# 15     Exploring the World

## By the end of this chapter you will have:

- developed your own knowledge of the world as a key area of learning;
- understood your role in supporting children in their learning about knowledge and understanding of the world;
- recognised the need to develop your subject knowledge to support children's learning.

## Introduction

This chapter explores the nature, content and practice associated with developing children's knowledge and understanding of the world (KUW). We look first at the holistic development of knowledge and understanding of the world and possible approaches before examining different ways that the environment and community can contribute to children's learning about their world. After examining curriculum provision across the four countries of the UK, we explore the implications for your practice and the need for you to develop subject knowledge and expertise in this area.

## What is knowledge and understanding of the world?

The following quotes from three children, of different ages, struggling to makes sense of their world provide insight into their attempts to understand different aspects of time.

'Mummy, in the olden days when dinosaurs were alive, what did you do?'
'Are we nearly there yet? It's a very long time', asks a child in a minibus, having just left their nursery on their way to Kew Gardens.

'I can't say Rose but when I am big I can say Rose.' Child reading *The King* by Dick Bruna with a practitioner.

Each of the children is questioning what is happening and attempting to clarify their ideas. In trying to sort out complex ideas they are making links between the knowledge they already have and new experiences and are developing their knowledge and understanding of the world. The quotes provide a useful starting point to consider what you, as a practitioner, understand knowledge and understanding of the world to be about.

## Activity 15.1  Pirate treasure

Read the following short case study. Think about what the children are doing and the potential for learning in this experience.

### Case Study: The pirate treasure

Three children are digging in the sand pit at a nursery school they attend five days a week. All three children appear focused on digging as deep as they can. Each child is digging their own hole but engaging in conversation with each other as they work. It is only by listening to their conversation that Paul, a practitioner, is able to anticipate what they are trying to do. Graham, the youngest of the three diggers, at three years and seven months, is struggling to dig deep without the walls of his hole falling in. Marvin (four years and two months) suggests he stands in the hole now as he is going 'downer' more. Graham jumps into the hole and begins to dig again but finds the space confining. He comments to Marvin that it is harder to dig like this and Marvin quickly suggests he makes his hole fatter: 'Do it like Nik's.'

Nik (four years five months) is digging at the opposite side of the sand pit to the other two and has a much wider hole. Nik's digging is not as deep as Marvin's but he is able to work from inside his hole more easily.

Graham goes over to have a look and watches Nik digging for a while but says nothing. He goes back to his hole and jumps gently into the bottom and tries to widen his hole, working on one side of the hole. Gradually he makes a long narrow hole into a wider rectangle and shouts to Nik, 'This is better, cos I can turn. I'll soon find the treasure.'

'No, I'm first' says Marvin. 'It's my story so I'm first. If I find it first then you can get it next! I'm going to find a box with gold in it like pirates do.

You can find some jewels and Nik can find some gold. My box will have lots of maps of treasure islands.'

'I'm hot. I want a drink,' says Graham.

Marvin replies 'When I find the treasure we can all have a drink 'cos we've got to read the map to see where to go.'

'Do it quick' says Graham.

Now answer the following questions.

Which areas of learning do you think were involved in this child-initiated activity?

What kind of skills were the children developing?

Which areas of learning that you have noted down would you include in knowledge and understanding of the world?

In enacting their story about pirates, these children were exploring materials and their properties and structures. Through digging holes, they were sharing techniques about how to dig. They were learning how to relate events in the past to activities in the present, and were beginning to think about how distances and locations can be pinpointed using maps. In retelling stories about pirates, the children engaged in what Rose Turner-Bisset (2004) calls 'meaningful history':

- they were using a story to develop an understanding of what people did in the past;
- they were communicating and socialising with each other as they acted out their story;
- they were helping each other to develop their skills and understanding of digging and making holes.

They were exploring historical, geographical and scientific ideas about their world but they were not yet aware of this. Finding the treasure was their target and the developing knowledge and understanding of the world came from a meaningful experience; an exploratory approach that captured their interest and helped them to enjoy learning while providing the tools for learning and opportunities to think about their learning.

## Curriculum guidance

The Curriculum guidance for the foundation stage in England (2000) suggests:

> Children acquire a range of skills, knowledge and attitudes related to knowledge and understanding of the world in many ways . . . They learn by encountering creatures, people, plants and objects in their natural environments and in real life situations, for example in the shop or the garden. They learn effectively by doing things, for example by using pulleys to raise heavy objects or observing the effect of an increasing incline of a slope on how fast a vehicle travels.
>
> (QCA/DfEE 2000: 82)

This quote exemplifies the kind of approach best adopted with young children, with the emphasis on learning by doing, using contexts and activities that interest and have meaning for children and are initiated by them.

Knowledge and understanding of the world, in making sense of personal and shared experiences, observations and ideas, involves exploring things we notice for ourselves, and responding to things others present to us. These interests may be immediate, spontaneous, ongoing or persistent concerns and are part of a lifelong quest to make sense of our world.

Rosie Turner Bisset (2004) describes the nature of historical experiences for young children, stressing how important it is to draw on children's interests to develop their understanding of their place in the world. She suggests that finding and using artefacts that are appropriate, and linked to the kinds of experience they have already had, help children develop their ideas about time past, present and future. Liaison with parents about children's experiences and home cultures and practices also helps them to move from the familiar to the wider environment. It encourages them to begin to understand their place in the world and the differences in each person's experiences. Scoffham (1999) suggests that, by providing appropriate experiences at an early stage, it is possible to raise children's awareness and respect for different cultures, races and ways of living before any stereotypical and prejudiced ideas have time to form.

## Themes or projects

Many settings encourage the use of themes to plan provision and activities. If these are broad enough, they allow the opportunity to follow children's interests, to provide new experiences and challenge children's ideas in a holistic way.

The 'spider' chart shown in Figure 15.1 shows how one nursery setting explored the kinds of activities that they could develop around the theme 'Toys'. From this initial collection of ideas, the practitioners selected particular aspects that, based on their knowledge of their children, would interest and challenge the children's current thinking and ideas. The chart is driven by questions that indicate the kind of experiences and investigations that could follow.

**Figure 15.1** Spider chart of toys

Other settings use different kinds of themes where concepts such as 'pattern' or 'change' can cater for a wider variety of interests within their group of children. As Katz and Chard (1989) suggest, using wider themes that relate to children's interests is important if children are to engage meaningfully in learning. When using themes, it is important not to exclude the normal provision, such as sand and water play, as many children will still need the opportunity to use these resources regularly.

Developing an area of provision like the role-play area around a theme such as a shop, hospital, post office or café can be a great stimulus for learning with children, engaging in play that extends their understanding about the jobs that people do and the processes and systems that operate in such workplaces. One early years unit in a primary school developed the role-play area into a post office. As Christmas drew near they extended the role-play to the outside area by turning the shed into a sorting office to handle the parcels and cards. Children who did not usually voluntarily become absorbed in writing activities became involved in writing cards and posting them and going outside to sort the parcels. Practitioners were astounded at how much the provision enabled shy and timid children to take risks and undertake different kinds of activities. One five-year-old girl, who rarely went outside, was enticed across to the shed to be chief sorter. By the end of the term, she was confident enough to go out and ride the bikes and deliver the mail to the 'sorting office' without reference to an adult. The children's ideas about places, roads and maps, what people do at work, and about money were extended.

## Developing a curriculum for knowledge and understanding of the world

A curriculum refers to the planned activities and resources that are provided to help children develop their understanding, thinking and knowledge about a wide range of areas of learning. Each UK country has defined what it understands by knowledge and understanding of the world and which areas of learning are included.

According to the curriculum guidance for the foundation stage in England (QCA/DfEE 2000), the following areas of learning are included in Knowledge and Understanding of the World:

- Scientific
- Geographical
- Historical
- Design technology
- Information and communication technology (ICT).

All four countries of the UK include the areas listed above in some form or another. Scotland, however, also includes mathematical experiences within knowledge and understanding of the world. Northern Ireland guidance (CCEA/DENI 1997) does not have an area called KUW but includes this within:

- Early experiences in science and technology
- Knowledge and appreciation of the environment.

Northern Ireland, Scotland and Wales do not refer to specific subjects explicitly but articulate the nature of the key areas of learning and link these to holistic experiences that children should have, which are similar to those from the English *Early Learning Goals* (QCA/DfEE 1999).

By the end of the Foundation Stage children should be able to:

- investigate objects and materials by using all their senses as appropriate;
- find out about, and identify some features of, living things, objects and events as they observe;
- look closely at similarities, differences, patterns and change;

- ask questions about why things happen and how things work;
- build and construct with a wide range of objects, selecting appropriate resources and adapting their work where necessary;
- select tools and techniques they need to shape, assemble and join the materials they are using;
- find out about and identify the uses of everyday technology and use information and communication technology and programmable toys to support their learning;
- find out about past and present events in their own lives, and in those of their families and other people they know;
- observe, find out about, and identify features in the place they live and the natural world;
- begin to know about their own cultures and beliefs and those of other people;
- find out about their environment, and talk about those features they like and dislike.

(QCA/DfEE 1999: 35)

As practitioners, it is necessary to integrate the areas, providing holistic and meaningful contexts for children to learn. Figure 15.2 below, taken from the Northern Ireland document (CCEA/DENI 1997) about hospital play, shows how to plan for holistic experiences around a theme and illustrates how different areas of learning can be included in hospital play.

As children in England, Wales and Northern Ireland move from early education settings into statutory schooling, knowledge and understanding of the world is described in terms of the separate subject areas of history, geography, science, information and communication technology and design technology. This is the start of the development of children's more formal understanding of the distinctive nature of each subject area, although much work is still carried out through themes and projects that link subjects together.

## Challenges for practitioners

Scoffham (1999) suggests that historical and geographical experiences seem to give early years practitioners most problems, especially in terms of planning. Children need help to develop their understanding of the process skills involved in acting out or engaging in historical or geographical events. These skills include questioning, searching, investigating, hypothesising and evaluating what they have found out.

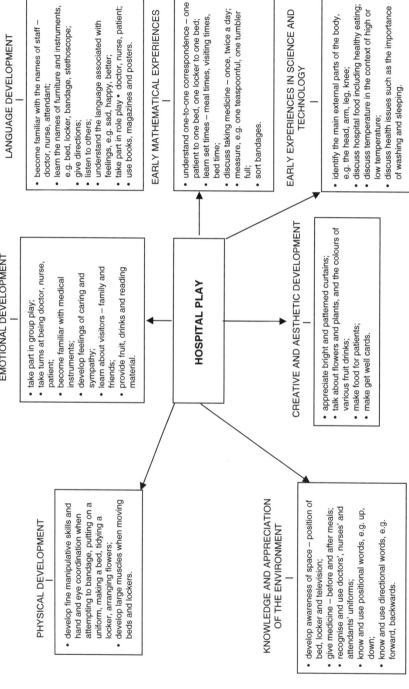

**LANGUAGE DEVELOPMENT**

- become familiar with the names of staff – doctor, nurse, attendant;
- learn the names of furniture and instruments, e.g. bed, locker, bandage, stethoscope;
- give directions;
- listen to others;
- understand the language associated with feelings, e.g. sad, happy, better;
- take part in role play • doctor, nurse, patient;
- use books, magazines and posters.

**EARLY MATHEMATICAL EXPERIENCES**

- understand one-to-one correspondence – one patient to one bed, one locker to one bed;
- learn set times – meal times, visiting times, bed time;
- discuss taking medicine – once, twice a day;
- measure, e.g. one teaspoonful, one tumbler full;
- sort bandages.

**EARLY EXPERIENCES IN SCIENCE AND TECHNOLOGY**

- identify the main external parts of the body, e.g. the head, arm, leg, knee;
- discuss hospital food including healthy eating;
- discuss temperature in the context of high or low temperature;
- discuss health issues such as the importance of washing and sleeping.

**PERSONAL, SOCIAL AND EMOTIONAL DEVELOPMENT**

- take part in group play;
- take turns at being doctor, nurse, patient;
- become familiar with medical instruments;
- develop feelings of caring and sympathy;
- learn about visitors – family and friends;
- provide fruit, drinks and reading material.

**HOSPITAL PLAY**

**CREATIVE AND AESTHETIC DEVELOPMENT**

- appreciate bright and patterned curtains;
- talk about flowers and plants, and the colours of various fruit drinks;
- make food for patients;
- make get well cards.

**PHYSICAL DEVELOPMENT**

- develop fine manipulative skills and hand and eye coordination when attempting to bandage, putting on a uniform, making a bed, tidying a locker, arranging flowers;
- develop large muscles when moving beds and lockers.

**KNOWLEDGE AND APPRECIATION OF THE ENVIRONMENT**

- develop awareness of space – position of bed, locker and television;
- give medicine – before and after meals;
- recognise and use doctors', nurses' and attendants' uniforms;
- know and use positional words, e.g. up, down;
- know and use directional words, e.g. forward, backwards.

**Figure 15.2** Hospital Play

## Exploring geographical ideas and skills

Exploration of route ways and maps is one way to extend geographical understanding. Setting up and developing routes and pathways around the grounds for large wheeled toys, and the use of signs with pictures and words, help children to develop the kind of language needed for reading maps and the skills necessary for understanding place and movement. Billet and Matusiak (1988) suggest three stages to developing mapping skills:

1  when children are developing elementary skills of plan or map making;

2  children becoming more accurate in their representation;

3  being able to draw their own plans.

Children need many different activities to develop their directional skills and understanding. Planning to use a range of games, such as 'Twister' or 'Snakes and Ladders', where children have to move themselves or move objects to help them build models in their head of directions and place, can support children's learning. There are many stories that help, such as *Rosie's Walk* by Pat Hutchings and *Alfie's Feet* by Shirley Hughes. Going outside the setting provides opportunities for children to develop their directional understanding and ideas about places and distance.

Rodgers (1999) suggests that children should also be given opportunities to engage with their environment and think about how to act as a conscientious user of resources both locally and globally. These ideas are far-reaching in terms of the sustainability of the Earth and may seem beyond the reach of young children. Yet to prepare children for life in the 21st century, it is important to support children in developing positive attitudes early by 'thinking globally and acting locally', as the Friends of the Earth motto encourages. By planning experiences that start with the child's immediate environment and involve watching daily changes that happen, of both a permanent and transient nature, it is possible to sow the seeds of awareness from an early age. There are many storybooks that raise some of these big environmental issues in ways that are meaningful to children and provide starting points and contexts for such learning. Examples include Helen Cowcher's *Rainforest*, and *The People who Hugged the Trees* by Deborah Lee Rose.

## Using the environment and the community

As young children grow and develop and become more mobile, it is possible to extend their world. As practitioners and carers go about their daily lives, this in itself brings children into contact with other people and experiences. With the move from their home environment, children can be provided with opportunities to see familiar activities and actions carried out in different ways and contexts.

## Visits and environmental walks

A trip to the park is fun for most children, whether they go with a parent or practitioner, and often stimulates curiosity and questions. Taking children out involves preparation both in terms of risk assessment and to ensure safety and purpose.

Environmental walks are effective in stimulating children's developing knowledge and understanding of the world. Examples of environmental walks may include a sound or smell walk, looking at street furniture, shops, trees, plants, buildings, or using and following directions. Matching the kind of walk to the age, stage of development and needs of the child or group is important, and briefing the children beforehand about purpose and expectations will help them to focus on the task and keep safe.

Using both the indoor and outdoor environment to develop children's knowledge and understanding of the world is, as Edgington (1998) suggests, another way to engage children more actively in their learning. The development of small trails or treasure hunts, inside and outside, leads children on a path of discovery and stimulates children's interest and learning.

## Involving others

Inviting experts into a setting can be a great way to stimulate children's interest. For example, in one nursery class one of the parents brought in two binocular microscopes so that the children were able to look at pond animals they had found that morning. Having been given guidance on how to collect the animals and treat them with respect, it was impressive to see the gentle way in which they handled the small creatures. It was notable how accurate the children's observations were, and the language they used to describe how some of the creatures moved was very apposite. As one child, Joel, said of the leech, 'it is stretching and curling and it wiggles about'. The head teacher was very impressed with the level of talk and the quality of children's drawings.

Although these children were experiencing several different aspects of learning within knowledge and understanding of the world, scientific experiences were the driving force in this instance. Siraj-Blatchford and Macleod-Brudenell (1999) suggest 'we all use science and technology and we are all practising scientists and technologists' (1999: 2) but we are not always aware how much we know, understand and can do in these areas. However, the authors go on to say, 'If we are to encourage young children to grow up to be good at these things we must start by trying to see the world through their eyes and support them in their own inquiries and projects' (1999: 2). This means we have often to explore our own understanding or call on those who know more both within our local family and community and more widely if necessary. Involving those who are experts in their field and who can engage with very young children adds a dynamic dimension to learning. Extending children's experience from the familiar to the wider, less familiar world is part of our role as practitioners. As Devereux (2002) says, 'actively working to sustain and nurture children's natural curiosity should be a priority' (2002: 59). If we are aware of this, it is not difficult to expand the experiences of children in our care, but it is important to provide time for them to absorb and think about what they see and know.

---

### Activity 15.2  Using my environment and community

Think about the activities you do weekly with the children in your care.

How often do the children have contact with people in the community?

How often do they go out to see and visit people and places?

How often do people come in to share their expertise or work alongside the children?

What do you think children might gain from such experiences in terms of knowledge and understanding of the world?

What skills would they develop? Are there ways you could extend, develop and improve your inclusion of the community in the children's learning?

---

Arranging any kind of visit to a place of interest, or someone visiting your setting, involves careful planning and thought if it is to be successful. Besides safety, the most important consideration is what you want the children to gain from the experience.

## Exploring cultural difference

In a multicultural community such as the UK, misunderstandings between communities can arise from lack of, or inaccurate, information. We need to welcome new experiences into the setting that will extend both adult and children's understanding of different cultures and lifestyles. It is not possible to be knowledgeable about every different country, religion, lifestyle and culture, but it is important to acknowledge when there are gaps in your knowledge and to search out accurate information. Most people are more than happy to talk about their different values and beliefs and share ideas with those who are interested. Early years settings do not operate in isolation from the local community or society as a whole and making links, be it on a small individual basis, or a larger more formal basis, can only help children broaden their understanding of the diverse community in which they live.

Parents, visitors and experts within the community are a rich source of information and expertise. When organising visits, it is important that people are well briefed about the needs and interests of the children and their stage of development and understanding. Many experts need support and guidance in how to interact with very young children, so that a rapport is built between the children and adult, based on mutual respect for each other's expertise and understanding.

Roden (1999), in talking about scientific experiences in particular (but it could apply to all aspects of knowledge and understanding of the world), suggests that young children are natural scientists and show some talent for scientific enquiry. Young children are intelligent, thoughtful and sensitive people who just lack the wider experience of life that adults have.

## Activity 15.3 Your strengths and areas for development

Read the following questions and think about what you do to support the development of children's knowledge and understanding of the world.

What areas of learning do you feel confident in supporting?

What strengths do you have in supporting children's learning in this area?

What areas of provision in your setting best support children's learning in this area?

What areas of your understanding do you think you need to develop?

Your answers to the above questions will differ but should indicate your strengths and positive aspects of your provision. The areas for development reflect your ability to evaluate critically what you do. It is important that you take time to consider how you might meet some of these targets in a realistic timescale. This might include studying relevant textbooks, attending a relevant course, asking someone more knowledgeable, searching the Internet and working alongside the children to solve the problem with an expert invited in to support you all learning together.

Exploring and reflecting on what we provide for knowledge and understanding of the world includes, as for any curriculum area:

- finding out what children already know and can do;
- providing a range of common resources on a regular basis;
- developing your own subject knowledge of the different areas;
- understanding how children 'come to know' in each area;
- understanding how young children learn, especially the children in your care;
- developing your ways of interacting with children as they try to make sense of the world;
- working with others with particular expertise, e.g. garden designer, your local practice nurse, local shopkeeper or librarian.

## Activity 15.4  Practitioner skills and knowledge

Read through the case study below, taken from a workplace day-care nursery, and as you read make a note of the key issues for you as a practitioner.

## Case Study: Lifting the buckets of sand

The children were filling buckets of sand from the indoor sand tray and carrying them out to the outdoor sand pit as part of their building game to make a castle outside. It was hard work and the sand was heavy and lifting it into the little wheelbarrow was difficult. Much sand was spilt on the floor, making it slippery when pushing the wheelbarrow. The children were tiring but had identified the problem and asked for something to help them lift the bucket.

There are times for finding out from first-hand experience and there are times for dipping into the pot of human knowledge and finding out how to use someone else's ideas to help solve your problem. It was suggested to the children that pulleys were a way of shifting heavy loads.

The practitioners had to mug up on how pulleys worked! They did not expect children to know about pulleys, nor did they expect them to reinvent them. As the practitioners set up a simple pulley system, they explained to the children how it worked. The children's interest in how this would make their work of lifting easier was exciting. They were eager to try it out. The children filled and lifted the buckets with considerably more ease using the pulley. Having emptied the indoor sand tray, they then brought back half-filled buckets to refill the indoor tray, before repeating the process.

From this moment on, the pulley system was often used by the children to lift objects in all kinds of role-play. The pulley was fixed to the ceiling in an area where children who were seen as transporters (Schema was one approach to learning used in this day-care centre) could move and lift things into containers or wheeled vehicles freely and safely. Several of the children were able to tell others how the pulley worked and could set it up themselves.

Being willing and able to work alongside children as you find out the answers provides a good role model for the children and supports their learning. As we discussed in Chapter 8, acting as guiding participant or a learning or apprenticeship partner and providing joint involvement episodes, enables children to see that it is acceptable not to know something or to make mistakes. Knowing this will enable the children to seek support and help when they need it, without losing face.

At times you may be more knowledgeable, the expert; at other times, you may take on the role of the supported learner. Such role modelling provides children with good examples of how it is acceptable to be open about what you can do and what you do not know – it is part of learning. Learning how to share ideas and, in so doing, develop their thinking enables children to grow intellectually. To think about ways of solving problems and to take risks and learn from these is, as Costello (2000) suggests, a vital part of developing as a confident and competent learner in later life.

## Review

The children digging for treasure at the start of this chapter exemplify the way children learn through play and how deep and meaningful that learning can be if the context in which they work or play is real. They show how young children struggle to make sense of their world and extend their knowledge and understanding of the world, geographically, historically, scientifically and technologically. Your role as a practitioner is to support children by becoming involved in their play or by initiating activities that will extend their ideas and help them develop their skills and understand the process of learning. Using curriculum documents to inform your planning, including the local environment and community, bringing in experts and developing your own subject knowledge and expertise will all add value to the learning experiences you provide for children.

## Questions for reflection

1 Which areas of your provision best support children's learning in knowledge and understanding of the world?

2 Which areas need further development?

3 Which areas of subject knowledge in this area of learning do you need to develop most?

## References

Billet, S. and Matusiak, C. (1988) 'Nursery children as mapmakers', *Education 3–13*, March.

CCEA/DENI (1997) *Curriculum Guidance for Pre-School Education*, Belfast: Northern Ireland Council.

Costello, P. (2000) *Thinking Skills and Early Years Education*, London: David Fulton Publishers.

Devereux, J. (2002) 'Developing thinking skills through scientific and mathematical experiences in the early years', in Miller, L., Drury, R. and Campbell, R. (eds) *Exploring Early Years Education and Care*, London: David Fulton Publishers.

Edgington, M. (1998) *The Nursery Teacher in Action*, London: Paul Chapman Publishing.

Katz, L. and Chard, S. (1989) *Engaging Children's Minds: The Project Approach*, Norwood, NJ: Ablex Publishing Corporation.

Qualifications and Curriculum Authority/Department for Education and Employment (1999) *Early Learning Goals*, London: QCA/DfEE.

Qualifications and Curriculum Authority (QCA)/Department for Education and Employment (DfEE) (2000) *Curriculum Guidance for the Foundation Stage*, London: Qualifications and Curriculum Authority/Department for Education and Employment.

Roden, J. (1999) 'Young children are natural scientists', in David, T. (ed.) *Young Children Learning*, London: Paul Chapman Publishing.

Rodgers, R. (1999) *Planning an Appropriate Curriculum for the Under Fives*, London: David Fulton Publishers.

Scoffham, S. (1999) 'Young children's perceptions of the world', in David, T. (ed.) *Teaching Young Children*, London: Paul Chapman Publishing.

Siraj-Blatchford, J. and Macleod-Brudnell, I. (1999) *Supporting Science, Design and Technology in the Early Years*, Buckingham: Open University Press.

Turner-Bisset, R. (2004) 'Meaningful history with young children', in Miller, L. and Devereux, J. (eds) *Supporting Children's Learning in the Early Years*, London: David Fulton Publishers.

## Children's books:

Bruna, D., (1964) *The King*, London: Methuen.

Cowcher, H. (1992) *Rainforest*, Leamington Spa: Scholastic.

Hughes, S. (1982) *Alfie's Feet*, London: Bodley Head.

Hutchings, P. (1996) *Rosie's Walk*, London: Red Fox.

Rose, D.L. *(1995) The People who Hugged the Trees*, Boulder, CO: Roberts Rinehart Publishers.

## Further reading

Bloomfield, P., de Boo, M. and Rawlings, B. (2000) 'Exploring our world', in Drury, R., Miller, L. and Campbell, R. (eds) *Looking at Early Years Education and Care*, London: David Fulton Publishers.

# 16 Perspectives on Curricula

## By the end of this chapter you will have:

■ explored five different approaches to teaching and learning;

■ understood how these approaches support children's learning and development;

■ considered the implications of these approaches for your practice.

## Introduction

In recent years, practitioners in all four countries of the United Kingdom have responded to changes and challenges posed by new curriculum policy initiatives. In this demanding climate it is easy to lose sight of the assumptions that underpin day-to-day practice, and to 'get on with the job' without building in time to think or reflect. Moss (1999) alerts practitioners to the importance of taking time to reflect on practice. He suggests that one way of doing this is by looking at the ways in which other practitioners approach teaching and learning, as this 'provides us with a sort of lens for looking at our own situations' (Moss 1999: 8). Taking time to look at the ways in which others work with young children will help you to reflect on and gain insights into your own practice, and to see what you do in a new light. In this chapter we explore five approaches to early childhood curricula: Steiner, Montessori, Schema, Reggio Emilia and Te Whāriki. The first four examples have been chosen because of their impact on practice in the UK. Te Whāriki is included as an example of national curricula for early childhood. These examples illustrate how and why different ideas about teaching and learning have developed, and how practitioners successfully weave and synthesise a range of ideas into their practice alongside published guidance.

# Influences in early childhood curricula

Laevers (2004) has said that curricula are the ways in which society expresses what it wants from education. The Organisation for Economic Cooperation and Development (OECD) Thematic Review of Early Childhood Education and Care (Bennett 2001) found that:

- most countries develop national curricula for young children;
- most agree on the utility of these frameworks;
- most agree about curricula principles and aspirations;
- most agree about subject areas;
- most cover children aged 3–6;
- there is a growing interest in curricula for children from birth to three.

Developing curricula for young children involves making important decisions and choices about what and how they learn. However, differences arise in terms of length, detail, level of prescription and orientation; also, in terms of structural implementation, pedagogical practice, different traditions and different conceptions of early childhood. In recent times, curriculum development has become increasingly centralised in some countries, including the UK, and has involved different 'stakeholders' such as early years practitioners, educational experts and policy makers. However, some approaches to curricula – both historical and contemporary – have stemmed from the beliefs or vision of one person. Below we briefly outline the origins of five different approaches to curricula. We also introduce the perspectives of five practitioners we interviewed for this chapter.

# Five approaches to teaching and learning

## The Steiner approach

The first Steiner school opened in Stuttgart, Germany, in 1919, just after the First World War. Rudolf Steiner, as a leading figure in a movement for social renewal (Chalibi 2001), wanted to create a system of education that would produce young adults who could act with intelligence, compassion and social conscience. With more than 770 Rudolph Steiner Waldorf schools and 1,200 kindergartens worldwide, as well as training courses for teachers, the curriculum places a heavy emphasis on the arts, including 'Eurythmy' (a form of movement involving simple rhythms and exercises). Seasonal festivals are celebrated as they reflect the rhythms of nature. Modern-day interpretation of his philosophy discourages the use of television and computers. Steiner principles emphasise the importance of unstructured play and the role of the teacher, who 'works' at activities as a model for children (Stedall 1992). Formal teaching is delayed until age seven.

## The Montessori approach

Maria Montessori, born in Rome in 1870, became the first woman in Italy to train as a doctor. Through her medical work, she developed an interest in children with special educational needs. She was influenced by the work of Edouard Seguin, whose education programme used graded equipment designed to stimulate children's senses (May 1997). Montessori's maxim was first to educate the senses and then the intellect, and she extended her methods to children who were developing normally. She opened her first *Casa dei Bambini* (children's house) for pre-school age children in Rome in 1907. Montessori developed a range of teaching apparatus and exercises, such as graduated rods, cylinders, geometric insets, and sandpaper letters and numbers, to develop the basics of reading and writing. She developed frames for buttoning, lacing and tying, and 'practical life exercises' such as sweeping floors and pouring liquids from one container into another. The approach emphasised children working individually rather than in groups. Equipment and exercises were 'self-correcting' so that children could independently correct their mistakes. The role of the adult, or 'directress', was to observe, support and guide. Montessori's approach emphasised children's 'work', with definite expectations of what children should do with the equipment, and tasks rather than free or imaginative play (May 1997). Standing describes the method as 'based on the principle of freedom in a prepared environment' (1966: 8). More recently her methods have been open to wider interpretation.

## Reggio Emilia

Loris Malaguzzi founded the Reggio Emilia system of early childhood education in Italy after his experiences of fascism in the Second World War. His system was based on the image of children as rich, strong, and powerful, with rights rather than needs, and who can think and act for themselves (Malaguzzi 1995). He referred to 'the hundred languages' through which he believed children express themselves, for example through play, language, drama and the written word. Adults are seen as more able others, who co-construct knowledge alongside children and support their learning. Abbot and Nutbrown (2001), reflecting on a visit to Reggio Emilia, note the presence of three successful prerequisites for 'successful' play – space, time and materials.

The Reggio Emilia network of early childhood services is situated in a small town in northern Italy, and is supported by the local community; it co-exists alongside a publicly funded system of pre-schools. Within Reggio Emilia centres there is no written curriculum; rather, the child is seen as a starting point (Rinaldi 1995). Educators in Reggio Emilia strongly believe that their 'localised' approach cannot be readily transferred to another culture or context. However, the system has become internationally known through the touring exhibition *The Hundred Languages of Children* (Malaguzzi 1996), and through visits to the region from practitioners and authorities concerned with early childhood education.

## Schema

Schema stems from Chris Athey's Early Education Project at the Froebel Institute (now the University of Surrey) in Roehampton, London. Athey was strongly influenced by the work of Jean Piaget, the Swiss psychologist and educationalist who attempted to explain how knowledge develops in young children. Piaget developed the concept of schema or mental representations into which we organise our knowledge about the world. Building on Piaget's ideas, Athey identified how children between the ages of two and five show repeatable patterns of behaviour or actions (schema), which they apply to everyday objects and events, and which manifest themselves in play. Examples of schema are:

- Trajectory – interest in up-and-down and along-and-back movements;
- Rotation – interest in things that rotate;
- Enclosure – interest in boundaries;
- Enveloping and containing – interest in covering and putting objects in containers;
- Connecting – interest in joining things together in various ways and forms;
- Transporting – interest in moving things about in different ways.

(Athey 1990: 37).

Athey developed a framework for teaching and learning that nourished and extended children's schema through the provision of resources, visits and other curriculum experiences. Play was seen to have an important role in children's learning: 'Playfulness implies knowledge that is so well assimilated it can be played with' (Athey 1990: 76).

## Te Whāriki

Te Whāriki (Ministry of Education 1996) is the New Zealand national curriculum framework for early childhood. It is a government-led initiative, developed by Margaret Carr and Helen May who worked with diverse groups of practitioners and representatives from different types of early childhood services, to create a curriculum that was acceptable to all parties. The published document is written in both English and Maori, and incorporates Maori perspectives (Smith 2002).

The words 'Te Whāriki' mean a woven mat on which everyone can stand, thus reflecting the inclusive nature of the curriculum. The curriculum document interweaves central 'principles', 'strands' and 'goals' into different patterns or programmes, which each early childhood centre is expected to weave into its own curriculum. The curriculum document states that children's play is 'valued as meaningful learning and the importance of spontaneous play is recognized' (Ministry of Education 1996: 16). Four principles form the foundation of Te Whāriki:

- **empowerment**: of families and children – children's sense of cultural and social identity, and their identity as learners;
- **holistic development**: the curriculum will not be divided up into physical, intellectual, emotional and social skills; children will be developing learning dispositions, which include skills and knowledge;
- **family and community**: the notion that funds of knowledge and people from the home community are seen as central to the well-being of the child;
- **relationships**: children learn through responsive and reciprocal relationships with people, places and things.

We know that learning is enriched when informed and sensitive practitioners reflect on their own practice. In the next section we explore the roles of practitioners within each curriculum approach.

## Practitioners' perspectives

In this section we draw on interviews with four practitioners and an early childhood authority, each of whom has worked with one of the approaches we discuss. They are:

Sally Jenkinson, a former Steiner-Waldorf teacher, and now a lecturer and writer on Rudolph Steiner;

Maggie Weber, owner and manager of the Milton Keynes Montessori Kindergarten;

Cindy Willey, head teacher of the former Wall Hall Nursery School in Hertfordshire, which worked with Schema;

Cynthia Knight, director of St Thomas Centre, a nursery in Birmingham influenced by the Reggio Emilia approach;

Margaret Carr – Professor of Early Childhood, University of Waikato, New Zealand.

Below we provide summaries of the practitioners' descriptions of the influence of a particular approach on their practice. These accounts reflect the personal perspectives and experiences of the people interviewed about the approaches they work with. Even settings that work within the same curriculum guidance will vary in the ways in which they interpret and implement that guidance. For example, no two Montessori or Steiner settings will operate in exactly the same way.

Four of the practitioners explained how they were looking for something different or better than the approach they had learnt about either during their training or more recently. Cindy Willey and Cynthia Knight had each experienced a 'eureka' moment, which had consolidated their thinking or seemed to match aspects of their existing practice, and helped them to see children's learning in a new way.

**Sally Jenkinson** was attracted to the Steiner approach because it seemed to offer an alternative value system to the more formal approaches to learning which, she believes, emphasise the achievement of short-term goals and fixed targets. She welcomed a system that allows children to play and that values children for who they are rather than what they might achieve. She liked the approach because it places emphasis on a childhood that is free from the stresses imposed by some aspects of mainstream schooling and because formal learning is delayed.

**Maggie Weber** sees the Montessori approach as synonymous with what she believes to be 'good practice', which in her view involves practitioners standing back to observe children, and then guiding their learning appropriately. She also emphasises the distinctive approach of the Montessori curriculum, including the teaching materials, the prepared environment, and the practical life exercises.

**Cindy Willey** describes how the Schema approach connected with her thinking and significantly changed her ideas about practice, as it explained a great deal about the behaviour and play of the children she was working with. She feels that the approach offers a distinctive way of identifying patterns of children's behaviour as a framework for teaching and learning.

**Cynthia Knight** explained how a visit to the Reggio Emilia exhibition *The Hundred Languages of Children* changed her approach to practice. The staff in St Thomas Centre adapted aspects of the approach, for example by having an artist working alongside the staff to support the children's creativity, and the use of mirrors and light to reflect and enhance the environment. Features of the approach that Knight sees as distinctive include its project emphasis, the documentation of children's learning through photographs, displays of their work, and written records and the emphasis on the environment.

**Margaret Carr** had an important role in developing a new early childhood curriculum that embraced the values and beliefs of the bicultural community of New Zealand. She sees the bicultural and bilingual nature of Te Whāriki as its most distinctive feature.

You may already work with one of these approaches in your setting. It is also likely that your approach to teaching and learning is governed by particular curriculum guidance for your setting, or by published national guidance, which requires you to work towards particular educational outcomes. Even if a setting has goals and outcomes to work towards, the methods it uses may incorporate or 'weave in' aspects of the approaches described in this chapter. Most practitioners take a creative approach to their work and develop their own ways of working, even within common guidelines.

## Main features of the approaches

Each of the approaches discussed in this chapter has exerted some influence on the early years curriculum in the UK. Listed below are some of the reasons why a particular approach may, or may not, appeal to practitioners.

Some people are attracted to the use of natural objects within the **Steiner** approach. However, others may think that this does not reflect the real world of childhood today, in which commercial products and TV characters powerfully influence children. Items such as books, jigsaw puzzles, and electronic toys and games can be important tools for children's learning.

The emphasis of the **Montessori** approach on social and emotional development is appealing, but the prepared environment and structured materials for teaching can seem too inflexible to some practitioners.

**Schema** offers a useful tool for observing children's play and gaining insights into their interests and ways of learning, but it can rely heavily on adult interpretation.

The idea of the environment as the 'third educator' and as a source for exploration and learning, as in the nurseries of **Reggio Emilia**, seems appealing, but some practitioners may feel insecure with the very open-ended approach to curriculum planning.

In the first activity in this chapter we invite you to think about the approach to teaching and learning in your setting.

In thinking about your own approach to teaching and learning, it may be that you affirmed aspects of your practice, or wondered about changes you might make. For example, Reggio Emilia may have prompted you to think about changes to your physical surroundings. However, you may have no immediate influence over these changes.

## The role of practitioners

We know that practitioners take on different roles and responsibilities across diverse settings. In this section we explore the different roles of practitioners within each curriculum approach.

Within **Steiner** settings, practitioners (educators and teachers) are seen as children's mentors whose role is to nurture individuality and creativity, guide children through activities, and to act as a model for learning. As Sally Jenkinson comments, 'The teacher is a learning resource to be freely imitated. If the child can see an adult working with patience and perseverance, this is a model to imitate'. In her interview, Jenkinson drew attention to the educational opportunities for children of observing adults, even when they are performing everyday tasks such as gardening or are experiencing difficulties. She argues that this kind of observation enables children to use and act out what they have learnt during their play and work experiences.

**Montessori** saw the role of the practitioner as 'directress', who observes, supports and guides, but does not intervene unnecessarily in children's learning (May 1997). In her interview, Maggie Weber noted that, although thinking about the role of Montessori practitioners has changed in recent times, it is important to draw on Montessori principles, in particular, as Weber says, 'her respect for the child, her knowledge of the child and the recognition of the child as an active learner'. Weber also draws attention to Montessori's belief that children have specific times when they learn to acquire particular skills, such as language and movement, and work hard towards gaining these skills. Weber talks about how Montessori practitioners help to direct children's learning during these sensitive periods to encourage them to develop their capacities for learning. She notes, 'We are looking for capacities as well as skills, kindness is something that you can work at in your early years and have as a quality in your total education'.

Athey viewed the role of the practitioner as an observer and researcher. Cindy Willey discusses how Athey's work translates into practice in her setting: '**Schemas** give us a very good shorthand in terms of trying to identify children's interests, and planning to meet those interests and their learning needs'. Willey describes how schema has become an important focus in planning meetings: 'While we may be thinking about the kinds of topics or focuses of interests that we may want the children to have access to, we'll also be thinking about how we can plan for the different schema activities that will help all of the children have access to them'.

In **Reggio Emilia** nurseries, practitioners (referred to as teachers) take on the role of children's learning partners. As projects develop, the teacher acts as the group's 'memory' by documenting visits and children's work through photographs, tape recordings and written notes. The children and teachers can than reconstruct, revisit and reflect on what they have learnt. The teachers pose problems and questions to be explored. Cynthia Knight noted that the practitioner's role is to enable children to use their 'hundred languages', and to encourage them to 'revisit and reflect on their experiences'. She explains the role of specific staff members in this child–adult partnership:

- a senior or advisory teacher (*a pedagogista*), who supports children's reflection on their learning and who meets regularly with other staff to share knowledge and ideas;

- a practising artist (an *atelierista*), who helps to develop and promote children's artistic skills and takes an important role in planning activities within the setting.

**Te Whāriki** supports the cultural identity of all children, and affirms and celebrates cultural differences to help children gain a positive awareness of their own and other cultures. The curriculum document stresses that adults working in early childhood provision must ensure that the curriculum is sensitively implemented, and is responsive to the different cultures and heritages of the children and families using the service (Ministry of Education 1996). Margaret Carr sees the child–adult relationship as an essential part of the process of fostering children's sense of identity:

> The idea of children developing a sense of identity as a learner means that one of the things that adults will be doing is to get to know the children very well. The teacher will also engage children in reciprocal communication – encouraging them to express their ideas. And remember we're talking about babies as well here. So a lot of that communication will be non-verbal, and a good teacher will recognise the signals of a non-verbal communication. The adult will be giving the child more and more responsibility, and encouraging a sense of community, a sense of justice, a sense of things being fair. We're not saying that learning is something that happens in the head of the child only. It happens as part of that relationship.
>
> (Carr 2001)

## Activity 16.2 Practitioners' roles

For this activity we have summarised the role of practitioners within the different approaches in Table 16.1. Compare these descriptions to your own role. Think about whether you take on any of these roles in your practice.

**Table 16.1**  Practitioners' roles

| Approach | Role of adults | Implications for your practice |
|---|---|---|
| Steiner | Model and mentor | |
| Montessori | Guide | |
| Schema | Observe and research | |
| Reggio Emilia | Learning partner | |
| Te Whāriki | Support and extend learning | |

It is likely that in your work you move between all the roles identified. You may have recognised your role as a gentle guide or perhaps as a more active learning partner. There may be times when you assume a more directive role or act as a model for children's learning. You may have thought about ways in which your role might be extended as a result of reading this section.

## Implications for practice

We now consider how the five approaches work in practice.

Since the introduction of the Foundation Stage guidance in England, Sally Jenkinson's setting has worked to make the learning experiences within the Steiner approach more explicit. The setting provides children with incidental learning experiences through activities such as baking, which requires the children to use a range of skills, including maths in the weighing and counting, and science in the baking process. She notes that, 'Our teachers have learned to tease out the learning outcomes necessary for the requirements of the Foundation Stage'.

In her interview, Maggie Weber recognises the importance of 'making the paperwork fit with national guidelines' but notes that they just don't 'fit neatly'. She explains how the curriculum works in action, drawing particular attention to its emphasis on *processes* rather than *results*: 'Once children have settled into the nursery, we put them in touch with practical life activities. We then really just follow their learning and see where their interests lie, and work with them, and put them in touch with those activities'. Weber notes that parents often comment on the children's independence and confidence in their own abilities.

Practitioners in Cindy Willey's setting try to plan the schemas that children may want to explore by standing back and observing. Willey notes how, even when the children seem involved in a particular task, they have opportunities to be covering the areas of learning in the Foundation Stage. She gives the example of a child creating a collage, which involves cutting and sticking, selecting and manipulating materials, and considering size and shape. In this one activity, the child may use and develop motor skills, maths, language and literacy, and knowledge and understanding of the world.

A key change to practice that Cynthia Knight's setting has made since learning about the Reggio Emilia approach relates to how children's learning is planned. Planning starts at the beginning of the year, instead of the start of each term as previously. The practitioners observe the children and identify their individual interests. They then consider ways to help the children develop their skills and interests throughout the year. Knight talks about how this child-centred approach facilitates the six areas of learning in the Foundation Stage: 'We found that when the children are very motivated and interested in a topic, it's very easy to develop that interest, which will follow all six areas of learning'.

In each of the accounts above, the practitioners seem to work comfortably within published curriculum guidelines yet manage to weave into this framework their own beliefs and understandings, and to form their own approaches to early childhood education and care.

Margaret Carr, in discussing some of the difficulties that practitioners in New Zealand experienced as the new Te Whāriki curriculum was introduced, explains how some were disappointed that there were no 'recipes' to follow. In addition, both the curriculum and the curriculum document are quite complex, which meant that some staff required more support and training in order to implement the curriculum. As she notes, 'One of the characteristics of an early childhood profession is that not everyone working with young children is qualified'.

You may already recognise similar challenges for practitioners when working with new and different guidelines.

---

### Activity 16.3 Thinking about practice

Now that you have seen how the practitioners featured in this chapter have each taken elements of a distinctive approach and adapted these to suit their ways of working, we would like you to think again about your practice. Make notes in response to the questions below.

1 Would you want to include any parts of these approaches in your curriculum? If so, which elements would you use and why?

2 Are there any changes you would like to make in your setting as a result of reading this chapter? If so, note down what these are.

3 How might you share your ideas with colleagues or parents?

---

Reading this chapter may have affirmed ideas and practices that already exist in your setting. You may have found many of the ideas interesting, but don't feel there is a place for them in your practice. On the other hand, you may have thought of a change that you would like to implement. You may like to develop your notes into a plan that you can discuss with a colleague or someone who knows you and your setting well.

## Review

In this chapter you have explored five approaches to teaching and learning in the early years, and considered the roles of practitioners within each approach. You will have thought about the main features of each approach and the implications for your practice. We hope that this chapter has encouraged you to stand back from your familiar practices and look at some of them in a new light. Reflecting on your learning is an important aspect of your professional development and part of the process of 'moving on' as an early years practitioner. This process of reflection and evaluation, together with appropriate development and planning for your own professional development, has been an ongoing theme within this chapter and throughout this book.

## Questions for reflection

1  Which of the five approaches in this chapter has had most influence in helping you to think about and reflect on your practice? Can you say why?

2  As a result of reading this book, what changes, if any, would you wish to make in relation to:
   ■ the curriculum in your setting
   ■ your practice?

3  Can you identify one or more possible next steps in your professional development?

## References

Abbott, L. and Nutbrown, C. (eds) (2001) *Experiencing Reggio Emilia: Implications for pre-school provision*, Buckingham: Open University Press.

Athey, C. (1990) *Extending Thought in Young Children: A parent–teacher partnership*, London: Paul Chapman Publishing.

Bennett, J. (2001) 'Goals and curricula in early childhood', in Kamerman, S. (ed.) *Early Childhood Education and Care: International perspectives*, The Institute for Child and Family Policy at Columbia University.

Carr, M. (2001) *The Te Whāriki Curriculum*, unpublished interview with Janet Soler, Milton Keynes, Open University/BBC.

Chalibi, M. (2001) *Waldorf: Awakening to tomorrow*, Berlin: Freunde der Erziehungskunst.

Drummond, M.J., Lally, M. and Pugh, G. (1989) *Working with Children: Developing a curriculum for the early years*, London: National Children's Bureau.

Laevers, F. (2004) 'The curriculum as a means to raise the quality of early childhood education: a critical analysis of the impact of policy', Keynote lecture, European Early Childhood Education Research Association, 14th annual conference, *Quality Curricula: The influence of research, policy and praxis*, University of Malta, 1–4 September.

Malaguzzi, L. (1995) 'History, ideas and basic philosophy: an interview with Lella Gandini', in Edwards, C., Gandini, L. and Forman, G. (eds) *The Hundred Languages of Children: The Reggio Emilia approach to early childhood education*, Norwood, NJ: Ablex Publishing Corporation.

May, H. (1997) *The Discovery of Early Childhood*, New Zealand: Bridget Williams Books/Auckland University Press/New Zealand Council for Educational Research.

Ministry of Education (1996) *Te Whāriki: He Whāriki Matauranga mo nga Mokopuna o Aotearoa*, Wellington: Learning Media.

Moss, P. (1999) *Difference, Dissensus and Debate: Some possibilities of learning from Reggio*, Stockholm: Reggio Emilia Institutet.

Rinaldi, C. (1995) 'The emergent curriculum and social constructivism: an interview with Lella Gandini', in Edwards, C., Gandini, L. and Forman, G. (eds) *The Hundred Languages of Children: The Reggio Emilia approach to early childhood education*, Norwood, NJ: Ablex Publishing Corporation.

Smith, A.B. (2002) 'Promoting diversity rather than uniformity: theoretical and practical perspectives', in Ffthenakis, W.E. and Oberhuemer, P. (eds) *Early Childhood Curricular Issues: International perspectives*, Leverkusen, Germany: Leske and Budrich.

Standing, E.M. (1966) *The Montessori Revolution in Education*, New York: Schocken Books.

Stedall, J. (1992) *Time to Learn: A film about Rudolf Steiner Waldorf Education*, Forest Row, Sussex: Hermes Films.

## Further reading

Fleer, M., Anning, A. and Cullen, J. (2004) 'A framework for conceptualising early childhood education', in Anning, A., Cullen, J. and Fleer, M. (eds) *Early Childhood Education: society and culture*, London: Sage Publications Ltd.

Members of the British Education Research Association Early Years Special Interest Group (2003) *Early Years Research: Early Years Pedagogy, Curriculum and Adult Roles, Training and Professionalism*, Notts: British Educational Research Association.

Miller, L. and Soler, J. (2003) 'Adult conceptualizations of early childhood curricula: a comparison of the English Foundation Stage Curriculum, Te

Whāriki and Reggio Emilia', *International Journal of Early Years Education*, 11 (1), 53–64.

Miller, L. Devereux, J., Paige-Smith, A. and Soler, J. (2004) 'Approaches to curricula in the early years', in Devereux, J. and Miller, L. (eds) *Working with Children in the Early Years*, London: David Fulton Publishers/The Open University.

## Website references

www.montessori.ac.uk – for information about the Montessori Centre International.

www.learningmedia.co.nz – for information about Te Whāriki.

www.steinercollege.org – for information about the Rudolf Steiner College.

# Index